INTRICATE LAUGHTER IN THE SATIRE OF SWIFT AND POPE

INTRICATE LAUGHTER IN THE SATIRE OF SWIFT AND POPE

Allan Ingram

St. Martin's Press   New York

First published in the United States of America in 1986

Printed in Hong Kong

ISBN 0-312-42540-6

Library of Congress Cataloging-in-Publication Data
Ingram, Allan.
Intricate laughter in the satire of Swift and Pope.
Bibliography: p.
Includes index.
1. Satire, English–History and criticism.
2. English literature–18th century–History and
criticism. 3. Laughter in literature. 4. Swift,
Jonathan, 1667-1745–Criticism and interpretation.
5. Pope, Alexander, 1688-1744–Criticism and
interpretation. I. Title.
PR935.I54   1986   821'.07'09   85-25000
ISBN 0-312-42540-6

*To My Mother
and the Memory of My Father*

Contents

Preface

The metaphysical solace (with which, I wish to say at once, all true tragedy sends us away) that, despite every phenomenal change, life is at bottom indestructibly joyful and powerful, was expressed most concretely in the chorus of satyrs, nature beings who dwell behind all civilization and preserve their identity through every change of generation and historical movement.

(Friedrich Nietzsche, *Birth of Tragedy*)

King! King! Dead faces laugh.
(W. B. Yeats, *The King's Threshold*)

Pack up your troubles in your old kit bag and smile, smile, smile. . . .
(popular song)

They know that Hamlet and Lear are gay;
Gaiety transfiguring all that dread.
(W. B. Yeats, 'Lapis Lazuli')

    A Barnacle goose
Far up in the stretches of night; night splits and
   the dawn breaks loose;
I, through the terrible novelty of light, stalk on,
   stalk on;
Those great sea-horses bare their teeth and laugh at
   the dawn.
(W. B. Yeats, 'High Talk')

I am grateful, as always, to my wife Glynis and to my daughters, Sarah and Ruth, for their immense patience and support. Without their help and understanding this book would have remained unwritten. My warmest thanks, too, are due to those friends who have been prepared to talk over my ideas and to make valuable suggestions for improvement. In particular I should like to thank Shelagh Frawley who was kind enough to decipher my handwriting and to offer intelligent criticism and constructive encouragement. They, however, will know where I have chosen to go my own headstrong way, and will laugh, silently, in their sleeves.

Newcastle   A.S.I.

1 The Uneasy Chair: Laughter, Satire and the Eighteenth Century

In January 1721, from 'obscurity' in Dublin, Swift composed a long letter to Pope (a letter which, according to Pope, 'Mr. Pope never received') designed to explain and justify his behaviour during the final period of Queen Anne's reign, and during the first years of the new ministry after her death. He begins: 'A Thousand things have vex'd me of late years, upon which I am determined to lay open my mind to you.'[1] Among the vexations he goes on to treat are the 'incurable breach' between Oxford and Bolingbroke, the treatment of his 'discourse' on Irish manufactures by the Chief Justice, and the libels written against him by the government pamphleteers.[2] He also speaks, however, of his frequent intercessions, when in a position of influence with the late ministry, in favour of his Whig friends.

> But, whatever opportunities a constant attendance of four years might have given me for endeavouring to do good offices to particular persons, I deserve at least to find tolerable quarter from those of the other Party; for many of which I was a constant advocate with the Earl of Oxford, and for this I appeal to his Lordship: He knows how often I press'd him in favour of Mr. Addison, Mr. Congreve, Mr. Row, and Mr. Steel, although I freely confess that his Lordship's kindness to them was altogether owing to his generous notions, and the esteem he had for their wit and parts, of which I could only pretend to be a remembrancer. . . . I remember it was in those times a usual subject of raillery towards me among the Ministers, that I never came to them without a Whig in my sleeve.[3]

1

Raillery from ministers, though, was not all Swift had to suffer 'in those times'. On 13 May, 1713, he wrote a letter of strong complaint to Addison.

> I was told yesterday, by several persons, that Mr. Steele had reflected upon me in his Guardian, which I could hardly believe, until, sending for the paper of the day, I found he had, in several parts of it, insinuated with the utmost malice, that I was author of the Examiner; and abused me in the grossest manner he could possibly invent, and set his name to what he had written. Now, Sir, if I am not author of the Examiner, how will Mr. Steele be able to defend himself from the imputation of the highest degree of baseness, ingratitude, and injustice?

Swift goes on to deny all connection with the *Examiner* (of which he had certainly not been editor since June, 1711), and to make more precise his charge of ingratitude.[4]

> Has he never heard that the author of the Examiner (to whom I am altogether a stranger) did a month or two ago vindicate me from having any concern in it? Should not Mr. Steele have first expostulated with me as a friend? Have I deserved this usage from Mr. Steele, who knows very well that my Lord Treasurer has kept him in his employment upon my intreaty and intercession?[5]

Relations between Swift and the two Whig essayists, and particularly those with Steele, had been deteriorating since Swift's change of parties during the autumn of 1710.[6] The reflection in *Guardian* 53 arose from an attack in the *Examiner* on the Earl of Nottingham and his daughter, but Swift's tone of injured astonishment, while ostensibly concerned to deny authorship, is clearly designed to appeal at a personal level to Addison's and Steele's sense of the enormity of friendship betrayed and obligation spurned. Such a tone, and such bland denial, made Swift a ripe target for the cruelty of Steele's reply. On 19 May, Steele wrote briefly to Swift.

> Mr. Addison shewed me your letter, wherein you mention me. They laugh at you, if they make you believe your interposition has kept me thus long in office. If you have spoken in my behalf

at any time, I am glad I have always treated you with respect;
though I believe you an accomplice of the Examiner's. . . . You
do not in direct terms say you are not concerned with him; but
make it an argument of your innocence that the Examiner has
declared you have nothing to do with him. I believe I could
prevail upon the Guardian to say there was a mistake in putting
my name in his paper: But the English would laugh at us,
should we argue in so Irish a manner. I am heartily glad of your
being made Dean of St. Patrick's.[7]

Ministerial rallying is one thing, a sign of the familiar acceptance
by 'great Ministers or men of Wit and Learning'[8] that Swift so
valued. To be laughed at behind his back by those same 'great
Ministers', however, means immediate exclusion, the immediate
undermining of almost three years of apparently rising favour,
and, moreover, the striking demonstration of Steele's superior
state of knowledge, his glorification at the cost of Swift's
sudden humiliation. Steele's 'interpretation', as Swift calls it in his
reply,[9] would effectively demolish both his standing in the world
and his private self-esteem before the awful spectre of friends and
enemies joining together to laugh at him. In the context of the
letter, Steele's congratulations on the preferment to a minor Irish
vacancy can only have been designed to add insult.
    As Bertrand Goldgar nicely understates it, 'Steele's phrase
"they laugh at you" stung Swift's pride'.[10] In his reply, written on
23 May,[11] he returns again and again to the claim: he summarizes
'the history of what you think fit to call, in the spirit of insulting,
"their laughing at me"', and continues:

Next I desire to know, whether the greatest services ever done
by one man to another, may not have the same turn as properly
applied to them? And, once more, suppose they did laugh at
me, I ask whether my inclinations to serve you merit to be
rewarded by the vilest treatment, whether they succeeded or
no? If your interpretation were true, I was laughed at only for
your sake; which, I think, is going pretty far to serve a friend.

Finally, after denying at length once more his connection with
the *Examiner*, Swift suggests a series of questions that Steele
should put to himself.

If Dr. Swift be entirely innocent of what I accuse him, how shall I be able to make him satisfaction? And how do I know but he may be entirely innocent? If he was laughed at only because he solicited for me, is that a sufficient reason for me to say the vilest things of him in print under my hand, without any provocation? And, how do I know but he may be in the right, when he says I was kept in my employment at his interposition? If he never once reflected on me the least in any paper, and hath hindered many others from doing it; how can I justify myself, for endeavouring in mine to ruin his credit as a Christian and a clergyman?[12]

The tone of injured innocence does not come easily to Swift, and he is clearly finding it of limited effectiveness against the aggressive Steele. Swift has only two arguments – that he did not write the *Examiner* and that Steele owes him a debt of gratitude – and he can do little more than repeat them with slight changes in emphasis. Having begun as the injured party in his letter to Addison, however, as the good Christian and clergyman, he has to make the best of it, even though the added vexation of being laughed at might make him feel the want of more equal weapons. On other occasions, of course, unhampered by this particular stance, and most notably in *The Publick Spirit of the Whigs*, published in February, 1714, Swift was able to treat Steele to far greater damage. For the present bout, Steele had with apparently little effort seriously discomposed his former friend, inflicting an injury which, while perhaps not entirely ruining Swift's 'credit' with the world, had certainly rankled with the private correspondent.[13]

Nor does this seem to have been an accidental blow on Steele's part. Only a month before, in his paper of 14 April, Steele devoted an entire *Guardian* to the subject of laughter.[14] Not unexpectedly, the author of *The Christian Hero* begins by describing laughter as an 'agreeable kind of Convulsion' during which people are 'so much unguarded' that 'then, if ever, we may believe the Face'. He concludes, too, by underlining the joyful and the natural in the act of laughing.

The Poets make use of this Metaphor when they would describe Nature in her richest Dress, for Beauty is never so lovely as when adorned with the Smile, and Conversation never sets easier upon us, than when we now and then discharge our selves in a Symphony of Laughter, which may not improperly be called *The Chorus of Conversation.*

His apparent design in the paper is to treat laughter with an easy blend of frivolity and genuine celebration. To laugh is to be a rational creature, and Steele quotes Milton in support of this commonplace contention. But there are remarks, too, in the body of the paper, in which Steele implies serious reservations about the laugh. The laugh of 'Men of Wit', for example, 'is for the most part but a faint constrained kind of Half-Laugh', while it is only the fool's laugh that is 'the most honest, natural, open Laugh in the World', which would appear to contradict the spirit of the easy symphony of laughter in conversation. Nor are all conversational choruses equally expressive of either good nature or candour.

The *Horse-Laugh*, or the *Sardonic*, is made use of with great Success in all kinds of Disputation. The Proficients in this Kind, by a well-timed Laugh, will baffle the most solid Argument. This upon all Occasions supplies the want of Reason, is always received with great Applause in Coffee-house Disputes, and that Side the Laugh joins with, is generally observed to get the better of his Antagonist.

The laugh, in fact, far from being a sign of unguarded honesty, is adapted for a whole range of social stratagems and disguises. 'The *Grin*' is 'made use of to display a beautiful Set of Teeth'; the 'Effeminate Fop, who by the long Exercise of his Countenance at the Glass, hath reduced it to an exact Discipline' will 'give Spirit to his Discourse' and 'admire his own Eloquence by a Dimple'; the 'Beau . . . practises the Smile the better to sympathize with the Fair. He will sometimes join in a *Laugh* to humour the Spleen of a Lady, or applaud a piece of Wit of his own, but always takes care to confine his Mouth within the Rules of Good-breeding'; and the '*Ionic* Laugh is of universal Use to Men of Power at their Levées; and is esteemed by judicious Place-Hunters a more particular Mark of Distinction than the Whisper'.

The laugh, then, when Steele looks aside from the principles of benevolism and from literary allusion to the world about him, is seen not as an expression of openness but as a device for display, for posing, an invitation to admire, a mark of rank complacent in the possession of favours to bestow. What should be a reminder of man's former innocence, his having nothing to hide, has itself degenerated to an instrument to be manipulated in pursuit of all those depraved, self-seeking impulses that mark his fallen state. And the worst of such laughers, in Steele's description (ironically, in view of the strategem he adopts in his letter to Swift), are the 'kind of *Grinners*' called by the Ancients '*Megarics*', and by the Moderns 'Snearers'.

> These always indulge their Mirth at the Expence of their Friends, and all their Ridicule consists in unseasonable Ill-nature. I could wish these Laughers would consider, that let 'em do what they can, there is no laughing away their own Follies by laughing at other People's.

A sense of serious unease, then, underlies Steele's treatment of laughter in *Guardian* 29 (a sense that may be found, too, in many other eighteenth-century discussions of laughter and of such associated topics as raillery, ridicule, humour, wit and satire[15]). His general assumptions are not borne out by the evidence. The 'inward Satisfaction' of which laughter is 'a visible Symptom' usually means not that 'we may believe the Face' but quite the opposite. Inward satisfaction is so often achieved at the expense of others, securing their admiration or accomplishing their discomfiture, that we should instinctively mistrust the face that wears a laugh. Steele's examples, flippant though his tone may be, quite demolish his case for the benevolence of laughter.

In a later essay, *Guardian* 72 (published 3 June, 1713, only a week after the final exchange of letters with Swift), Steele makes an attempt to locate the period of laughter's degeneracy in the reign of Charles II. He had already made a suggestion to this effect in an earlier *Spectator* paper, written in September 1711,[16] on the subject of 'Wenching'. Corresponding as an anonymous 'Man of Pleasure about Town', then imprisoned in the Round-house 'for Theft when I designed only Fornication', Steele asserts:

> The World is so altered of late Years, that there was not a Man who would knock down a Watchman in my Behalf, but I was

carried off with as much Triumph as if I had been a Pick-pocket. At this Rate there is an End of all the Wit and Humour in the World. . . . If Fornication is to be scandalous, half the fine Things that have been Writ by most of the Wits of the last Age may be burnt by the common Hangman.

It was not an unusual opinion. In a later *Spectator*,[17] occupying the serious Saturday slot for 1 November, 1712, John Hughes (dismissed by Swift in 1735 as 'among the *mediocribus* in Prose as well as Verse'[18]) elaborates on the subject. The *Spectator* has been accused, he says, of 'attempting to make a Revolution in the World of Gallantry, and that the Consequence of it will be, that a great deal of the sprightliest Wit and Satyr of the last Age will be lost'. It has, he confesses, 'been my Ambition, in the Course of my Writings, to restore, as well as I was able, the proper Ideas of Things', and he takes the opportunity to launch into a detailed attack upon the values of 'the last Age'.

Indeed if I may speak my Opinion of great part of the Writings which once prevailed among us under the Notion of Humour, they are such as would tempt one to think there had been an Association among the Wits of those Times to rally Legitimacy out of our Island. A State of Wedlock was the common Mark for all the Adventurers in Farce and Comedy, as well as the Essayers in Lampoon and Satyr, to shoot at; and nothing was a more standing Jest in all Clubs of fashionable Mirth and gay Conversation. It was determined among those airy Criticks, that the Appellation of a *Sober Man* should signifie a *Spiritless Fellow*. And I am apt to think it was about the same time, that *Good-nature*, a Word so peculiarly elegant in our Language, that some have affirmed it cannot well be expressed in any other, came first to be rendered Suspicious, and in danger of being transferred from its original Sense, to so distant an Idea as that of *Folly*.

Hughes sets against such values 'the wise *Benevolus*' who converses with 'good Sense and good Humour among all his Friends' and whose 'Satisfaction' at home 'settles in to an habitual Complacency, which shines in his Countenance, enlivens his Wit, and seasons his Conversation'.

In *Guardian* 72, Steele, writing as the aged Nestor Ironside (born, as he relates in *Guardian* 2, in 1642, and admitted to '*Magdalen-Hall* in *Oxford*' at sixteen), claims actually to have witnessed the degeneracy of laughter. He has heard from Oxford of a forthcoming '*Publick ACT*' in which a '*Terra-filius* . . . is to lash and sting all the World in a Satyrical Speech'. Ironside declares that the university should not permit such a thing, and recalls his own time there when

> a *Terra-filius* contented himself with being bitter upon the Pope, or chastising the *Turk*; and raised a serious and manly Mirth, and adapted to the Dignity of his Auditory, by exposing the false Reasoning of the Heretick, or ridiculing the clumsie Pretenders to Genius and Politeness.

The wit that flourished under the restored monarchy, however, raised mirth that was neither serious nor manly.

> In the jovial Reign of King *Charles* the Second, wherein never did more Wit or more Ribaldry abound, the Fashion of being arch upon all that was Grave, and waggish upon the Ladies, crept into our Seats of Learning upon these Occasions. . . . It is to me amazing, that ever any Man bred up in the Knowledge of Virtue and Humanity, should so far cast off all Shame and Tenderness, as to stand up in the Face of Thousands, and utter such Contumelies as I have read and heard of. Let such an one know that he is making Fools merry, and wise Men sick; and that in the Eye of considering Persons, he hath less Compunction than the common Hangman, and less Shame than a Prostitute.

Steele, then, writing as a man thirty years his senior, places humour's age of innocence as lasting until the end of the Commonwealth. To laugh at such a time was to be aware of man's dignity as a rational creature capable of exercising judgment in matters of religion and society, fit to breathe the same air as Milton. The fallen laugh, however, demonstrates only the irresponsibility of the emptiness, shamelessness and self-regard of one capable of standing up 'in the Face of Thousands'. The laugh, at one time the sign of man's fitness for redemption, is now the measure of his irredeemable corruption. And Steele, making it 'the Business of this paper, to show how base and ungenerous it is to traduce the Women', may well have the Earl of Nottingham's daughter and the *Examiner* in mind, and behind them, of course, Swift.

The personality of Charles II and the character of his court are held up for blame by Hughes and Steele for the degenerate state of wit and humour, and this degeneracy goes some way to explain Steele's unease in dealing with the subject of laughter. If there was one man, however, whose influence produced profound unease not only in Steele but in almost every other examiner of laughter, it was Thomas Hobbes. Hobbes, through his remarks on laughter in particular, and his view of the nature of man and of society in general, haunts discussions of wit, humour, satire and associated subjects well on into the eighteenth century, from Addison, Steele and Shaftesbury, through Francis Hutcheson's *Reflections upon Laughter*, first published in 1728 (though not collected until 1750), and Anthony Collins' *Discourse concerning Ridicule and Irony in Writing* in 1729, to Corbyn Morris' 1744 *Essay Towards Fixing the True Standards of Wit, Humour, Raillery, Satire, and Ridicule*, and beyond. Hobbes made it impossible to touch upon the subject of laughter without making some attempt to come to terms with him.[19]

Hobbes, says Swift, 'clearly proves that ev'ry Creature / Lives in a State of War by Nature'.[20] The laugh, after Hobbes, is one weapon in this war. And Swift also remarks, in the *Discourse Concerning the Mechanical Operation of the Spirit*, that

> it is the Opinion of Choice *Virtuosi*, that the Brain is only a Crowd of little Animals, but with Teeth and Claws extremely sharp, and therefore, cling together in the Contexture we behold, like the Picture of *Hobbes*'s *Leviathan*, or like Bees in perpendicular swarm upon a Tree, or like a Carrion corrupted into Vermin, still preserving the Shape and Figure of the Mother Animal. (*Tale of a Tub*, p.277)

Man, after Hobbes, still clings to his fellow to preserve the 'Shape and Figure' of the Commonwealth, but as he does so he receives and inflicts constant pain from the 'Teeth and Claws' of his nature. Animals, as Rochester writes,

> With Teeth and Claws by Nature Arm'd, they hunt
> Nature's Allowance, to supply their Want;
> But man, with Smiles, Embraces, Friendships praise
> Unhumanly his Fellows Life betrays.[21]

The laugh, after Hobbes, measures the amount of pain inflicted, imposing as it does so a spurious impression of jovial unity.

What Hobbes has to say on the subject of laughter is mainly contained in chapter VI of *Leviathan*, 'Of the Interior Beginnings of Voluntary Motions, commonly called the Passions; and the Speeches by which they are expressed', though reworked from his earlier *Elements of Law*, part 1, chapter 9, 'Of the passions of the mind'.[22] His remarks in *Leviathan*, however, are surprisingly brief.

> *Sudden glory*, is the passion which maketh those *grimaces* called LAUGHTER; and is caused either by some sudden act of their own, that pleaseth them; or by the apprehension of some deformed thing in another, by comparison whereof they suddenly applaud themselves. And it is incident to most of them, that are conscious of the fewest abilities in themselves; who are forced to keep themselves in their own favour, by observing the imperfections of other men. And therefore much laughter at the defects of others, is a sign of pusillanimity. For of great minds, one of the proper works is, to help and free others from scorn; and compare themselves only with the most able.[23]

He devotes more space to the subject in *Elements of Law*, calling laughter 'a passion which hath no name' and referring not to its '*grimaces*' but to 'distortion of the countenance'. He denies that the 'joy' and 'triumph' of laughter arise from wit, 'for men laugh at mischances and indecencies, wherein there lieth no wit or jest at all'. We do not, however, laugh 'when a jest is broken upon ourselves, or friends of whose dishonour we participate', though 'men laugh at the follies of themselves past, when they come suddenly to remembrance, except they bring with them any present dishonour'. Hobbes considers, too, something of the mechanics of group laughter, starting with the man who is laughed at.

It is no wonder therefore that men take it heinously to be laughed at or derided, that is, triumphed over. Laughter without offence, must be at absurdities and infirmities abstracted from persons, and where all the company may laugh together. For laughing to one's self putteth all the rest to a jealousy and examination of themselves.[24]

Man, here, is a creature trapped not only in the 'passions of the mind' but, as a consequence, also in a perpetual present. His self-esteem is so fragile that he must be permanently alert lest it be shattered by some unlooked-for stimulus to self-examination. Remembering 'suddenly' himself past can only be tolerated when it brings enjoyment with no fear of 'present dishonour'. As to the future, as Hobbes had already argued in chapter 4, this is frequently seen in terms of present appetite, 'the appetite of them, who, having a conception of the end, have next unto it a conception of the next means to that end'.[25] The 'end' chosen as an example is 'honour', one measure of which, we may conclude, is to avoid being laughed at.

The Elements of Law, as M. M. Goldsmith explains in his introduction to the Tönnies edition, was printed in 1649 and 1650 in a corrupt edition, from which the copy for the 1750 *Works* was taken.[26] The discussion of laughter in *De Homine*, published in Latin in 1658, adds only a little to earlier versions, including the introduction of the 'stranger'. The passion of laughter arises 'from any word, deed or thought of one's own that is seemly, or of a stranger that is unseemly'.[27] The phrase 'sudden glory' has been replaced by 'sudden self-commendation resulting from a stranger's unseemliness'. Therefore, concludes Hobbes, 'there are three things conjoined that move one to laughter: unseemliness, strangers and suddenness'.

These two works are helpful in providing amplification of Hobbes' views on laughter, but it was by *Leviathan* that he was principally influential, and it was against the view of man expressed in *Leviathan* that later writers such as Shaftesbury and Hutcheson argued. The brevity of the *'Sudden glory'* passage, if anything, adds to its disparaging assessment of man. The softening edges of the longer versions are sharpened, extenuating material, like the admission that men may laugh at 'themselves past', is excised. Man, the laughing animal, stands out stark and completely self-centred, his inner nature suddenly revealed in the 'grimaces' distorting his countenance. Yet it is not only what Hobbes had to say on laughter that so disturbed later writers on the subject. Man the laugher was only a small part of man 'in a State of War by Nature'. The terms Hobbes uses in discussing laughter are pointed by his use of them elsewhere in *Leviathan*, and his opinions make far more damaging sense when taken in the context of his overall analysis of mankind.

'Glory', for example, is defined shortly before Hobbes turns to laughter, and is given in both its true and its false, or 'vain', aspects.

> *Joy*, arising from imagination of a man's own power and ability, is that exultation of the mind which is called GLORYING: which if grounded upon the experience of his own former actions, is the same with *confidence*: but if grounded on the flattery of others; or only supposed by himself, for delight in the consequences of it, is called VAIN-GLORY.[28]

Similarly 'pusillanimity' is '*Desire* of things that conduce but a little to our ends, and fear of things that are but of little hindrance'.[29] Even 'sudden' is used when describing anger as 'Sudden courage', that false courage apparently distinguishable from the true by its moving without consideration of any likely 'hope of avoiding . . . hurt by resistance'.[30] Opposed to laughter, we have '*sudden dejection*', which is 'the passion that causeth WEEPING; and is caused by such accidents, as suddenly take away some vehement hope, or some prop of their power: and they are most subject to it, that rely principally on helps external, such as women, and children'.[31]

The crucial factor, though, underlying all of Hobbes' remarks on the various characteristics of the passions is man's inescapable appetite for power, that 'general inclination of all mankind, a perpetual and restless desire of power after power, that ceaseth only in death'.[32] Glory and laughter proceed from the sudden affirmation of power, weeping from sudden disappointment of it. And just as laughter only has meaning in the context of public interaction, so power is properly measured only in terms of society, as Hobbes makes quite clear in chapter X, 'Of Power, Worth, Dignity, Honour, and Worthiness'.

> The *value*, or WORTH of a man, is as of all other things, his price; that is to say, so much as would be given for the use of his power: and therefore is not absolute; but a thing dependant on the need and judgment of another. . . . And as in other things, so in men, not the seller, but the buyer determines the price. For let a man, as most men do, rate themselves at the highest value they can; yet their true value is no more than it is esteemed by others.[33]

To be laughed at – or, as Steele knew, to be put in fear of it – is one way of knowing how far one is valued by others. Market forces, then, govern what is considered to be of worth, or honourable. Nothing can be taken as 'absolute'. And when we recall that each individual 'buyer' is himself governed entirely by appetite, we realize the true horror of Hobbes' vision for those of his successors who would see man as a creature capable of benevolence, and the laugh as a sign of a fundamentally good rather than ill nature. For Hobbes is quite unequivocal on values.

> But whatsoever is the object of any man's appetite or desire, that is it which he for his part calleth *good*: and the object of his hate and aversion, *evil*: and of his contempt, *vile* and *inconsiderable*. For these words of good, evil and contemptible, are ever used with relation to the person that useth them: there being nothing simply and absolutely so; nor any common rule of good and evil, to be taken from the nature of the objects themselves.

Moreover, 'because the constitution of a man's body is in continual mutation, it is impossible that all the same things should always cause in him the same appetites, and aversions: much less can all men consent, in the desire of almost any one and the same object'.[34] In this context, to be laughed at is to experience the unpleasant truth of a sudden mutual agreement among one's fellows on an object of aversion.

There is one further aspect of Hobbes' analysis of man to be noted here, and that is to be found in chapter VIII, 'Of the

Virtues, commonly called Intellectual; and their contrary Defects', where he turns his attention to madness. Madness, for Hobbes, arises from some 'extraordinary and extravagant passion', but the passions he goes on to cite are precisely those he has brought together in his remarks on laughter, or has associated with laughter through careful placing of his terms: glory, self-commendation and dejection.

> The passion, whose violence, or continuance, maketh madness, is either great *vain-glory*; which is commonly called *pride*, and *self-conceit*; or great *dejection* of mind.[35]

Again, the underlying factor is man's appetite for power, expressed either with the certainty of 'some man in Bedlam' who 'should tell you, he were God the Father', or with the excessive anger of one who is denying the knowledge that his power is uncertain or non-existent. So, 'Pride subjecteth a man to anger, the excess whereof, is the madness called RAGE and FURY', such as 'excessive desire of revenge', 'excessive love, with jealousy', 'excessive opinion of a man's own self, for divine inspiration, for wisdom', and 'vehement opinion of the truth of any thing, contradicted by others'. The contrary condition, dejection, which Hobbes has already defined as being 'caused by such accidents, as suddenly take away some vehement hope, or some prop of their power', he now aligns with pusillanimity in that it 'subjects a man to causeless fears; which is a madness, commonly called MELANCHOLY'.[36]

The laugh, then, in the form Hobbes' discussion of it takes, already suggests the terms of the madness which arises from some excess in our normal passions. We may laugh in 'sudden glory', but our very laughter betrays the vanity of that glory, our little triumph is evidence of our genuine pusillanimity. Madness and melancholy beckon whenever we show our teeth, distort our countenances in 'those' *grimaces* called LAUGHTER'. And the laugh traditionally attributed to the madman is laughter at its most raw, for the madman laughs at everything and nothing, affirming no sudden sense of superiority, yet laughing still as if superior to all the world. Excluded from society, he laughs at that very society which has denied his estimate of himself, has persecuted and humiliated him. He laughs to scorn society's values, as if they are mad as he is. But in laughing he seems, too, to set at nothing his own miserable condition. He is no longer in himself, but laughing with society at his own antics and delusions, at the self which has been humiliated, persecuted and denied. His laugh is an act of judgment both of society and of himself, and yet his judgment is worth nothing, for he is mad.

Shaftesbury, one of the major thinkers writing in the shadow of Hobbes, comes close to conceding the case on such disturbing associations to laughter when, in his *Essay on the Freedom of Wit and Humour*, first published in 1709, he describes 'those grave gentlemen' who would write against the use of raillery and 'at the same time have upon every turn made use of that weapon'. There is nothing so ridiculous, he says, 'as this Janus-face of writers, who with one countenance force a smile, and with another show nothing beside rage and fury'. He continues, alluding to the laughter and tears that are so close that they are virtually meaningless, that affirm and deny everything and nothing. He is referring, through, not to madmen but to children. These writers, says Shaftesbury, are like

> an executioner and a merry-Andrew acting their part upon the same stage. . . . They are no more masters of gravity than they are of good-humour. The first always runs into harsh severity, and the latter into an awkward buffoonery. And thus between anger and pleasure, zeal and drollery, their writing has much such a grace as the play of humorsome children, who, at the same instant, are both peevish and wanton, and can laugh and cry almost in one and the same breath.[37]

There is no sense of unease, however, in Shaftesbury at this uneasy proximity. The 'monstrous' products of the 'jumbled' brains of such writers, in fact, are so 'ridiculous to the world' that they are themselves fit objects for laughter.[38] And the 'zealous gentlemen' who might in their turn rail at Shaftesbury himself, far from being 'terrible', are actually as comical as 'those grotesque figures and dragon-faces, which are seen often in the frontispiece and on the corner-stones of old buildings'. They, 'with all their grimace', are both 'harmless' and 'useless', serving only for 'pleasantry and farce' and making 'the highest ridicule'.[39]

Shaftesbury alludes to much that is Hobbesian in the laugh – the Janus-face, executioner and jester on the same stage, the grotesque grimace that is a source of pleasure – but his clear intention in the treatise is to recommend wit and humour, and in so doing to strip the laugh of its post-*Leviathan* accumulations. 'Good-humour', as he declares at the beginning of his *Letter Concerning Enthusiasm*, 'is not only the best security against enthusiasm, but the best foundation of piety and true religion', for 'Nothing beside ill-humour, either natural or forced, can bring a man to think seriously that the world is governed by any devilish or malicious power.' Ill-humour may even 'be the cause of atheism'.[40] Shaftesbury acknowledges in his *Essay* that he is disturbed by 'that gross sort of raillery which is so offensive in good company'. This he regards as 'the most scurrilous buffoonery'. However, true 'freedom of conversation' will banish this species of humour.[41] Similarly, 'We have seen in our own time the decline and ruin of a false sort of wit, which so much delighted our ancestors', the quibble and the pun. 'All politeness', he says, 'is owing to liberty', and so 'wit will mend upon our hands, and humour will refine itself, if we take care not to tamper with it, and bring it under constraint, by severe usage and rigorous prescriptions'. And he moves to a conclusion on the workings of social intercourse that is diametrically opposed to Hobbes' view of group humour.

> We polish one another, and rub off our corners and rough sides by a sort of amicable collision. To restrain this, is inevitably to bring a rust upon men's understandings. 'Tis a destroying of civility, good breeding, and even charity itself, under pretence of maintaining it.[42]

What for Hobbes was an occasion of potential offence, of jealously guarded self-esteem and anxious seeking for signs of personal superiority, becomes for Shaftesbury the means by which understanding is kept bright and the civilized values advanced.

Shaftesbury would have some restrictions placed upon the freedom of public intercourse, however. 'Common society' is to be respected, which means that nothing should give occasion for 'scandal or disturbance'. In particular, 'The public is not, on any account, to be laughed at to its face; nor so reprehended for its follies as to make it think itself contemned.'[43] We must 'learn to temper and regulate that humour which nature has given us as a more lenitive remedy against vice, and a kind of specific against superstition and melancholy delusion'. There is proper and improper laughter, and 'a great difference between seeking how to raise a laugh from everything, and seeking in everything what justly may be laughed at'. Fortunately, however, it is apparently very simple to tell what is and is not a fit subject for laughter, 'For nothing is ridiculous except what is deformed, nor is anything proof against raillery except what is handsome and just.'[44] There are, he argues, ingredients such as bravery, generosity and temperance which go to 'make up a virtuous character', and those such as cowardice, avarice and gluttony which make a vicious one. One cannot laugh at both, for 'To laugh both ways is nonsensical.' Therefore 'One may defy the world to turn real bravery or generosity into ridicule', and only 'the grossest and most contemptible of mankind' would make 'an unaffected temperance' the subject of contempt. In this way laughter may be seen as proper or improper, genuine or itself ridiculous and therefore false, for 'A man must be soundly ridiculous who, with all the wit imaginable, would go about to ridicule wisdom, or laugh at honesty, or good manners.'[45]

With such arguments up his sleeve, Shaftesbury can deny the 'common saying, that interest governs the world', and is able to scorn those 'modern projectors' who, like Hobbes, 'would new-frame the human heart, and have a mighty fancy to reduce all its motions, balances, and weights, to that one principle and foundation of a cool and deliberate selfishness'.[46] Shaftesbury and the 'friend' he addresses 'can laugh at such maxims as these' and 'divert' themselves 'with the improved selfishness and philosophical cowardice of these fashionable moralists'.[47] And here we see actually operating in the treatise the truth-test which Shaftesbury had proposed at the very outset of his letter. Speaking of the validity or otherwise of opinions, he attempts to distinguish between 'sacred truths' and 'monsters'. We may be imposed upon, he says, by spectres,

> whilst we refuse to turn them every way, and view their shapes and complexions in every light. For that which can be shown only in a certain light is questionable. Truth, 'tis supposed, may bear all lights; and one of those principal lights, or

natural mediums, by which things are to be viewed, in order
to a thorough recognition, is ridicule itself, or that manner of
proof by which we discern whatever is liable to just raillery in
any subject.[48]

The laughter of Shaftesbury and his 'friend', then, at these
'modern projectors' is itself proof of how ridiculous their
arguments in favour of 'deliberate selfishness' are. The case put
forward by Hobbes and others may be highly plausible until it is
looked at with good humour, when it immediately becomes
laughable, and therefore nonsense. Similarly, Shaftesbury
himself ends his treatise by declaring that he has 'taken the
liberty... to laugh upon some occasions'. He expects to have
his own truth-test applied to his work, and 'if I have either
laughed wrong, or been impertinently serious, I can be content to
be laughed at in my turn'.[49]

Mutual laughing, the laugher laughed at, however, is also
part of the truth-test. At the opening of Part II of the *Essay*,
Shaftesbury imagines an Ethiopian suddenly transported to
Paris or Venice at carnival time 'when the general face of
mankind was disguised, and almost every creature wore a mask'.
Unused to such fantastic behaviour, the Ethiopian would
probably 'for some time be at a stand, before he discovered the
cheat'. He would not at first understand how a whole people
could 'make it a solemn practice to impose on one another, by
this universal confusion of characters and persons'. Lack of
understanding, however, would soon give way to laughter.

> Though he might at first perhaps have looked on this with a
> serious eye, it would be hardly possible for him to hold his
> countenance when he had perceived what was carrying on.
> The Europeans, on their side, might laugh perhaps at this
> simplicity. But our Ethiopian would certainly laugh with
> better reason. 'Tis easy to see which of the two would be
> ridiculous. For he who laughs and is himself ridiculous, bears a
> double share of ridicule.

Social conventions and assumptions may blind us to what is
truly ridiculous, may blind us even to the perception of what is
ridiculous in our behaviour by a more clear-sighted observer,
whom we repay for his clear-sightedness by ridicule. Here it is

obviously the laugh of the Europeans that qualifies as the false or improper laugh, the laugh based upon nonsense, while the Ethiopian laughs 'with better reason' for his judgment. Shaftesbury does not leave it here, however, but continues the argument.

> However, should it so happen that in the transport of ridicule, our Ethiopian, having his head still running upon masks, and knowing nothing of the fair complexion and common dress of Europeans, should upon the sight of a natural face and habit, laugh just as heartily as before, would not he in his turn become ridiculous, by carrying the jest too far; when by a silly presumption he took nature for mere art, and mistook perhaps a man of sobriety and sense for one of those ridiculous mummers?[50]

Shaftesbury's main interest in his subsequent discussion of this example is in distinguishing between 'the face of Truth' and 'all the counterfeit vizards which have been put upon her'.[51] What is intriguing, however, is the prospect of increasingly proper grounds for ridicule by which each justifiable laugher is himself more justifiably laughed at. Each frame of judgment, while perfectly adequate in the circumstance which gives rise to the laugh, is itself rendered inadequate when placed in the context of a wider frame and a more expansive laugh. We cannot with conviction conclude that the 'man of sobriety and sense' will laugh at the Ethiopian – he may even mistake him for a mummer. His 'sense', however, will itself be placed, sooner or later, and justifiably laughed at by some contemporary Democritus, feeding 'th' eternal jest'.[52] Our laughter may be a sign of our godlike vision, our freedom from the short-sightedness and narrow-mindedness of our fellows. It may also be the object of someone else's laughter.

We do not need to accept Shaftesbury's rather easy arguments on the reliability of man's good nature, his ability to perceive the distinction between the true and the ridiculous, to see that his case depends upon the rejection of virtually everything that Hobbes had to say on the nature of man. Even the form of Shaftesbury's work, 'In A Letter to a Friend', and the written style that this necessarily imposes, stands as a denial of the clinical 'Matter, Forme and Power of A Commonwealth

Ecclesiastical and Civil' with its unrelentingly analytical prose. Where Hobbes had insisted upon the laugh as both sign and instrument of man's ultimately self-interested nature, Shaftesbury treats mankind as capable of folly but equally capable of seeing the light of divine benevolence. The laugh, in the context of Shaftesbury's work, is a signal not of condemnation for the human race but of optimism. Followers of Shaftesbury, too, shared his antipathy for the Hobbesian and his approval of the redefined laugh. For Francis Hutcheson, our ability to laugh is a mark of God's favour on fallen mankind, for the implanting of 'a sense of the ridiculous, in our nature, was giving us an avenue to pleasure, and an easy remedy for discontent and sorrow'. Moreover, laughter is 'very contagious' so that 'one merry countenance may diffuse chearfulness to many'.[53] And Anthony Collins, in his *Discourse concerning Ridicule and Irony in Writing*, argues for the importance of mockery in matters of religion, where men's opinions and practices 'are generally so absurd and ridiculous'. The laughter aroused will remove from men's minds 'all bigotry contracted by ignorance and an evil education, all peevishness, hatred, and ill-nature towards one another, on account of different sentiments in religion' and will 'form in them the natural principles of moderation, humanity, affection and friendship'.[54] The laugh, it would seem, is truly Janus-faced, encapsulating on one side all the inevitable vices of our fallen nature, and on the other expressing and aiding all the virtues towards which redeemable man may aspire.

Within the context of such differing views of the nature of man, and of such opposing interpretations of man's capacity for genuinely disinterested judgment, the satirist, whose very existence depends upon the arousing of laughter, or something very like it, clearly finds himself in a dilemma. Satire demands, with Shaftesbury, that man should be ultimately redeemable, otherwise the entire moral basis of the satiric stance is demolished. The satirist becomes, in that case, a creature operating from motives of envy and spite, and is consequently as corrupt and damnable as his victims and his readers. The satirist has no alternative but to assume readers capable of making moral judgments, even if he has to lead them carefully to such judgments by means of laughter. And yet the legacy of Hobbes lays the laugh open to profoundly disturbing questions, and

ones which Shaftesbury comes nowhere near facing. After
Hobbes, does not the satirist's invitation to laugh merely mean
an invitation to express and indulge all the most vicious and self-
interested instincts of human nature?

Paul Elkin, in his invaluable book *The Augustan Defence of
Satire*, draws on a wide range of contemporary treatises and
pamphlets as he explores the various threads of the early
eighteenth-century debate on the nature of satire. Critics such
as Corbyn Morris, says Elkin, in preferring Shakespeare's '*Joy,
Frolic* and *Happiness*' to Ben Jonson's exposure and ridicule of
folly and vice, were asking for 'comedy without satire' and
'laughter free of any tincture of contempt'.[55] Dryden was
anxious to consider the feelings of those laughed at, who should
ideally enjoy the joke as much as anyone. And on the nature of
the laugh itself, Elkin observes:

> Addison and Hutcheson and certain other critics, such as
> Anthony Collins, succeeded in establishing a distinction
> between two sorts of laughter, the comic and the satiric,
> between 'innocent' laughter, on the one hand, and 'judicial' or
> 'derisive' laughter, on the other; and the opponents of satire
> used this destinction to express their distaste for ridicule in all
> its manifestations.[56]

To be content with drawing such a distinction, however, is to
dodge the issue, and still leaves the reader to decide the nature of
his laughter at the clearly satiric works of major writers like
Swift and Pope, as well as the political satires of Steele and, to a
lesser extent, of Addison himself in, for example, *The Tatler*.
Once we have stripped away comic or 'innocent' laughter at one
side, and personal ridicule, or 'rationalized spite',[57] at the other,
we are still left with a daunting mass of work, plainly satiric,
undeniably important, and quite clearly demanding a response in
which laughter is expected to be a prominent feature.

One significant work which does attempt to face the issue of the
nature of satire, and within that broad field the fundamental
question of what we are doing when we laugh at certain things, is
Dryden's *Discourse concerning the Original and Progress of
Satire*. From the very opening of the *Discourse*, the paragraphs
of dedication 'To The Right Honourable Charles, Earl of
Dorset and Middlesex', Dryden is clear that mankind, at least in

certain shining examples, is capable of the highest standards of judgment and benevolence. While the form, of course, and much of the content of his address to Dorset is dictated by convention, Dryden does direct his encomium in a way that is particularly appropriate not only to satire but to a well-defined view of satire. Dorset, generous to all is beloved of all, second to none living is nevertheless envied by none. But Dorset also displays those very qualities of honesty and sympathy in judgment which, as we may infer from the body of the discourse, the ideal satirist would wish to find in his ideal reader.

> Good sense and good nature, are never separated, though the ignorant world has thought otherwise. Good nature, by which I mean beneficence and candour, is the product of right reason which of necessity will give allowance to the failings of others, by considering that there is nothing perfect in mankind; and by distinguishing that which comes nearest to excellency, though not absolutely free from faults, will certainly produce a candour in the judge.[58]

Moreover, with even one isolated example of the perfection human nature can achieve set before our eyes so early, Dryden makes it impossible for himself to follow the Hobbesian view of mankind or of society, or to endorse the implications of that view for the nature of satire. He can speak of 'the ignorant world', but for the moment the thoughts of the ignorant are kept safely different in kind, removed to the realms of 'otherwise'. The 'beneficence and candour' of right-reasoning men like Dorset, however, allow these 'others' to be judged as wrong yet forgiven as human. And these qualities are, says Dryden, what has made Dorset's own satires so 'inimitable', themselves supreme examples of ideal satire.

> There is much more of salt in all your verses, than I have seen in any of the Moderns, or even of the Ancients. But you have been sparing of the gall; by which means you have pleased all readers, and offended none.[59]

Much of what Dryden has to say about the nature of satire in the discourse expands on the terms he has used in the flattery of Dorset – salt and gall, pleasure and offence. In particular, as he discusses the work of various classical satirists who preceded Horace and Juvenal, he wants to know their intended effect upon their readers. Did they wish primarily to entertain or to instruct? Were they seeking to arouse laughter or thought? Of Varro, for example, he quotes 'Tully himself' as observing:

> And you yourself have composed a most elegant and complete poem; you have begun philosophy in many places: sufficient to incite us, though too little to instruct us.

Varro, concludes Dryden, was therefore 'studious of laughter; and that, learned as he was, his business was more to divert his reader than to teach him'. The laughter he aroused owed something to his model, Menippus, but 'avoids his impudence and filthiness, and only expresses his witty pleasantry'.[60] Andronicus, on the other hand, Dryden speculates, 'expressed the way of Aristophanes, Eupolis, and the rest, which was to call some persons by their own names, and to expose their defects to the laughter of the people'.[61] (The people, adds Dryden, 'ran in crowds to these new entertainments'.[62]) Persius, however (and here Dryden is paraphrasing Casaubon), 'was not good at turning things into a pleasant ridicule, or in other words, . . . he was not a laughable writer'.[63] Being unable, therefore, to 'laugh with a becoming grace', it is 'moral doctrine' that we find first and foremost in the satires of Persius. Admirers such as Casaubon demote 'well-mannered wit' and elevate 'the scourging of vice, and exhortation to virtue' as 'the very soul' of satire, which, being 'of the nature of moral philosophy; as being instructive: he therefore, who instructs most usefully, will carry the palm'.[64] Dryden concludes:

> There is a spirit of sincerity in all he says. You may easily discern that he is in earnest, and is persuaded of that truth which he inculcates. In this I am of opinion, that he excels Horace, who is commonly in jest, and laughs while he instructs; and is equal to Juvenal, who was as honest and serious as Persius, and more he could not be.[65]

This most fundamental issue, the debate about what satire should be doing, underlies Dryden's attempt to distinguish between and evaluate the qualities of Horace and Juvenal. There is a distinction to be made, for example, in terms of satiric tone – whether we expect to laugh with the author or to be preached at by him.

> Juvenal exhorts to particular virtues, as they are opposed to those vices against which he declaims, but Horace laughs to shame all follies, and insinuates virtue rather by familiar examples than by the severity of precepts.[66]

There is a distinction, too, for Dryden, in terms of the reactions aroused in the reader. Horace, where he

> barely grins himself, and, as Scaliger says, only shows his white teeth, he cannot provoke me to any laughter. His urbanity, that is, his good manners, are to be commended, but his wit is faint, and his salt, if I may dare to say so, almost insipid. Juvenal is of a more vigorous and masculine wit, he gives me as much pleasure as I can bear. He fully satisfies my expectation, he treats his subject home. His spleen is raised, and he raises mine.[67]

In placing laughter and 'spleen' thus in competition as satiric responses, Dryden, at this stage in his argument, is clearly not ready to countenance the possibility of a genuine satire that would combine these two satisfactions, the laugh rendered malicious, or Hobbesian, by spleen, or spleen softened, made socially acceptable, by laughter. The laughter Horace would arouse is at objects insufficiently strong for the proper moral force of the satiric form. Only the full weight of spleen, in this competition, satisfies the emotional and moral demands of satire. So, while Horace is acknowledged as 'the more general philosopher', Juvenal is finally the greater satiric poet.

> His thoughts are sharper, his indignation against vice is more vehement; his spirit has more of the commonwealth genius; he treats tyranny, and all the vices attending it, as they deserve, with the utmost rigour, and consequently, a noble soul is better pleased with a zealous vindicator of Roman liberty, than with a temporizing poet, a well mannered court slave, and a man who is often afraid of laughing in the right place, who is never decent, because he is naturally servile.[68]

Dryden is aggressively decisive here, but such decisiveness belies the true pattern of his debate. In one light he has been more than careful to allow the merits of each poet. As Paul Elkin remarks, though, the *Discourse* demonstrates Dryden's 'vacillations and inconsistencies regarding the respective merits of Horace and Juvenal', a 'being in two minds' that was 'entirely representative of the period – that is, the period from Dryden to Johnson'.[69] Elkin goes on to cite a variety of eighteenth-century critics and satirists – Swift, Young, Steele, Dennis, Beattie and Johnson among others – who contributed to the Horace–Juvenal debate, usually declaring for Horace, but equally displaying, like Johnson, the surviving influence of Juvenal in their own work. What we have, in fact, is a profound uncertainty over the true nature of satire and the satiric response, an uncertainty that finds expression in the very need to present a competition in the first place, and, in Dryden's case, in his continual hedging and qualifying, his over anxiety to be scrupulously just to both competitors. That this uncertainty is rooted in a correspondingly profound unease over what happens when we laugh, is made clear by the direction the remainder of Dryden's *Discourse* takes.

What Dryden says he will go on to consider before ending his essay is 'somewhat of their particular manner belonging to all of them', to Horace, Juvenal and Persius.[70] Almost immediately, however, having awarded satiric pre-eminence to Juvenal, he turns to discussing the question of what we laugh at. And here Dryden is quick to fall back upon personal reactions. Having established that, while Horace is the more laughter-seeking writer, nevertheless 'Juvenal has railed more wittily than Horace has railed', Dryden continues:

> Horace means to make his reader laugh; but he is not sure of his experiment. Juvenal always intends to move your indignation; and he always brings about his purpose. Horace, for aught I know, might have tickled the people of his age; but amongst the Moderns he is not so successful.

Admirers of Horace's humour may, perhaps, 'see a jest farther off than other men' and 'may find occasion of laughter, in the wit-battle of the two buffoons, Sarmentus and Cicerrus, and hold their sides for fear of bursting, when Rupilius and Persius are scolding'. Dryden himself, however, 'cannot so much as smile at their insipid raillery'. He has heard better puns from 'honest Mr. Swan ... and yet have had the grace to hold my countenance'. For Dryden, laughter thus aroused is wholly distasteful, and though he is 'sorry to say it, for the sake of Horace', nevertheless 'he has no fine palate who can feed so heartily on garbage'.[71]

So far it would appear that Dryden is so uneasy in the act of laughing that he would wish to hold his countenance in the face of the strongest provocation. The objects that laughing satirists such as Horace hold up to us are mild, trivial, scarcely fit for satire at all, and 'of a lower nature'[72] than the subjects Juvenal has treated. Moreover, we cannot be 'sure' of Horace: a writer who sets out to make us laugh and frequently fails lays himself open to question. Not only do we doubt his sense of humour, but we may also begin to doubt his moral judgment, especially in comparison with one like Juvenal who, intending to move our indignation, always succeeds. Artistic certainty and moral trust go hand in hand. And yet Dryden, despite his thinly veiled contempt for the 'well mannered court slave' and the 'garbage' of laughter at unworthy objects, cannot bring himself to agree with 'that learned critic Barten Holyday' when he says that 'A perpetual grin, like that of Horace, rather angers than amends a man.' Rather, he moves straight from Holyday's remark to the most influential passage of the whole *Discourse*, and one which depends upon the manner not of instructors and declaimers like Persius and Juvenal but of the laughing Horace.

Significantly, Dryden begins this 'fine raillery' passage with a reminder to the reader of the addressee of the *Discourse*, Charles, Earl of Dorset.

Let the chastisements of Juvenal be never so necessary for his new kind of satire; let him declaim as wittily and sharply as he pleases, yet still the nicest and most delicate touches of satire consist in fine raillery. This, my Lord, is your particular talent, to which even Juvenal could not arrive.

That such a reminder is not merely a piece of bonus flattery is made clear by the following two sentences, so often omitted when this familiar passage is quoted.

'Tis not reading, 'tis not imitation of an author, which can produce this fineness. It must be inborn, it must proceed from a genius, and particular way of thinking, which is not to be taught; and therefore not to be imitated by him who has it not from nature.

Dryden is quite deliberately asking us to recall those qualities which at the very outset he took care to associate with Dorset: good sense and good nature, such as make for 'beneficence and candour' in judgment. These are the qualities which, for Dryden, are equally essential for the ideal satirist and his ideal reader. It is in the context of these qualities 'from nature' that 'fine raillery' is to be understood, for it is only by means of 'fine raillery' that Dryden will permit laughter as a valid satiric response. Only through the 'fine raillery' that is made possible by good sense and good nature can the laugh be rendered more significant than just a taste for 'garbage' and yet remain unpolluted by malice or bitterness. It is through 'fine raillery' that laughter and spleen may be combined in a single balanced response to proper satiric art.

How easy it is to call rogue and villain, and that wittily! But how hard to make a man appear a fool, a blockhead, or a knave, without using any of those opprobrious terms! To spare the grossness of the names, and to do the thing yet more severely, is to draw a full face, and to make the nose and cheeks stand out, and yet not to employ any depth of shadowing. This is the mastery of that noble trade, which yet no master can teach to his apprentice. He may give the rules, but the scholar is never the nearer in his practice. Neither is it true, that this fineness of raillery is offensive. A witty man is tickled while he is hurt in this manner; and a fool feels it not. The occasion of an offence may possibly be given, but he cannot take it. If it be granted that in effect this way does more mischief; that a man is secretly wounded, and though he be not sensible himself, yet the malicious world will find it for him; yet there is still a vast difference betwixt the slovenly butchering of a man, and the fineness of a stroke that separates the head from the body, and leaves it standing in its place.[73]

This, then, is Dryden's attempted solution to the dilemma of the nature of the satiric laugh – his attempt to have things both ways. We may laugh, but only if we are sure that we laugh from good nature, and at sufficiently serious objects, and that the victim of our laughter, far from being pained, is himself 'tickled' by the jest. Such a laugh is both the expression of our own good nature and the delighted recognition of the good nature of the satirist, who allows us to judge and sympathise in the same act. Yet the very need to judge is acknowledgement of the Hobbesian legacy, for in laughing the satiric laugh we recognise, too, the fallen nature of man, his capacity for ignorance and folly which the same laugh forgives. Whereas in Hobbes, however, the laugh is an expression of our own viciousness, here the laugh produced by 'fine raillery' is the redeemed laugh of a nature capable of 'right reason'.

Even as we read, though, we become aware that Dryden's solution will not do. It depends on the assumpion that there are not only ideal satirists and readers, like the Earl of Dorset, but ideal victims, too, whose own wittiness cannot let them take offence. That Dryden actually gives us an example of the ideal victim, 'Zimri in my *Absalom*', who 'was too witty to resent it as an injury',[74] is no reassurance. Not all victims are the Duke of Buckingham, just as all readers are not the Earl of Dorset and Middlesex. There is indeed 'nothing perfect in mankind', least of all its laughter, and Dryden himself, as he develops his 'fine raillery' ideal, begins to acknowledge that other pressures may intervene to spoil the fineness. The 'malicious world', those multitudes who are neither witty nor fools, will make sure that the victim feels his offence. The secret wound will not be allowed to stay secret. It may be necessary to grant 'that in effect this way does more mischief'. Dryden rushes on to make his celebrated distinction betwen 'slovenly butchering' and skilful decapitation, a proper and important distinction to make, but one having no logical connection with the admissions of the first part of his sentence. His triumphant 'yet there is still' does not complete 'If it be granted', though grammatically it would seem to. The satirist might reconcile himself to his killing trade by admiring the fineness of his own strokes – the victim might even seek consolation in being less slovenly butchered than he could have been. The satire itself, though, is still given to the 'ignorant', 'malicious' world to arouse its ignorant, malicious laughter. And how can the satirist know that in admiring his own skill he is not merely avoiding the recognition of his fundamentally ill nature? Is he not, perhaps, equally malicious as those 'others' of the world, but possessing the ability to make better jokes? Dryden evades such questions by addressing ideal satirist, citing ideal victim, but he has redeemed the satiric laugh only by denying the nature of laughter itself.

Writers and critics throughout the eighteenth century pick up this problem of the motives of the satirist. Pope, Ambrose Philips, Defoe, Bentley, Whitehead, Shenstone and Cowper among countless others[75] accuse the satirist of malice, envy, self-love, love of scandal and a perverted taste for nastiness of every kind, all concealed beneath a hypocritical cloak of public good. In the periodical essay, too, Addison and Steel return over and over again to the attack, keeping the matter well in the public eye. In *Spectator* 23, Addison is quite decisive on the subject of ill-natured and ill-directed satires.

> There is nothing that more betrays a base ungenerous Spirit than the giving of secret Stabs to a Man's Reputation. Lampoons and Satyrs, that are written with Wit and Spirit, are like poisoned Darts, which not only inflict a Wound, but make it incurable. For this Reason I am very much troubled when I see the Talents of Humour and Ridicule in the Possession of an ill-natured Man.

Such a man will find the greatest gratification in stirring up sorrow and exposing to derision while himself remaining 'unseen and undiscovered'. Moreover, if a witty and ill-natured man

> is vicious into the bargain, he is one of the most mischievous Creatures that can enter into a Civil Society. His Satyr will then chiefly fall upon those who ought to be the most exempt from it. Virtue, Merit, and every thing that is Praiseworthy, will be made the subject of Ridicule and Buffoonry.

There is nothing, he concludes, so pernicious as 'Wit, when it is not tempered with Virtue and Humanity', and it is 'infinitely more honourable to be a good-natured Man, than a Wit'. Writers of 'Libels and Lampoons' are described in *Spectator* 451, again by Addison, as a 'Race of Vermin, that are a Scandal to

Government, and a Reproach to Human Nature'. Even 'the finest Strokes of Satyr' that are 'aimed at particular Persons, and which are supported even with the Appearances of Truth' are 'the Marks of an evil Mind, and highly Criminal in themselves'. Such writers, says Addison, whose 'pernicious Arts' make us appear 'a Nation of Monsters', should be ranked 'with the Murderer and Assassin', and he cites with approval what 'we learn from a Fragment of *Cicero*, that tho' there were very few Capital Punishments in the twelve Tables, a Libel or Lampoon which took away the good Name of another, was to be punished by Death'.

It is Steele, however, in *Tatler* 242, who pronounces most fully on the question of the motives of the satirist, his design being 'to tell some Coxcombs that run about this Town with the Name of Smart Satirical Fellows, that they are by no means qualified for the Characters they pretend to, of being severe upon other Men, for they want Good-nature'. Personal spite, he argues, either as a consequence of having suffered injury, or as a result of simple ill nature, has no place in true raillery and satire. On the contrary, having reflected upon 'the great and excellent Persons that were admired for Talents in this Way', he has concluded with the at first sight 'unaccountable' assertion

> that Good-nature was an essential Quality in a Satirist, and that all the Sentiments which are beautiful in this Way of Writing must proceed from that Quality in the Author. Good-nature produces a Disdain of all Baseness, Vice and Folly, which prompts them to express themselves with Smartness against the Errors of Men, without Bitterness towards their Persons. This Quality keeps the Mind in Equanimity, and never lets an Offence unseasonably throw a Man out of his Character.

Only 'Backbiters assign their Descriptions to private Men', while it is the business of the satirist to 'describe the Age'. Whoever writes 'from personal Hatred or Passion' will be unable to make his cause 'the Cause of Mankind', but 'the Representations of a Good natured Man bear a Pleasantry in them, which shews there is no Malignity at Heart, and by Consequence are attended to by his Hearers or Readers, because they are unprejudiced'. To be regarded, Steele concludes, satire must be made 'the Concern of Society in general', for there is 'no possibility of succeeding in a Satirical Way of Writing or Speaking, except a Man throws himself quite out of the Question'.

Addison's and Steele's suspicion of the true motives of satirical writers extends, too, to their opinion of the readers of satires. A man of good sense and good nature may read a satire, even one apparently directed against himself, and react in a way that enhances, rather than diminishes, his dignity as a human being capable of redemption. In *Spectator* 355, Addison speaks of 'those who have detracted from my works, or spoken in Derogation of my Person'. He describes his conduct:

> when I hear of a Satyrical Speech or Writing that is aimed at me, I examine my own Heart, whether I deserve it or not. If I bring in a Verdict against my self, I endeavour to rectify my Conduct for the future in those Particulars which have drawn the Censure upon me; but if the whole Invective be grounded upon a Falshood, I trouble my self no further about it.

Other readers, though, whose characters are not the object of attack, should be equally vigilant in examining their responses to satirical writing. In such a reader, we may assume, a spurious impression of disinterestedness may blind him to the secret gratification these works afford his unacknowledged malicious nature. Addison, in *Spectator* 451, condemns those 'who take Pleasure in the reading and dispersing' of libels as 'very little short of the Guilt of the first Composers', and he goes on to quote 'the words of Monsieur *Bayle*, who was a Man of great Freedom of Thought, as well as of exquisite Learning and Judgment'. For Bayle, the taking of pleasure 'in the reading of a Defamatory Libel' is 'an heinous Sin in the Sight of God'. It is 'a Joy which we conceive from the Dishonour of the Person who is defamed'. Moreover,

> it is a Sign that we are not displeased with the Ill-nature of the Satyrist, but are glad to see him defame his Enemy by all kinds of Stories; and then we deserve the Punishment to which the Writer of Libel is subject . . . It is an uncontested Maxim, that they who approve an Action would certainly do it if they could; that is, if some Reason of Self-love did not hinder them.

To indulge in satiric laughter, then, may be to indulge many of the vices which characterise Hobbesian fallen mankind.

So strong a desire to regulate for the taking of pleasure, such inquiry for the true motives of both satirist and reader, together with a determined indifference to personal attack by those 'troublesome Insects' the 'common Fry of Scribblers'[76] (and we may here recall Pope's declared unconcern at the vermin who would aggravate his 'long Disease'), should not surprise us in a generation of writers who found themselves unable to come to terms with what it meant to laugh. We have seen in Steele, Shaftesbury and Dryden the evidence of unease in the act of laughing. It is perhaps in the opinions and example of Addison, however, that the conflict concerning the Janus face of laughter is most revealingly exposed, and particularly in his two early *Spectator* essays on the subject. In the first, No. 47, there is little evidence of conflict. Addison docilely follows the Hobbes line, even quoting the 'sudden Glory' passage from 'the best of all his Works', and adding:

> Thus every one diverts himself with some Person or other that is below him in Point of Understanding, and triumphs in the Superiority of his Genius, whilst he has such Objects of Derision before his Eyes.

Far from expressing concern at this unflattering view of human nature, however, Addison proceeds to discourse in a jocular manner, covering such topics as the keeping of fools, the describing of 'merry Drolls' in terms of some favoured dish – '*Pickled herrings*', '*Jack Puddings*' – and that 'little Triumph of the Understanding, under the Disguise of Laughter' that customarily prevails on April Fools' Day. There is no real disapproval even at the '*Biters*: a Race of Men that are perpetually employed in laughing at those Mistakes which are of their own Production'. Addison picks up the Hobbesian terms again when he refers to 'That secret Elation and Pride of Heart which is generally called Laughter', but nowhere does he use the clear, denunciatory language of, for example, his paper on satire and lampoons. It is as though he is content to accept, or has not considered the implications of, the Hobbesian account of laughter. To read *Spectator* 47 is to believe that all is innocent and easy in the world of eighteenth-century humour. Addison even concludes the essay by writing in praise of *'Butts'*, those 'particular sort of Men who are such Provokers of Mirth in Conversation, that it is impossible for a Club or Merry-meeting to subsist without them'. Men who might elsewhere be described as scapegoats, the most miserably excluded of mankind, are here only 'honest Gentlemen' who are 'exposed', 'pelted' and shot at. And the greatest *'Butt'* of all, Sir John Falstaff, is 'an Hero of this Species'. It is with Falstaff's lines that Addison concludes.

> *Men of all sorts* (says that merry Knight) *take a Pride to gird at me. The Brain of Man is not able to invent any thing that tends to Laughter more than I invent, or is invented on me. I am not only Witty in my self, but the Cause that Wit is in other Men.*

Such is not the case in *Spectator* 249. While in his third paragraph Addison does refer back to his earlier paper, reaffirming his agreement with Hobbes, the treatment of laughter is far from the facetious levity of *Spectator* 47. To begin with, he carefully singles man out as the only laughing creature, for 'all above and below him are serious'. This means that man 'sees things in a different light from other Beings, and finds his Mirth rising from Objects which perhaps cause something like Pity or Displeasure in higher Natures'. Such emphasis on laughter as a sign of the baseness of man's nature, his uniqueness amid an unfallen creation, together with his assertion two paragraphs later 'that Laughter was the Effect of Original Sin, and that *Adam* could not laugh before the Fall', makes it clear that Addison's opinions have hardened. Laughter is no longer a harmless, even a civilized diversion. Rather, he has taken the full implications of the Hobbesian views he had overlooked in the earlier paper. The consequence is that Addison, quite clearly, can no longer approve of laughter. At best it is to be defended as 'receiving Joy from what is no real Good to us', or relief from 'the Gloom which is apt to depress the Mind and damp our Spirits'. Its general character, though, is even less comfortable.

> Laughter, while it lasts, slackens and unbraces the Mind, weakens the Faculties, and causes a Kind of Remissness, and Dissolution in all the Powers of the Soul: And thus far it may be looked upon as a Weakness in the Composition of human Nature.

To expose others to laughter 'is the Qualification of little ungenerous Tempers', and one who does so 'cuts himself off from all manner of Improvement'. It is to be so blind to our own good that we seek to use a man's faults 'for the Sport of others' rather than observing his virtues 'for our own Improvement'. And Addison follows Hobbes to his 'fewest abilities' claim, declaring that 'Persons the most accomplished in Ridicule, are those who are very shrewd at hitting a Blot, without exerting any thing Masterly in themselves'. In fact, the uses to which laughter is put virtually cancel those few benefits Addison was prepared to grant it.

> If the Talent of Ridicule were employed to laugh Men out of Vice and Folly, it might be of some Use to the World; but instead of this, we find that it is generally made Use of to laugh Men out of Virtue and good Sense, by attacking every thing that is Solemn and Serious, Decent and Praise-worthy in human Life.

Only by imagining some golden age of laughter can Addison reconcile himself at all to so obvious a mark of man's degeneracy. He describes, to the detraction of the modern world, the laudable innocence of the Ancients.

> We may observe, that in the First Ages of the World, when the great Souls and Master-pieces of human Nature were produced, Men shined by a noble Simplicity of Behaviour, and were Strangers to those little Embellishments which are so fashionable in our present Conversation.

The Ancients excelled us in virtually every known art and science, but 'we excel them as much in Doggerel, Humour, Burlesque, and all the trivial Arts of Ridicule'. However, although it is used as further proof of modern culpability, Addison does seem to find his vision of a blameless golden age sufficiently inspiring to enable him to close his essay with a brief glimpse of an innocent, non-Hobbesian laughter. This, he makes clear, is how we 'naturally' regard laughter, stripped of the accretions of a debased modern civilization. To speak of such laughter, however, he has to resort to the evidence of metaphor.

I shall conclude this Essay upon Laughter with observing that the Metaphor of Laughing, applied to Fields and Meadows when they are in Flower, or to Trees when they are in Blossom, runs through all Languages.... This shews that we naturally regard Laughter, as what is both in it self amiable and beautiful.

He concludes by drawing, like Steele in *Guardian* 29, the dignity and authority of Milton to his side, quoting his 'very poetical Figure of Laughter', and thus leaving the reader with the safely remote world of 'L'Allegro' in his mind.

We find, then, in *Spectator* 249, what had been noticeably absent from No. 47, an awareness of the baseness of human nature that Hobbes' analysis of laughter must imply. Addison corrects the inconsistency of his earlier paper, not by retracting his agreement with Hobbes, but by turning against laughter itself, by observing it everywhere in the modern world as the expression of man's idleness and of his capacity for folly and viciousness. This diagnosis, however, is not one he can accept as universally true, and so we have the classical–pastoral–mirthical vision with which he ends the essay as evidence of the possibility of a laugh of pristine innocence.

Such laughter, though, is not to be found in the world of Addison and Steele, and nor is there a great deal of evidence for it in their periodical essays. Perhaps the most consistently joyful kind of laughter we are invited to witness and share is that which again and again is proposed against the free-thinkers, for such laughter becomes the assertion of a belief in a divine creation which they would deny. They are described, quite typically, at the opening of *Guardian* 27, the paper for Saturday, 11 April, 1713, as 'those gloomy Mortals, who by their Unbelief are rendered incapable of feeling those Impressions of Joy and Hope, which the Celebration of the late glorious Festival naturally leaves on the Mind of a Christian'. Their characteristic gloom is itself, according to *Tatler* 135, a fit object for laughter, for 'There is indeed nothing in the World so ridiculous as one of these grave Philosophical Free-Thinkers.' Having 'neither Passions nor Appetites', and 'no Heats of Blood nor Vigour of Constitution', such men are scarcely human, certainly not capable of the ordinary motions of human thought. A free-thinker 'has neither Wit, Gallantry, Mirth or Youth' but only 'a poor, joyless, uncomfortable Vanity of distinguishing himself from the rest of Mankind'. As such he is 'rather to be regarded as a mischievous Lunatick, than a mistaken Philosopher'. As the essay proceeds, it emerges that the free-thinker stands for all that is least admirable in mankind, his position representing human nature at its most fallen.

> These Apostates from Reason and good Sense, can look at the glorious Frame of Nature, without paying an Adoration to him that raised it; can consider the great Revolutions in the Universe, without lifting up their Minds to that superior Power which hath the Direction of it; can presume to censure the Deity in his Ways towards men; can level Mankind with the Beasts that perish; can extinguish in their own Minds all the pleasing Hopes of a future State, and lull themselves into a stupid Security against the Terrors of it.

In laughing such men to scorn, we are also asserting all those values which are denied by the free-thinkers' very existence. To laugh is not merely to enjoy the ridiculous, it is the duty of every redeemable human being. This laugh would approach Addison's ideal laugh, while the laugh of the free-thinker himself is the very opposite, the Hobbesian expression of man at his most ignorant and selfish. This laugh is described at the end of Addison's religious wax-work display in *Tatler* 257.

> Just opposite to this Row of Religions, there was a Statue dressed in a Fool's Coat, with a Cap of Bells upon his Head, laughing and pointing at the Figures that stood before him. This Ideot is supposed to say in his Heart, what *David*'s Fool did some Thousands of Years ago, and was therefore designed as a proper Representative of those among us who are called Atheists and Infidels by others, and Free-thinkers by themselves.

Laughter is proper, then, when its object is those men who at the same time exclude themselves from and deny the common hope of mankind. Similarly, the laugh at its most improper is expressed by the sound the free-thinker would make if such gloomy creatures could be conceived of as laughing. When Addison and Steele turn to the laughter they see going on around them, however, the matter is less clear cut. Here the range and kinds of laughing are enormous – Mrs Gatty, the successful toast, laughing at her lovers in *Tatler* 24; Humphry Slyboots, in No. 63, arguing against the good-natured Will. Truby that 'Risibility being the Effect of Reason' no man should laugh without it; Addison's description of the 'Immoral as well as Ridiculous' grinning matches in *Spectator* 173; the laughter, in *Guardian* 68, of the arrogant 'Town Lady' at her country neighbours 'to whom she her self is equally ridiculous'. Laughter is raised at Isaac Bickerstaff's expense when he meets 'the comical Actor', Tom Mirrour, in *Tatler* 51. Puzzled as to why 'all that sat near us laughed', Bickerstaff is told that Mirrour 'assumed your Air and Countenance so exactly, that all fell a laughing to see how little you knew yourself, and how much you were enamour'd with your own Image'. And in *Spectator* 468 Steele pays tribute to 'poor Dick Eastcourt', the comedian, who is praised for the kinds of laughter he raised.

> He had so exquisite a Discerning of what was defective in any Object before him, that in an Instant he could shew you the ridiculous Side of what would pass for beautiful and just, even to men of no ill Judgment, before he had pointed at the Failure. ... He had the Knack to raise up a pensive Temper, and mortifie an impertinently gay one, with the most agreeable Skill imaginable.

His talents made him an ideal figure in company, so 'qualified for Conversation' that he could 'keep the Discourse to himself ... and maintain his good Humour with a Countenance, in a Language so delightful, without Offence to any Person or Thing upon Earth'. We should spare, says Steele, 'one Gush of Tears for so many Bursts of Laughter'.

The place of the laugh in company is of particular significance in these essays, for, as *Guardian* 29 suggested, it is in company that a man's attitude to others and himself becomes clearest. The laugh, both proper and improper, can reveal, therefore, something of the true nature of our companions. Callisthenes, in Steele's *Spectator* 422, like Dick Eastcourt, combines wit and judgment, and so is able to rally 'the best of any Man I know, for he forms his Ridicule upon a Circumstance which you are in your Heart not unwilling to grant him, to wit, that you are

Guilty of an Excess in something which is in it self laudable'. He is a truly agreeable man, making 'his Friends enjoy themselves, rather than him, while he is in their Company'. Acetus, on the other hand, 'has no regard to the Modesty or Weakness of the Person he raillies' and 'can be pleased to see his best Friend out of Countenance, while the Laugh is loud in his own Applause'. The consequence is that

> His Raillery always puts the Company into little Divisions and separate Interests, while that of *Callisthenes* cements it, and makes every Man not only better pleased with himself, but also with all the rest in the Conversation . . . *Acetus* ought to be banished human Society, because he raises his Mirth upon giving Pain to the Person upon whom he is pleasant.

The laugh raised by Callisthenes, then, increases our estimation of human nature, denies the Hobbesian view of the way society works, while Acetus only confirms the laugh as an implement of destruction and selfishness.

> Nothing but the Malevolence, which is too general towards those who excell, could make his Company tolerated; but they, with whom he converses, are sure to see some Man sacrificed where he is admitted, and all the Credit he has for Wit is owing to the Gratification it gives to other Men's Ill-nature.

The laugh can save, but it can also kill, and what it can kill is our belief in the fellowship of mankind. To be laughed at, as Swift undoubtedly realised, is not merely to be the subject of a joke, of harmless diversion, but to be ruthlessly excluded from a fellowship that had only existed in one's own gullible imagination, and which now has a spurious vindictive unity at your expense alone. For Swift, too, Steele, the former friend delivering the blow, putting the doubt in his mind, was living proof of man's fundamental viciousness – as Steele must himself have been aware, if only from having been characterised by Swift as base, ungrateful and unjust. The good-natured man, the writer of papers intended to ensure that society did not operate in the way that Hobbes said it did, was willing, when under attack, to stand himself as the type of Hobbesian man. That

Swift's own satires have often been taken, both by contemporaries and ever since, as underlining with savage laughter man's fundamental viciousness, is one further entanglement in this perplexing debate: what do we do when we laugh? what do we do to others? what do we do to ourselves? Above all, what care can we observe in the art of the writer who would attempt to handle the laugh?

In *Tatler* 82 there is related an incident in which an engaged couple retired for a while to the groom's chamber shortly before the hour of their wedding. They indulged in 'a little fond Raillery on the Subject of their Courtship', after which

the Lover took up a Pistol, which he knew he had unloaded the Night before, and presenting it to her, said, with the most graceful Air, whilst she look'd pleased at his agreeable Flattery; Now, Madam, repent of all those Cruelties you have been guilty of to me; consider before you die, how often you have made a poor Wretch freeze under your Casement; you shall die, you Tyrant, you shall die, with all those Instruments of Death and Destruction about you, with that inchanting Smile, those killing Ringlets of your Hair _____ Give Fire, said she, laughing. He did so, and shot her dead.

2 Acts of Exclusion: Laughter and the Satiric Victim

It is in the work of Swift that we find, through his careful handling of his readers' laughter, the most convincing evidence that one writer of satire, at least, had given serious thought to the question of what we do when we laugh. *A Beautiful Young Nymph Going to Bed*, as Irvin Ehrenpreis suggests, has traditionally been taken as representing Swift 'at his most damnable',[1] and yet such a poem, pushing as it apparently does beyond all limits of good taste what we are expected to laugh at, nevertheless, because of that very pushing, is able to confront the reader successfully with the nature of his own laughter.

Denis Donoghue has described the 'eminently Swiftian' device of treating 'the organic as if it were mechanical'. Corinna is 'a machine, her bedroom a factory; when she goes to bed, the factory is shut down'.[2] And it is indeed crucial for the working of the poem that we are lulled into accepting as mechanically predictable the nightly behaviour of Corinna. She is predictable from the joke of the opening couplet, in which the anticipated statement of her loneliness – 'For whom no Shepherd sighs' (l.2) – is safely turned, for the moment, into a glance at her availability: she is, as her association with *'Drury-Lane'* (l.1) will already have indicated, always available, predictably merciful to languishing shepherds, and, as a beautiful and young nymph, is presumably rarely alone. Such a reversal in the opening lines of the poem should make us suspect that here all is not as it seems, especially as we then learn that, contrary to our expectation, Corinna does habitually find herself alone, 'Returning at the Midnight Hour' (l.7). Swift, though, in having already offered us a fleeting opportunity to sympathise with the apparent loneliness of Corinna, only to deny it in a joke, has made it harder for us to feel anything for her real isolation as she climbs 'Four Stories . . . to her Bow'r' (l.8). She has been offered to us as an object of laughter, and of laughter in particular at her ready sexual availability. The reader's enjoyment of the poem is prepared: it will depend upon permitted sexual encroachment rendered safe by encouraged laughter. Corinna will be, quite literally, the object of both. Her body/machine is there only to please the reader. It has no feeling of its own, Corinna is too predictable to think. The dismantling of the machine, once the reader has grasped the pattern, provides the momentum of the poem and of the joke. For twenty lines we are encouraged to overlook the possibility of there being a person beneath the relentlessly removed layers of contrivance. By the last of the twenty lines Corinna is reduced to the single mechanical hand that works, by now, so predictably on.

> Proceeding on, the lovely Goddess
> Unlaces next her Steel-Rib'd Bodice;
> Which by the Operator's Skill,
> Press down the Lumps, the Hollows fill,
> Up goes her Hand, and off she slips
> The Bolsters that supply her Hips. (ll.23–8)

Where can the poem go from here? What else is there to be removed? The reader has by now exhausted his inclination to laugh, his sexual interest no longer seeks gratification, but the poem shows no sign of ending. What, after such predictability, can happen next?

What does happen next is that Swift, in anticipation of Corinna's own task at the close of the poem, proceeds to put together the person he has just encouraged the reader to conspire with him to dismantle, to treat as object. Having willingly suspended the inclination to sympathise, preferring the poet's offer of easy pleasure through sex and laughter, the reader is now compelled by Swift's change of focus to face up to the possibility of Corinna's being a real living and feeling person after all. The 'Hand' that has just removed the last article of artifice is now sent 'With gentlest Touch' to explore 'Her Shankers, Issues, running Sores' (ll.29–30). The information, casually given, that these are the 'Effects of many a sad Disaster' (l.31) begins to sketch in a past for her, suggests that she is capable of remembering – that she must remember, over and over again, as she each night reads the record of that past on her own body. The hand that is now capable of 'gentlest Touch' is capable too of applying the few pitiful remedies to the body that, at last, is really Corinna: the 'Plaister', the 'greasy Paper', the '*Bolus*' (l.32, 36, 37). The machine that had been running down for the night is now seen as no machine, for only now can what is real be appreciated. We are brought face to face with a body habitually in pain and, as Corinna 'between two Blankets creeps' (l.38), Swift begins, too, to show us and make us feel with the habitually anguished mind.

Deane Swift praised Swift's imaginative ability to 'dream in the character of an old battered strumpet',[3] and it is through the dream that he at last forces us to enter Corinna's mind, convincing the reader first that there is a mind to enter, and then, in the mechanically relentless alternatives his couplets present, drawing him into the fevered helplessness of personalised nightmare.

> Or if she chance to close her Eyes,
> Of *Bridewell* and the *Compter* dreams,
> And feels the Lash, and faintly screams;
> Or, by a faithless Bully drawn,
> At some Hedge-Tavern lies in Pawn;
> Or to *Jamaica* seems transported,
> Alone, and by no Planter courted;
> Or, near *Fleet-Ditch*'s oozy Brinks,
> Surrounded with a Hundred Stinks,
> Belated, seems on watch to lye,
> And snap some Cully passing by;
> Or, struck with Fear, her Fancy runs
> On Watchmen, Constables and Duns. . . .   (ll.40–52)

The predictable rhythm of the machine that was earlier used to help us to depersonalise Corinna has now been turned round and made into the device by which the reader, because he too has known the anguish of entrapment in the mechanical pattern of nightmare, must inevitably contribute to the process of reconstructing a personality from the dismantled remains of a woman, of piecing together a past, a memory, a set of assumptions and apprehensions – the faint dream scream at the feel of the lash, the dread of aloneness, not in the familiar surroundings of *'Fleet-Ditch'* but transported to the unknown fears of Jamaica. Seeing, now, as Corinna sees, feeling as she feels, the reader would not miss what he was encouraged by Swift to miss before, those small details of the mechanical dismantling which showed her capacity for care and self-concern, for finely controlled movements of a quite different class to those of the automatic hand that the poet rendered so prominently. The detail of Corinna 'seated on a three-legg'd Chair' (l.9), after its initial comic effect, leaves a far more enduring impression of a carefully maintained balance and of a self control capable of maintaining such a balance throughout the operations of dismantling. She 'picks' out the 'Crystal Eye' and 'wipes it clean' (ll.11–12), a detail at first distasteful but rendered, on second reading, poignant by the evident impossibility of keeping anything clean in such surroundings. The 'Art' with which she had 'Stuck on' her eyebrows, seen initially perhaps as a moral statement in warning against seduction by cosmetic beauty, now becomes a detail of the pathetic attempt to maintain sufficient face to practise the only occupation open to her. The 'Care' with which she pulls them off, 'displays 'em' and finally 'in a Play-Book smoothly lays 'em' (ll.15–16), is not, after all, to be attributed to vanity but to the appalling knowledge that tomorrow will be exactly the same as today, and that what has served in the past will have to be made to serve in the future. The life in Corinna had been there even in the terms of her dismantling, but Swift, concerned at the outset to seem to invite our laughter, deliberately set the pattern of the poem against her, so that such life went largely unnoticed.

By the end of the dream, however, the life is all too evident. When Corinna wakes, it is through her eyes that the reader surveys the wreckage of her room, having experienced through her dreaming mind 'the Ruins of the Night' (l.58), and by now knowing intimately the vital importance of each damaged item – the items whose removal was at one time anticipated to be for the reader's gratification.

A wicked Rat her Plaister stole,
Half eat, and dragg'd it to his Hole.
The Crystal Eye, alas, was miss't;
And *Puss* had on her Plumpers pisst.

A Pigeon pick'd her Issue-Peas;
And *Shock* her Tresses fill'd with Fleas.   (ll.59–64)

The injuries done during the night by rat, cat etc., are versions of those the reader was prepared to do by his attitude at the beginning of the poem. Corinna's identity, so hard to 'recollect' from the 'scatter'd Parts' (l.68) of her memory, has been abused by the reader's desire for thoughtless entertainment as by the trespasses of the vermin in her room. The reader has done penance, however, in contributing to the rebuilding of Corinna's identity through the medium of the dream. He does not need to have described the physical rebuilding of her body, the daily 'Arts' (l.67) of her reconstruction. He now has sufficient imaginative sympathy to know it for himself, 'the Anguish, Toil, and Pain' (l.69). In a most characteristic Swiftian gesture, the 'bashful Muse' withdraws, unwilling to 'interfere' (ll.71–2) where the prying reader had so readily interfered early in the poem. But the reader himself, having 'seen' first of all Corinna only in terms of her external reality, and then having 'seen' more properly exactly as she sees, has no choice but to see her now 'in the Morning dizen'd' (l.73). If to 'spew', to 'be poison'd' (l.74), therefore, is on one hand a measure of the distance between the reader's expectation of the 'beautiful young nymph' and the forcibly acknowledged reality, between the image of desire and what that desire is now found to be based on, it is also the physical consequence of knowing what it is to be Corinna, of seeing and smelling with her as she sees and smells each morning of her life. Fully and physically to realise the life in such a way is far from pleasant, but it is extreme just to the extent that our readiness for gratification, for denying the life, was also extreme. The greater the pleasure we allowed ourselves to expect from Corinna, the more abhorrent do we find the irresponsible nature of our own desires, and the more violent our confrontation with real 'Anguish, Toil, and Pain'.

   If the reader's expectation of a harmlessly erotic striptease gives this poem one of its dimensions, Irvin Ehrenpreis suggests another more precisely historical dimension when he refers to the indictment for rape faced by Dr Thomas Sawbridge, the Dean of Ferns, in the summer of 1730, a piece of news, says Ehrenpreis, 'which probably belongs among the provocations of [Swift's] most scatological satires'.

On Tuesday, 2 June, Sawbridge was arraigned for 'forcibly and feloniously ravishing' Susanna Runsard. The following Monday, although he was supposed to be tried, no evidence appeared against him, and the trial was put off a week. But again no evidence appeared; so he was acquitted. A report went out that Sawbridge would indict the girl for perjury.

Swift, continues Ehrenpreis, thought otherwise, and wrote to the Earl of Oxford:

> There is a fellow here from England, one Sawbridge, he was last term indicted for a rape. The plea he intended was his being drunk when he forced the woman; but he bought her off. He is a dean and I name him to your Lordship, because I am confident you will hear of his being a bishop.[4]

A second rape also came to public notice in 1730 to 'enlarge Swift's sense of outrage'. Colonel Francis Charteris, 'cheat and usurer, who had tricked his way into a fortune and married his daughter to an earl', was convicted of rape in February 'but soon received the king's pardon'.[5] Both Sawbridge and Charteris are featured, the first prominently, in Swift's poem of 1730, *An Excellent New Ballad: or, The True English Dean to be hang'd for a Rape* (a poem in which, on its political side, Steele is also glanced at): 'Shall a Subject so Loyal be hang'd by the Nape, / For no other Crime but committing a Rape' (ll.35-6). Evidence of Swift's strength of feeling over the subject of rape is to be found, too, as early as 1711, when he recounts for Stella his interest in a similar case.

> I was this forenoon with Mr. secretary at his office, and helped to hinder a man of his pardon, who is condemned for a rape. The under-secretary was willing to save him, upon an old notion that a woman cannot be ravished: but I told the secretary, he could not pardon him without a favourable report from the judge; . . . What; I must stand up for the honour of the fair sex? 'Tis true, the fellow had lain with her a hundred times before; but what care I for that? What! must a woman be ravished because she is a whore? (*Prose Writings*, XV, 319-20)

Swift's interest displays an attitude quite out of his time (if the opinion of Under-Secretary Hare is to be taken as typical), and quite in keeping with the underlying attitude of *A Beautiful Young Nymph*, in the assertion that a woman's being a whore does not make her rape excusable, and yet, to a modern mind, astonishingly barbaric in the insistence on the ultimate penalty for such a crime.

A Beautiful Young Nymph Going to Bed, probably written in 1731, should, then, like *The Lady's Dressing Room*, *Strephon and Chloe* and *Cassinus and Peter*, be seen as one of a series of poems arising in part from Swift's sense of outrage both at the rapes committed by fornicators such as Sawbridge and Charteris and at the ease with which they were able to evade punishment. Typically, though, Swift's treatment of rape is so controlled in *A Beautiful Young Nymph* that the subject at first seems not to be treated at all. How, after all, can a whore 'For whom no Shepherd sighs in vain' ever be in a position to be raped? To be prepared, though, as the reader is encouraged to be, for even the minor sexual gratification of voyeurism is to be guilty of looking upon another human being only as an object. That such an encroachment is here an imaginative rather than an actual indulgence prevents the transgression from being a rape as such, but the state of mind of the voyeur differs only in degree from that of the rapist. Neither is prepared to let his victim exist in her own right. To do so requires a revolution in thought, in being made to see, such as the poem itself provides.

More than this, though, Swift is interested in making us aware of the consequences of our own laughter. To be ready to laugh at, just as much as to rape or to watch as a spectacle, is to deny individuality and to treat as an object. To laugh is easy, but to be laughed at is to be instantly defined and limited as the object of someone's laughter. Corinna is presented as a machine in order to encourage our laughter at her, and as long as we laugh she can be nothing but a machine. Any life that is in her is overlooked in the search for fresh matter for laughter. Only when the poet has begun to make our laughter distasteful to us do we begin to notice those unperceived signs of life, of the real person behind the exterior we have been engaged in assaulting. To laugh at is to violate as completely as to rape, for both insist on treating the person as object, and neither will easily give up pleasure for the revolutionary acknowledgement that this object is really an individual with a unique and sensitive identity to be 'gathered up' once the violation is over. That is why Swift so often takes sexual squalor and scatalogical humour in the same glance, and why it needs a poem as aggressive as *A Beautiful Young Nymph Going to Bed* to compel the reader to take the responsibility for his own laughter. For only when we are aware of the power of laughter, of what it means to laugh at someone, can we be trusted to laugh only where laughter is deserved, and to offer to the rest of our kind the fully human response of compassion.

A Beautiful Young Nymph Going to Bed, however, is a rarity in the satire of the early eighteenth century. The art of the satirist is not normally engaged in redeeming his victim from the status of object, but rather in presenting in dehumanised terms some actual person against whom the writer wishes to arouse his readers' laughter. Hobbes had pointed to the importance of 'a stranger's unseemliness' in leading to the 'sudden self-commendation' of laughter. When Shadwell or Bentley, Theobald or Cibber is held up as principal victim in a work of satire, a large proportion of the effectiveness of such satire depends, of course, upon the very familiarity of the man himself to contemporary readers. Laughter will be most successfully aroused by presentation of the recognisable features and characteristics of the victim. And yet in a vital respect the Shadwell or Cibber being held up as object for laughter is not at all the Shadwell or Cibber who may be known and recognised in the street, for the figure in the satiric representation is known *solely* by his characteristic features and gestures. He *must* be depicted in terms of external reality only. Any glimpse into the real personality of the victim as he lives and breathes will at once destroy the satiric artifice. Shadwell of *Mac Flecknoe*, Cibber of *The Dunciad*, must be instantly recognisable versions of real men, but they must share nothing of the life of the men they resemble. They must be figures rendered only in terms of a mechanical predictability that can certainly be perceived in the features and behaviour of their models, but which in the satiric versions is the whole of the personality. The art of the satirist will arouse laughter to the extent that it keeps life from his victims as drawn, and the laughter aroused will itself be confirmation of the victim's status as object, a figure irredeemably excluded from the life. In this way, then, we may accept Hobbes' 'stranger' as the appropriate object of laughter, for in rendering Shadwell as fit for laughter, Dryden is giving the reader not the actual Shadwell but Shadwell as a stranger, familiar in externals but so complete a stranger to the real Shadwell, to any real person, that the principles of his existence share nothing of the principles of our own. Shadwell of *Mac Flecknoe* is man rendered mechanical, predictable, lifeless, a complete though recognisable stranger to all the familiar principles of human existence. Only when he is thus rendered can we properly laugh at him, and as long as we laugh the satiric victim will never be accepted into the human dimension, for the satiric victim, unless in the hands of an exceptional satirist such as Swift, is once a stranger always a stranger.

Both Bergson in his essay, *Laughter*, and Freud have paid considerable attention to the question of how laughter works, and in particular to the kind of relation there is between the laugher and the object of his laughter, what mechanical relation and what psychological relation. Bergson, for example, in considering what constitutes the comic, summarizes:

> Any arrangement of acts and events is comic which gives us, in a single combination, the illusion of life and the distinct impression of a mechanical arrangement.[6]

The art of the caricaturist, he suggests (to which it will be no violation to add the art of the satirist), is to render what is actually there in the life as if it were indeed a mechanical arrangement. In even the most harmonious features there exist 'the signs of some impending bias, the vague suggestion of a possible grimace, in short some favourite distortion towards which nature seems to be particularly inclined'. What the caricaturist does is to detect 'this, at times, imperceptible tendency' and to render it 'visible to all eyes by magnifying it'. He

> makes his models grimace, as they would do themselves if they went to the end of their tether. Beneath the skin-deep harmony of form, he divines the deep-seated recalcitrance of matter. He realises disproportions and deformations which must have existed in nature as mere inclinations, but which have not succeeded in coming to a head, being held in check by a higher force.[7]

This 'higher force', Bergson continues, is 'the effort of a soul which is shaping matter, a soul which is infinitely supple and perpetually in motion'. What the satirist does, we may add, is to deny in his victim the very existence of such a shaping spirit. Corinna is denied her soul in order that the reader may subsequently be brought to acknowledge it. Shadwell and Cibber, more typically, remain, in Bergson's words, 'immersed and absorbed in the materiality of some mechanical operation'. The dimension in which they are made to exist is that of 'matter', matter which is 'obstinate' and which 'draws to itself the ever-alert activity of this higher principle, would fain convert it to its own inertia and cause it to revert to mere automatism'.[8] The suggestion must be that the victim of caricature, the victim of satire, has the existence of 'a jointed puppet':

> The suggestion must be a clear one, for inside the person we must distinctly perceive, as through a glass, a set-up mechanism. But the suggestion must also be a subtle one, for the general appearance of the person, whose every limb has been made rigid as a machine, must continue to give us the impression of a living being.[9]

The control, however, is a very fine one, for this 'impression of a living being' must not for a moment allow the possibility of feeling on behalf of the victim. Laughter depends rather upon the artist's ability to achieve in his reader complete absence of feeling for the object of his attack. As Bergson argues,

> Indifference is its natural environment, for laughter has no greater foe than emotion. I do not mean that we could not laugh at a person who inspires us with pity, for instance, or even with affection, but in such a case we must, for the moment, put our affection out of court and impose silence upon our pity.[10]

The comic, he adds, 'demands something like a momentary anaesthesia of the heart'.[11] For this reason, any sign of conscious choice in the victim of laughter must be eliminated. Such a necessity lies behind Bergson's distinction between gesture, upon which comedy relies and would work to concentrate our attention, and action, which, for the successful arousing of laughter, comedy must work to avoid.

> By *gestures* we here mean the attitudes, the movements and even the language by which a mental state expresses itself outwardly without any aim or profit, from no other cause than a kind of inner itching. Gesture, thus defined, is profoundly different from action. Action is intentional or, at any rate, conscious; gesture slips out unawares, it is automatic. In action, the entire person is engaged; in gesture, an isolated part of the person is expressed, unknown to, or at least apart from, the whole of the personality.[12]

For Bergson, such absence of thought in the object of laughter, such irresponsible incapacity for proper action, is one major reason why we are so prepared to laugh at the victim who is thus skilfully rendered for our pleasure. A person who is incapable of choice has no moral dimension to his existence. Even a comic expression of face can signify an absence of the capacity for moral choice.

> One would say that the person's whole moral life has crystallised into this particular cast of features. This is the reason why a face is all the more comic, the more it suggests to us the idea of some simple mechanical action in which its personality would be for ever absorbed.[13]

Our laughter in these circumstances is our protection against a different form of existence, against the mechanical, the amoral which will always be a threat to the secure continuation of society. Not that Theobald or Cibber wish for the end of all human society: they have not that capacity for individual choice to wish for anything beyond immediate mechanical gratification. But their very existence, as rendered by Pope, is the existence of the anti-social, the threat of the stranger, of the irresponsibility that is the permanent presence of anarchy.

> Society will therefore be suspicious of all *inelasticity* of character, of mind and even of body, because it is the possible sign of a slumbering activity with separatist tendencies, that inclines us to swerve from the common centre round which

society gravitates: in short, because it is the sign of an eccentricity.[14]

Society's instinct for its own survival isolates

> a certain rigidity of body, mind and character, that society would still like to get rid of in order to obtain from its members the greatest possible degree of elasticity and sociability. This rigidity is the comic, and laughter is its corrective.[15]

This brings Bergson, as he approaches the end of his work, to his main conclusion on the function of laughter, and consequently upon the normal relation between the laugher and the person depicted as his object.

> Laughter is, above all, a corrective. Being intended to humiliate, it must make a painful impression on the person against whom it is directed. By laughter, society avenges itself for the liberties taken with it. It would fail in its object if it bore the stamp of sympathy or kindness.[16]

Laughter may be cruel, may even depend on the laugher denying for the moment that capacity for sympathy which is normally an essential feature of his humanity, but it is necessarily so, for the survival of society is of a higher priority than the feelings of those individuals who can be depicted as so real a danger to society that they must be rendered harmless, as non-persons, by the act of exclusion that is laughter.

Both Bergson and Freud agree, however, that the arousal of laughter at the victim's expense is something of a cheat. For Freud, 'A joke will allow us to exploit something ridiculous in our enemy which we could not, on account of obstacles in the way, bring forward openly or consciously.' The joke will 'bribe the hearer with its yield of pleasure into taking sides with us without any very close investigation'.[17] And such a 'yield of pleasure', as Bergson makes clear, does not rely upon the higher spirit of our own nature, but rather upon our readiness to become indifferent to 'our neighbour's personality'.[18] The function of laughter 'is to intimidate by humiliating' and it 'would not succeed in doing this had not nature implanted for that very purpose, even in the best of men, a spark of spitefulness or, at all events, of mischief'. Our laughter, then, cannot be 'kind-hearted' and nor can it be 'absolutely just'.[19] Rather it is always ready, at the mercy of the artist with the skill to draw us into endorsing the grinding of his particular axe.

Freud, though, is especially interested (and especially useful for the consideration of the laugh in satire) in discussing the way that jokes act as a medium of understanding between the maker of the joke and his listener. Humour arises, he argues,

> when a writer or narrator describes the behaviour of real or imaginary people in a humorous manner. There is no need for those people to display any humour themselves; the humorous attitude is solely the business of the person who is taking them as his object; and ... the reader or hearer shares in the enjoyment of the humour.[20]

The humorous attitude 'can be directed either towards the subject's own self or towards other people', it brings 'a yield of pleasure to the person who adopts it, and a similar yield of pleasure falls to the share of the non-participating onlooker'. And yet, as Freud had already demonstrated in his earlier *Jokes and their Relation to the Unconscious*, the onlooker is non-participating only insofar as he takes no part in the initiation of the humour. The onlooker does participate, however, to the extent that he more or less readily allows himself to become infected by the 'humorous attitude' and to endorse by his laughter the proposals of the joke-maker. This process is particularly crucial in what Freud calls the 'tendentious' joke.

> Generally speaking, a tendentious joke calls for three people: in addition to the one who makes the joke, there must be a second who is taken as the object of the hostile or sexual aggressiveness, and a third in whom the joke's aim of producing pleasure is fulfilled.[21]

Freud's association of the object of the joke with the object of sexual aggressiveness reinforces Swift's success in equating the reader's laughter at Corinna with actual rape. What is equally significant, however, is that laughter is used as a means of persuasion which works by rendering the opponent – or 'enemy', as Freud calls him – inconsiderable not in his own eyes necessarily but in the eyes of the onlooker.

> By making our enemy small, inferior, despicable or comic, we achieve in a roundabout way the enjoyment of overcoming him – to which the third person, who has made no efforts, bears witness by his laughter.[22]

In consequence, the hearer, 'who was indifferent to begin with', is turned into 'a co-hater or co-despiser', so creating 'for the enemy a host of opponents where at first there was only one'.[23] Such a 'host', to return for a moment to Bergson's argument, may eventually come to stand for society avenging itself upon the person who has been successfully depicted as a threat to its own security. The more widespread the laughter aroused by the satirist, therefore, then the more completely has he managed to mask the real Cibber or Curll under the features of the non-human figure that society has agreed should be excluded as a threat to its existence. And once laughter has been aroused no protest or argument is possible, for laughter 'upsets the critical judgement which would otherwise have examined the dispute', it 'endeavours to push the criticism out of sight'.[24]

From the point of view of the first person, the joke-maker or satirist, Freud devotes considerable time to the process and techniques of making people comic. 'The discovery', he suggests, 'that one has it in one's power to make someone else comic opens the way to an undreamt-of yield of comic pleasure and is the origin of a highly developed technique'. The comic can be found in people's

> movements, forms, actions and traits of character, originally in all probability only in their physical characteristics but later in their mental ones as well or, as the case may be, in the expression of those characteristics.

Methods of comic rendering include many of the traditional satiric techniques: 'putting them in a comic situation, mimicry, disguise, unmasking, caricature, parody, travesty, and so on'[25] – all of them, it should be added, techniques which must deny the reality of the victim in order to work at all. In fact, as Freud later adds, the comic works on other people 'without regard to the personal characteristics of the individual concerned – that is to say, by employing the comic of situation'. The comic situation itself 'may be a real one (a practical joke) . . . or it may be simulated by speech or play'. Provided that the pleasure of laughter is released, however, and through it the 'aggressiveness, to which making a person comic usually ministers', then the 'reality of the comic situation' does not matter.[26] The joke-maker's power, therefore, is immense, for not only is his listener ready to trade endorsement for the yield of pleasure of the joke, but his craft encourages him to take whatever liberties he wishes with the 'characteristics' of his victims. It is in the comic situation, real or simulated, that such conditions prevail as will rob the victim of his 'characteristics' and use them, not in their normal context of his whole human personality, but as features which must stand for him under the remorseless and dehumanising logic of the joke.[27] From here, Freud is able to cite and endorse Bergson's 'formula' of *'mécanisation de la vie'* and 'to include his view under our own formula'.[28]

What Freud adds in 1927, though, is a whole new dimension to the act of laughing, for now he is looking far more closely into the mental attitudes of the person who is laughing, the man who is possessed of 'the humorous attitude'. Humour, he argues, 'has something liberating about it; but it also has something of grandeur and elevation', which 'lies in the triumph of narcissism, the victorious assertion of the ego's invulnerability'. Freud clearly believes that the necessity for the laugh to ignore feeling in the object of laughter does not merely constitute a denial of a significant human dimension in the laugher but is, moreover, a positive assertion of the individual's selfish and asocial determination to survive.

> The ego refuses to be distressed by the provocations of reality, to let itself be compelled to suffer. It insists that it cannot be affected by the traumas of the external world: it shows, in fact, that such traumas are no more than occasions for it to gain pleasure.[29]

Humour, then, 'signifies not only the triumph of the ego but also of the pleasure principle, which is able here to assert itself against the unkindness of the real circumstances'. Such self-assertion, however, against what should be recognised as real, such denial in favour of the pleasure principle, brings us once again to a recognition of the proximity of laughter and madness. Humour, it seems, rejects 'the claims of reality'.

> Its fending off of the possibility of suffering places it among the great series of methods which the human mind has constructed in order to evade the compulsion to suffer – a series which begins with neurosis and culminates in madness and which includes intoxication, self-absorption and ecstasy.[30]

Our laughter, then, may echo that of the madman, whose self-absorption is so complete that he can laugh equally at the unreality of the world and the unreality of his own suffering. Whenever we laugh, we might therefore ask, do we not give spontaneous expression to a mind that welcomes any opportunity to retreat from reality? And yet Freud refuses to take such a step. He recognises that the humorous attitude remains outside the realms of madness, and is content to state the question:

> In what, then, does the humorous attitude consist, an attitude by means of which a person refuses to suffer, emphasizes the invincibility of his ego by the real world, victoriously maintains the pleasure principle – and all this, in contrast to other methods having the same purposes, without over-stepping the bounds of mental health? The two achievements seem incompatible.[31]

Bergson and Freud have interested themselves with what Freud calls the first and third persons in laughing, the initiator and the onlooker or onlookers who are drawn in to endorse the propositions of the joke-maker. We should also be interested, though, in the person who is under attack. What happens in the mental processes of the *real* person whose resemblance is being violated by satirist, caricaturist or joke-maker within a logic that is not only quite independent of the individual himself, but actually seems to threaten his human existence? What is it like, then, to be laughed at? What does it mean, in other words, to be treated as an object by other members of one's society?

'No more fiendish punishment could be devised, even were such a thing physically possible, than that one should be turned loose in society and remain absolutely unnoticed by all the members thereof.'[32] Thus R. D. Laing approvingly quotes William James as he begins his chapter on 'Confirmation and Disconfirmation' in *Self and Others*. For, as Laing later adds, 'Every human being, whether child or adult, seems to require *significance*, that is, *place in another person's world*.'[33] Such *'place'* is essential if one is to have any real sense of identity.

> A person's 'own' identity cannot be completely abstracted from his identity for others. His identity-for-himself; the identity others ascribe to him; the identities he attributes to them; the identity or identities he thinks they attribute to him; . . . 'Identity' is that whereby one feels one is *the same*, in this place, this time as at that time and at that place, past or future. . . .[34]

The individual who can manage the problems of his own identity without needing to think about them, who is instinctively assured of his own *'significance'*, qualifies as what Laing in *The Divided Self* refers to as the 'ontologically secure person'.

> A man may have a sense of his presence in the world as a real, alive, whole, and, in a temporal sense, a continuous person. As such, he can live out into the world and meet others: a world and others experienced as equally real, alive, whole, and continuous. Such a basically *ontologically* secure person will encounter all the hazards of life, social, ethical, spiritual, biological, from a centrally firm sense of his own and other people's reality and identity.

For such a person, moreover, it may be difficult 'to transpose himself into the world of an individual whose experiences may be utterly lacking in any unquestionable self-validating certainties'.[35] This latter is the state of mind of the ontologically insecure person who 'in the ordinary circumstances of living may feel more unreal than real', who may feel 'precariously differentiated from the rest of the world, so that his identity and autonomy are always in question'.[36]

It is the satirist, the joke-maker, whom we may see within the process of laughter-making as the ontologically secure person, confidently asserting the unquestionable reality of the structural assumptions of his satire or joke, while the victim, the second person, in being treated as object or machine, is being quite deliberately faced with loss of any real identity He is finding himself thrust into the role of the ontologically insecure person, confirmed as 'differentiated from the rest of the world'. And when Laing goes on to discuss 'the nature of the anxieties' to which the most extreme case of the ontologically insecure person, 'the schizoid individual', is subject, we see clearly the very terms already recognised as describing the techniques of creating an object of satire, for the schizoid individual suffers from 'the dread of losing inner autonomy, freedom; in short, being turned from a man with subjectivity to a thing, a mechanism, a stone, an it, being petrified'.[37] Such loss of autonomy is particularly threatened when the individual is apparently the object of another's consciousness, imprisoned in another's gaze. For

> consciousness has two main properties: its power to petrify (to turn to stone: to turn oneself or the other into things); and its power to penetrate. Thus, if it is in these terms that the gaze of others is experienced, there is a constant dread and resentment at being turned into someone else's thing, of being penetrated by him, and a sense of being in someone else's power and control.[38]

'Petrification' Laing has already described as the dread of being turned 'from a live person into a dead thing, into a stone, into a robot, an automaton, without personal autonomy of action, an *it* without subjectivity'. To this he adds 'depersonalization', in which one looks at the victim and 'no longer allows oneself to be responsive to his feelings', indeed one may even 'be prepared to regard him and treat him as though he had no feelings'[39] – the very consequence that Swift attributes to his readers' laughter at *A Beautiful Young Nymph Going to Bed*. The consequence for Laing, too, is that 'one is open to the possibility of experiencing oneself as an *object*' of another's experience, and 'thereby of feeling one's own subjectivity drained away'. In particular,

One is threatened with the possibility of becoming no more than a thing in the world of the other, without any life for oneself, without any being for oneself.[40]

The consequence for the real satiric victim, however, has an added complexity, for we must remember that while at one level, the level of his own identity, he is being denied, or at least ignored, treated as irrelevant, at another, in his being as the thing of the satirist, he finds 'himself' displayed to the public gaze and laughter, held up as an object, a machine or an it possessing neither feeling nor autonomy. It is the victim's real self that is being made 'ontologically insecure', but this insecurity can only be deepened by what Laing in *Self and Others* refers to as 'confirmation of a false self'. Genuine confirmation is an essential process between members of a society if that society is to remain healthy. Here Laing quotes from a paper by Martin Buber.

In human society, at all its levels, persons confirm one another in a practical way, to some extent or other, in their personal qualities and capacities, and a society may be termed human in the measure to which its members confirm one another.[41]

There is also, Laing adds, that 'lack of genuine confirmation' which 'takes the form of actively confirming a false self, so that the person whose false self is confirmed and real self disconfirmed is placed in a false position'.[42] One particular kind of disconfirmation, moreover, is the 'failure to recognize a person as agent', for the 'attribution of agency to human beings is one way we distinguish people from things set in motion by agents external to themselves'.[43] Again, the satiric victim finds his own feelings and actions, his own autonomous agency, overlooked, while a false self, a created thing 'set in motion' by the satirist and having neither life nor feelings, is confirmed as 'being' him by the recognition of his fellow members of society, and yet at the same time confirmed as being only an object by those fellow members' laughter. The 'false position' of the victim threatens not only ontological insecurity but, it would seem, the madness of schizophrenia, for, as Laing goes on to point out,

Some people are more sensitive than others to not being recognized as human beings. If someone is *very* sensitive in this respect, they stand a good chance of being diagnosed as schizophrenic.[44]

The greatest fear, Laing argues, for the schizoid individual, is the indifference of others, for he must prevent the 'fading away' of his identity. In order to exist there must be someone else to believe in his existence, otherwise his sense of his own identity will simply 'drain away'.[45] The threat presented by indifference is that 'the person or thing is treated with casualness, or callousness, as though he or it did not matter, ultimately as though he or it did not exist'.[46] When Addison, as quoted in chapter 1, describes his reaction to personal satire – 'If I bring in a Verdict against my self, I endeavour to rectify my Conduct . . . but if the whole Invective be grounded upon a Falshood, I trouble my self no further about it'[47] – he is describing the state of mind of a man of such commanding 'ontological security' that we may well wish to question the precise veracity of his claim. Addison's stance, like Dryden's ideal victim, stands at one remarkably secure extreme of possible responses to being confirmed as an it, of being placed in a 'false position'. At the other extreme, the schizoid individual will divert his 'whole effort' into striving 'to preserve his *self*', the self which is so 'precariously established' that 'he is subject to the dread of his own dissolution into non-being, into what William Blake described in the last resort as "chaotic non-entity"'. He must 'guard himself against losing his subjectivity and sense of being alive'.[48] But in that 'last resort' the schizoid individual is so reduced, so close to being a nothing, that he 'is precluded from having a direct relationship with real things and real people'. The 'final effect', says Laing,

> is an overall experience of everything having come to a stop. Nothing moves; nothing is alive; everything is dead, including the self. The self by its detachment is precluded from a full experience of realness and aliveness.[49]

I am not, of course, suggesting that all individuals who find themselves the victims of personal satire instantly become schizophrenic, or even that they inevitably begin to doubt their ontological autonomy. There may well be many victims who are able, like Addison, to shrug off the invective or, like Buckingham, to join in the laugh. What is clear, though, is that the art of the satirist consists in the successful denial of his victim's real living human identity in favour of the substitute object that is confirmed by the laughter of the onlookers. This process, moreover, involves subjecting the victim to treatment that, in ontologically insecure individuals, would normally be found to intensify such insecurity towards the crisis in identity which characterises schizophrenia. Such an attack and such laughter, such an exclusion from the usual fellowship of society, are a very real threat to the victim's sense of identity, and their tendency is to reduce his selfhood to that level of nothingness that is the particular feature of the state of mind of the schizophrenic. Robert C. Elliott ends his book, *The Power of Satire*, by speculating on the way in which satire can be said to 'kill' its victims. The verses of the Greek satirist Archilochus reputedly 'caused Lycambes and his daughter to hang themselves'.[50] Can such threats still be taken at all seriously? Do they have any meaning in the modern world?

> What does it mean to say that Jonson and Pope and Byron and Roy Campbell kill their enemies symbolically? What did it mean to John Partridge, the astrologer, to be ridiculed "to death" by Swift and his friends?[51]

Our increasing knowledge of the processes of mental illness does add a new dimension to the possibility of answering Elliott's questions. The victims of satire are being done to death in a very real psychological way, even if, unlike Lycambes and his daughter, they refrain from going off and hanging themselves. And who will not be struck by the extraordinary coincidence between the nature of Swift's attack on the Æolists in Section VIII of *Tale of a Tub*, and Laing's description of the state of mind of one schizoid patient?

> Another patient oscillated between moments when he felt as though he was bursting with power, and moments when he felt he had nothing inside and was lifeless. However, even his 'manic' feeling of himself was that he was a container full of air under tremendous pressure, in fact, nothing but hot air, and his sense of deflation came with this thought.

And, says Laing, this patient's feelings are far from unusual.

> The schizoid individual frequently speaks of himself in these
> terms, such that, phenomenologically, we are justified in
> speaking of the vacuum that the self feels itself to be.[52]

How, we might well ask, could Swift possibly have anticipated
so close a correspondence? Or should we not rather look to
Swift's reading of Robert Burton and of later commentators on
melancholy and mental illness[53] for the beginnings of an
explanation of how far the terms resorted to by modern
schizophrenic patients resemble those traditionally adopted by
sufferers from a wide variety of physical and psychological
maladies?

And yet we do not need to rely on the evidence of the inner
processes of schizoid individuals for confirmation of the nature
of any threat to the reality of the self, the threat that satire
ultimately makes actual on the identity of its victim. For the
horror of not being is one of man's basic primal fears – hence the
importance of mutual confirmation between members of a
healthy society – and our adult lives are secure and happy
largely insofar as we have discovered for ourselves ways to
overcome such a fear. Laing cites Freud's description of a little
boy's 'game' of 'disappearance and return'. During a

> long period of solitude the child had found a method of
> making himself disappear. He had discovered his reflection in
> a full-length mirror which did not quite reach the ground so
> that by crouching down he could make his mirror-image
> 'gone'.

The little boy, who had earlier been observed playing at making
his mother 'disappear', now 'plays also at making himself
disappear'. Freud, says Laing, 'suggests that both games are to
be understood as attempts to master the anxiety of a danger
situation by repeating it again and again in play'. And Laing
himself continues:

> If this is so, the fear of being invisible, of disappearing, is
> closely associated with the fear of his mother disappearing. It
> seems that loss of the mother, at a certain stage, threatens the

individual with loss of his self. The mother, however, is not simply a *thing* which the child can see, but a *person* who sees the child. Therefore, we suggest that a necessary component in the development of the self is the experience of oneself as a person under the loving eye of the mother.[54]

This fear, however, is far from peculiar to Freud's 'disappearing boy', for any child who, for example, 'cries when its mother disappears from the room is threatened with the disappearance of his own being, since for him . . . *percepi=esse*'. In the presence of his mother the child 'is able fully to *live* and *move* and *have his being*'. In going to sleep, too, the child experiences a loss of his own awareness of himself, which may be frightening unless he is being safely watched by a parent, or at least has a light to be seen by.

In sleep the 'inner' light that illumines one's own being is out. Leaving on the light not only provides assurance that if he wakes there are no terrors in the dark, but provides a magical assurance that during sleep he is being watched over by benign presences (parents, good fairies, angels). Even worse, perhaps, than the possible presence of bad things in the dark is the terror that in the dark is *nothing* and *no one*. Not to be conscious of oneself, therefore, may be equated with nonentity.[55]

In such a context we may recall Dryden's consecration of Shadwell with poppies and, of course, the mighty yawn which produces the universal non-being that ends *The Dunciad*. Dulness and sleep, by satiric convention, go hand in hand, and yet we should also be aware that the convention is not only literary. Sleep, as Laing points out, is that time when self-awareness, self responsibility is lost. It is that period of each day when we are all at our most vulnerable, returned to the helplessness of the child. The satirist's treatment of his victim, at heart, is directed precisely there, at producing the state of mind of the child fearful of non-being. The victim's real self, in being overlooked in favour of an object self, in being excluded from the accustomed reality of human society, is as if thrust back to those areas of childhood where his confidence in his own existence was by no means assured, and where the various devices subsequently discovered to serve as guarantors of his identity were all unlearned.

And is it not likely, too, to turn aside from the literary victim for a moment, that here we have one essential reason for the clown's and professional comic's traditional adoption of some costume or distinguishing mark – Chaplin's hat and stick,[56] Keaton's pasty face, the combination, even, of fat man and thin man? One function of such marks, of course, is the straight-forward one of recognition, the signal that the clown will behave in an expected manner, that this is the same Chaplin we have seen and admired before. But when, as Enid Welsford explains, the fool was once treated as a scapegoat to be 'killed' in folk rites – 'whether a living man or an effigy'[57] – or at least, in his stage version, was conventionally 'carried off . . . on the devil's back',[58] the clown's costume may actually be a defence against his real exclusion by society's laughter, the being 'killed' into non-existence that his traditional fates suggest. The clown, then, actually erects for himself that mechanical false self with which the satirist violates his victim, and is able to control it as a separate 'object' identity. The comic's real self will remain private and inviolate, assured of his own autonomous being, while the protective false 'object' self is given to the public gaze for laughing appreciation and for banishment. And from the point of view of the laughers, such a badge or costume is assurance that this laughter is safe laughter, part of an expected professional contract. It does not recognisably draw upon Bergson's 'spark of spitefulness', but rather follows Freud's pattern of the 'intentionally' comic.

> First and foremost, it is possible to produce the comic in relation to oneself in order to amuse other people – for instance, by making oneself out clumsy or stupid. In that way one produces a comic effect exactly as though one really were these things. . . . But one does not in this way make oneself ridiculous or contemptible, but may in some circumstances even achieve admiration. The feeling of superiority does not arise in the other person if he knows that one has only been pretending.[59]

Or rather, there is a feeling of superiority, but it is at the expense of the created self, not of the clown's real self. The fate of the victim of satire, the shaking of his ontological security and the attempted thrusting towards the terror of non-being of the child and the schizophrenic, is consequently avoided.

It is when we look at such a work of satire as Swift's *Bickerstaff Papers* that we find, as Elliott suggested, a genuine full-scale 'killing' of the satiric victim, and the killing here is not only the prediction of Partridge's actual death and its 'fulfilment', but also Swift's clear intention from the very beginning of the work to secure the astrologer's banishment from all human society. In the fourth paragraph, Partridge and his kind already find themselves excluded from the medium of society's common culture, the English Language.

> I will allow either of the Two I have mentioned, or any other of the Fraternity, to be not only Astrologers, but Conjurers too; if I do not produce an Hundred Instances in all their Almanacks, to convince any reasonable Man, that they do not so much as understand Grammar and Syntax; that they are not able to spell any Word out of the usual Road; nor even in their Prefaces to write common Sense, or intelligible *English*. (*Prose Writings*, II, 142)

Swift was to employ the same tactic in *The Publick Spirit of the Whigs*, where the target is Richard Steele, who is found to have

> Qualities enough to denominate him a Writer of a superior Class . . . provided he would a little regard the Propriety and Disposition of his Words, consult the Grammatical Part, and get some Information in the Subject he intends to handle. (*Prose Writings*, VIII, 32)

To write, moreover, in parody of a writer's style, as Swift does of Steele's in a section of his poem 'The First *Ode* of the Second Book of Horace Paraphras'd: And Address'd to *Richard Steele*, Esq', is to treat the victim's very medium of expression as a machine, so predictable that it can be captured and turned against its mechanically minded originator by any man of a reasonable and flexible intelligence. For Swift to adopt as Bickerstaff, then, the formal medium of an astrological seer is already to treat Partridge and his kind as mechanical objects insofar as their habitual modes of expression can be recognisably parodied.

When, however, we hear of Partridge's impending death, the first of Bickerstaff's predictions, it is in the appropriately dismissive tone that is to be characteristic of Swift's 'Bickerstaff' style, as if the removal from the race of one who is already no real member of it is a matter of concern to no one.

My first Prediction is but a Trifle; yet I will mention it, to shew how ignorant those sottish Pretenders to Astrology are in their own Concerns: It relates to *Partrige* the Almanack-Maker; I have consulted the Star of his Nativity by my own Rules; and find he will infallibly die upon the 29th of *March* next, about eleven at Night, of a raging Fever: Therefore I advise him to consider of it, and settle his Affairs in Time. (*Prose Writings,* II, 145)

The second voice of the papers, too, that of 'A Person of Quality',[60] treats Partridge's death as of interest only insofar as it would be a first sign of Bickerstaff's accuracy, for he

hath seven weeks good, during which time the world is to be kept in suspense; for it is so long before the almanack-maker is to die, which is the first prediction: And, if that fellow happens to be a splenetic visionary fop, or hath any faith in his own art, the prophesy may punctually come to pass by very natural means. (*Prose Writings,* II, 196)

Partridge, then, has two alternatives open to him: to die or not to die. Either way, however, he will render himself the mechanical object of society's laughter, for to die as predicted is by definition to be predictable, even though such dying could be a sign of Partridge's very human 'faith in his own art', while not to die exposes him as a hypocrite and therefore as a suitable object of society's recriminative derision. But Partridge's death would in itself be of no moment, though anticipating the reader's consuming interest in later events, in events post-Partridge, it would wonderfully raise Mr. Bickerstaff's reputation for a fortnight longer, until we could hear from France whether the Cardinal de Noailles were dead or alive upon the fourth of April, which is the second of his predictions. (*Prose Writings*, II, 196)

The 'Person of Quality' does take Partridge seriously as a real person insofar as he advises him to challenge the 'Squire to publish the calculation he hath made of Partridge's nativity' and suggests that 'in honour' Bickerstaff should 'give Mr. Partridge the same advantage of calculating *his*, by sending him an account of the time and place of his birth, with other particulars necessary for such a work' (*Prose Writings*, II, 197–8). To be placed on the same level of reality as Bickerstaff himself, though, is already to be regarded as having the same identity, the same kind of birth and death as a fiction who, as the 'Person of Quality' almost immediately conjectures, 'dropt out of the clouds about nine days ago, and, in about four hours after, mounted up thither again like a vapour' (*Prose Writings*, II, 199). Partridge, clearly, like Bickerstaff, has never been properly alive, and his death will merely be an acknowledgement that such objects are never truly part of the human race.

The *Letter to a Person of Honour* in which Partridge's death is described gives realistic circumstantial details of the scene – details manifestly more real, we may take it, than the man who is dying has ever been – including the comments of those about him to the effect that 'he had been for some Hours delirious', to which the letter-writer adds his own observation that 'when I saw him, he had his Understanding as well as ever I knew'. Partridge is now allowed, for the first time in the papers, to speak for 'himself'. This expression of autonomous identity, however, is used only to confirm Partridge as a machine, and as incapable of independent judgment. Like Lycambes and his daughter, Bickerstaff's prediction has, for the past fortnight, 'had the perpetual Possession of his Mind and Thoughts; and he did verily believe was the true natural Cause of his present Distemper'. What is more, he goes on to condemn himself as quite lacking in judgment in his profession of astrologer, being only 'a poor ignorant Fellow, bred to a mean Trade; yet I have Sense enough to know, that all Pretences of Astrology are Deceits', his predictions being 'my own Invention to make my

'Almanack sell'. Almanack-makers, far from relying upon independent judgment, 'have a common Form for all those Things' (*Prose Writings*, II, 154–5). The 'Wise and Learned', on the other hand,

> who can only judge whether there be any Truth in this Science, do all unanimously agree to laugh at and despise it; and none but the poor ignorant Vulgar give it any Credit, and that only upon the Word of such silly Wretches as I and my Fellows, who can hardly write or read. (*Prose Writings*, II, 154)

We who read and laugh, then, in so doing define ourselves as the 'Wise and Learned' community from which the self-condemning Partridge is excluded by his confessed ignorance, just as he is excluded from our common humanity by being held up – and by 'participating' in that holding up – as an object for our laughter.

Squire Bickerstaff Detected, which Swift allowed 'to appear in the *Miscellanies* of 1727, with a note that he had not written it', and at different times attributed to, among others, 'Nicholas Row Esq.', 'Dr. Yalden' and Congreve,[61] describes in Partridge's own voice the farcical consequences of the published account of his death. Ned the Sexton, 'come to know' details for the funeral, declares, against 'Partridge's' protests, that

> it is in Print, and the whole Town knows you are dead; why, there is Mr. *White* the Joiner, is but fitting Screws to your Coffin, he will be here with it in an Instant; he was afraid you would have wanted it before this Time.... Hist, hist, says another Rogue, that stood by him, away Doctor into your Flanel Gear as fast as you can; for here is a whole Pack of Dismals coming to you, with their black Equipage; and how indecent will it look for you to stand frightening Folks at your Window, when you should have been in your Coffin this three Hours? (*Prose Writings*, II, 220)

'Partridge's' proofs that he is in fact alive and well are ignored by popular opinion, he says, and 'Partridge', the 'real' man as he speaks and writes in *Squire Bickerstaff Detected*, finds himself treated as dead, as much an object as the 'it' Partridge of the other *Bickerstaff Papers*, for

Though I print Almanacks and publish Advertisements; although I produce Certificates under the Ministers and Church-Wardens hands, I am alive, and attest the same on Oath at Quarter-Sessions; out comes *A full and true Relation of the Death and Interment of* JOHN PARTRIGE; Truth is bore down, Attestations neglected, the Testimony of sober Persons despised, and a Man is looked upon by his Neighbours, as if he had been seven Years dead, and is buried alive in the Midst of his Friends and Acquaintance. (*Prose Writings*, II, 222)

An extra twist has been given to the usual predicament of the satiric victim, for the real Partridge who should feel himself under attack, with all the threats to his identity in the world that such attack brings with it, finds that someone, be it Swift, Congreve or another, has actually written into the satiric series a version of that real self to render laughable 'real' descriptions of and protests at the consequences of the joke. The real Partridge, then, has been given a voice and form, shown as farcically outraged, and so has become a second 'object' Partridge trapped in the logic of the satirist's work. Partridge himself, outside the world which has been created by the satirist and which is endorsed every time someone reads and laughs at him, has found himself excluded even from the victim's ground of protest by the encroachments of this model 'real' Partridge. Well might the real Partridge share the 'real' Partridge's complaint that

henceforward, to murder a Man by Way of Prophecy, and bury him in a printed Letter, either to a Lord or Commoner, shall as legally entitle him to the present Possession of *Tyburn*, as if he robbed on the Highway, or cut your Throat in Bed. (*Prose Writings*, II, 223)

Finally, Swift's own *Vindication of Isaac Bickerstaff, Esq.* completes the satiric demolition of Partridge by the calm assurance of its tone – the assurance of the ontologically secure satirist who knows by now that the taste of the town has been with him – and the audacity of its humour. Partridge, says Bickerstaff, has behaved indecently, and not at all in a manner designed to 'contribute to the Discovery of Truth'.

To call a Man *Fool* and *Villain*, and *impudent Fellow*, only for differing from him in a Point meerly speculative, is, in my humble Opinion, a very improper Stile for a Person of *his* Education. (*Prose Writings*, II, 159)

Partridge's 'Scurrility and Passion' in this 'Point meerly speculative' is, he hints, probably 'a tacit Confession of a weak Cause' (*Prose Writings*, II, 159). Few men have been readier to 'own their Errors' than Bickerstaff, and yet Partridge has made

no Objection against the Truth of my Predictions, except in one single Point, relating to himself: And to demonstrate how much Men are blinded by their own Partiality; I do solemnly assure the Reader, that he is the *only* Person from whom I ever heard that Objection offered. (*Prose Writings*, II, 161)

And Bickerstaff proceeds to justify his continued assertions of Partridge's death by proving, in 'the Eyes not only of *England*, but of all *Europe*', that 'Mr. *Partrige* is not alive'. The terms of these proofs, however, amount not only to a complete and amusing redefining of the meaning of death, but to a virtual withdrawal from the seriousness of the hoax, secure in the knowledge that Swift has won hands down and that Partridge, in terms of public standing, is well and truly 'dead'.

And my first Argument is thus: Above a Thousand Gentlemen having brought his Almanacks for this Year, meerly to find out what he said against me; at every Line they read, they would lift up their Eyes, and cry out, betwixt Rage and Laughter, *They were sure no Man* alive *ever writ such damned Stuff as this*. Neither did I ever hear that Opinion disputed.

With proofs at this level for argument, Swift is able both to give up the dispute and to continue to have his jest, declaring that

if an *uninformed* Carcass walks still about, and is pleased to call it self Partrige; Mr. *Bickerstaff* does not think himself any way answerable for that. Neither had the said Carcass any Right to beat the poor Boy, who happened to pass by it in the Street, crying, *A full and True Account of Dr.* Partrige's *Death*, & c. (*Prose Writings*, II, 162)

What we see in the series of pamphlets known as the *Bickerstaff Papers*, then, is a mock killing used to accomplish the very real 'killing' of a satiric victim, undertaken, or at least initiated, by a writer who was clearly adopting and shaping his techniques of attack in order to achieve the maximum sense of exclusion for the object of the satire. We may not be able still to answer precisely Elliott's question, 'What did it mean to John Partridge', but the kind of description I have given of the pressures experienced by those unfortunate enough to feel themselves, either permanently or spasmodically, under the threat of being overlooked by their fellows, can bring us close to appreciating what happens to the victim of satire. Moreover, our understanding of the way satire works, and of how a writer like Swift manages the many devices of offence at his disposal, is clarified by an awareness of the end towards which satiric attack tends, the ultimate and complete exclusion of the victim.

The Partridge jest, of course, did not end with the *Bickerstaff Papers*, but is taken up again by, among others, the 'Isaac Bickerstaff' that Swift lent to Steele for *The Tatler*. In the first number Partridge is again taken to task for pretending to be alive.

> For though the Legs and Arms and whole Body of that Man may still appear and perform their animal Functions; yet since, as I have elsewhere observed, his Art is gone, the Man is gone.

The aptness of the device of 'killing' the victim clearly appealed to writers of a satiric inclination, and Steele immediately proceeds to broaden the grounds on which a man may be declared 'dead'.

> I shall, as I see Occasion, proceed to confute other dead Men, who pretend to be in Being, that they are actually deceased. I therefore give all Men fair Warning to amend their Manners, for I shall from Time to Time print Bills of Mortality; and I beg the Pardon of all such who shall be named therein, if they who are good for nothing shall find themselves in the Number of the Deceased.

Steele's concluding remark (which also concludes *Tatler* 1), of course, makes explicit the grounds and effect of satiric attack: those who place themselves outside the bounds of human tolerance (bounds, however, defined by the satirist) will find their 'nothing' rewarded with the non-existence of being an object of human laughter – they will be rendered dead. And this is precisely the argument offered in *Tatler* 241 for the banishment of drunkards. While 'all the Vicious in general are in a State of Death', a drunkard is 'of all vicious Persons the most vicious'. The drunkard, more than any, should be considered as a machine,

> For if our Actions are to be weigh'd and considered according to the Intention of them, what can we think of him who puts himself into a Circumstance wherein he can have no Intention at all, but incapacitates himself for the Duties and Offices of Life, by a Suspension of all his Faculties?

The drunkard, who has 'banished himself from all that is dear, and given up all that is sacred to him', is already in a state of 'Non-Existence'. It is peculiarly fitting, then, that he should be pronounced dead.

It is Bergson who makes the suggestion that 'certain vices have the same relation to character that the rigidity of a fixed idea has to intellect'.[62] To portray a person under the grip of a predominant vice is to protray him in terms of a machine, for such a vice 'lends us its own rigidity instead of borrowing from us our flexibility. We do not render it more complicated; on the contrary, it simplifies us.' Vice in comedy, however 'intimately' it is 'associated with persons', will always retain 'its simple, independent existence', and consequently it 'plays on them as on an instrument or pulls the strings as though they were puppets'. This, says Bergson, 'is really a kind of automatism that makes us laugh'.[63]

Such a suggestion, while commonplace to the spectator of any conventional classical comedy (and Bergson looks particularly to Molière in support of his argument), does nevertheless point to alternative satiric ways of 'killing' a man than joking him to death in the Partridge manner. A single predominant vice or vicious characteristic, satirically treated, will be enough to secure the exclusion by laughter of the 'automaton' character with whom the vice has been identified – and we may here recall Bergson's corrective and avenging laughter by which society protects itself against those individuals who lack the elasticity necessary for proper social relations, or, in Laingian terms, for healthy mutual confirmation. The anonymous writer of the 1728 pamphlet, *An Essay upon the Taste and Writings of the Present Times... Occasion'd by a late Volume of Miscellanies by A. Pope, Esq: and Dr. Swift*, criticises Swift as 'a kind of *Midas* reversed' by whose 'Magick, whatsoever he touches immediately turns to brass'. So, 'he formerly proved the Duke of Marlborough to be no general; and thus he now proves a W——le no Statesman'.[64] Such 'Magick', though, far from turning a character to brass, contrives rather to bring out the 'brass' that is already there in the form of a vicious or harmful characteristic and to redefine the whole personality in terms of that single feature. This, indeed, would appear to be how Swift habitually thought of many of his victims – not as men capable of exercising individual choice, but as machines or animals, acting only by irresistible instinct. He is no more angry with Walpole, he writes to Pope, 'than I was with the kite that last week flew away with one of my chickens, and yet I was pleased when one of my servants shot him two days after'.[65] As a writer, too, he does not think of such people as men. He inquires of Pope:

> And who are all these enemies you hint at? I can only think of Curl, Gildon, Squire, Burnet, Blackmore, and a few others whose fame I have forgot: Tools in my opinion as necessary for a good writer, as pen, ink, and paper.[66]

Such a concentration upon one feature of a personality in order to deny personality is something we see over and over again in the work of Swift. In the *Elegy On the much lamented Death of Mr. Demar, the Famous rich Man*, our perception of Demar is gradually altered as the poem proceeds. The miserly Demar is described initially in terms of his lust for money and of the moral lesson to be drawn therefrom.

> He walk'd the Streets, and wore a Thread-bare Cloak;
> He Din'd and Sup'd at Charge of other Folk, ...
> He that cou'd once have half a Kingdon bought,
> In half a Minute is not worth a Groat;

His *Coffers* from the *Coffin* could not save,
Nor all his Int'rest keep him from the Grave.

(ll. 9–10, 19–22)

By the end of the poem, though, we realise that the language
Swift is now using of him is making us perceive Demar as
indistinguishable from his money – his whole personality, in
death as in life, has actually become his money: 'He who so long
was *Currant* 'twould be strange / If he shou'd now be *cry'd down*
since his *Change*' (ll.35–6). This, as the epitaph makes clear,
gives Demar a kind of life after death, but only in the sense that
as a man he has never been properly alive.

His *Heirs* that he might safely rest,
Have put his *Carcass* in a *Chest*.
The very *Chest*, in which they say
His *other Self*, his *Money* lay.
And if his *Heirs* continue kind,
To that dear *Self* he left behind;
I dare believe that Four in Five
Will think his *better Self* alive.

(ll.43–50)

What might have been only another poem on the moral folly of
hoarding has been given a new dimension by Swift's awareness of
the implications of the conventional ways of rendering a man as
an object. Demar undergoes a multiplicity of deaths – the actual,
the 'death' of never having been alive, and the 'death', too, of
being the object of laughter of Swift's poem.[67]

One of Swift's most devastating personal killings, though, is
accomplished by his *Short Character of his Excellency Thomas
Earl of Wharton, Lord Lieutenant of Ireland*, that 'damned
libellous pamphlet', as he described it to Stella (*Prose Writings*,
XV, 115). Wharton, whom Swift 'hated ... like a Toad',[68] is a
puppet or machine in that he is clearly in the grip of a
predominant vice, or rather, in his case, of three, for

He has three predominant Passions, which you will seldom
find united in the same Man, as arising from different
Dispositions of Mind, and naturally thwarting each other:
These are Love of Power, Love of Money, and Love of

Pleasure; they ride him sometimes by Turns, and sometimes all together. (*Prose Writings*, III, 180–1)

The 'Slavery' of the Irish people with mention of which Swift has begun the pamphlet, and which he attributes to the conduct of Ireland's series of English governors down to Wharton (*Prose Writings*, III, 177), is, we realise, to be proved in the pamphlet rather upon Wharton himself, both in the sense that he is a slave to his predominant vices, and insofar as Swift is enslaving his 'Character' by his satiric rendering. Such slavery to vice, moreover, means, as Denis Donoghue says, that Swift may advert to Wharton's activities in 'politics, religion and lechery, but only to say that in this case they are all one; there is no point in differentiating where the acts are indistinguishable'.[69] Wharton 'is a Presbyterian in Politics, and an Atheist in Religion; but he chuseth at present to whore with a Papist' (*Prose Writings*, III, 179).

Our inability to distinguish between what are normally separate identifiable strands of a man's personality is pushed by Swift to the extreme position where we are shown Wharton's mind working in the mechanical way such lack of discrimination implies, with the consequence that Wharton, lacking a proper rational dimension, can have his thoughts and motives described in terms of comic action:

> he seemeth to have transferred those Talents of his Youth for intriguing with Women, into public Affairs. For, as some vain young Fellows, to make a Gallantry appear of Consequence, will chuse to venture their Necks by climbing up a Wall or Window at Midnight to a common Wench, where they might as freely have gone in at the Door, and at Noon-Day; so his Excellency, either to keep himself in Practice, or advance the Fame of his Politics, affects the most obscure, troublesome, and winding Paths, even in the most common Affairs, those which would be brought about as well in the ordinary Forms, or would follow of Course whether he intervened or not. (*Prose Writings*, III, 180)

In that the 'Gallantry' is wholly appropriate to the 'character' of Wharton, he is easily identified by the reader as actually climbing the wall or window. When, however, we make the

necessary mental adjustment and realise that Swift is talking of
Wharton's political behaviour and motivation, his engulfment,
both physically and mentally, in the comic action of the analogy
is complete.

Other faculties, too, which are normally distinguishing
features of the dignified human being are, in Wharton, reduced
to the level of animal instinct.

> He is without the Sense of Shame or Glory, as some Men are
> without the Sense of Smelling; and, therefore, a good Name
> to him is no more than a precious Ointment would be to
> these. (*Prose Writings*, III, 178)

The activities he can engage in at his present age are those
normally expected 'of a young Man at five and twenty', and none
are distinguished by the necessity for thought, 'Whether he
walketh or whistleth, or sweareth, or talketh Bawdy, or calleth
names' (*Prose Writings*, III, 179). And when, late in the
pamphlet, we are shown Wharton exercising the faculty of
speech, we find here, too, all of Swift's assertions demonstrated
as true: 'Is he, by G—d? why then (G—d d—mn me) he shall
have the first Bishoprick that falls' (*Prose Writings*, III, 182).
Such a speaker exercises no rational choice in the pattern of his
words – which cannot properly even be called a pattern,
especially set as they are within the careful balance of Swift's
own style. Wharton simply throws together the fewest simple
words that will do, though varying them a little with the
unvarying and unthinking regularity of his oaths. We, who can
appreciate the wit of a writer who attributes such oaths to a man
planning the disposition of a bishopric, will not admit one
whose speech so nearly resembles the automatic grunting of
animals to any degree of kinship with our own nature.

Having produced so good a likeness of Wharton in his
pamphlet, to the exclusion of the real Wharton, Swift describes
for Stella a chance meeting with his victim in London some
months after the appearance of the *Short Character*. Swift's
instinct is to ignore this real Wharton, as he had effectively done
both in his pamphlet and in his *Examiner* papers against him,
and he clearly expects Wharton's attitude to be the same. The
reaction of the victim, however, is not to allow himself to be
excluded by Swift in person, but to demand recognition.

> I intended to dine with Mr. Masham to-day, and called at
> White's Chocolate-house to see if he was there. Lord
> Wharton saw me at the door, and I saw him, but took no
> notice, and was going away; but he came through the crowd,
> called after me, and asked me how I did, & c. This was pretty;
> and I believe he wished every word he spoke was a halter to
> hang me. (*Prose Writings*, XVI, 427)

Swift reads on Wharton's politeness the effects he expects his
satire to have had – the desire to render the satirist as dead as he
has rendered his victim. Wharton's first move is to attract
Swift's attention, his second to treat him as though nothing
untoward has happened between them – as if the satire itself, by
being ignored, can be rendered non-existent. Beneath the masks,
though, Swift detects the desire that animates the whole satiric
momentum of the early eighteenth century, the desire for
revenge.

Desire for revenge, however, by no means always takes the
form of a reply in kind. Robert Martin Adams has described
William Wotton's reaction to *A Tale of a Tub* as 'one of
unqualified horror',[70] and certainly such horror is easy to find in
the pages of Wotton's *Observations upon The Tale of a Tub*[71]
(which Wotton then believed to have been written by Temple).
For Wotton, the *Tale* is 'one of the Prophanest Banters upon
the Religion of *Jesus Christ*, as such, that ever yet appeared'
(*Tale of a Tub*, p.324), and, in short,

> God and Religion, Truth and Moral Honesty, Learning and
> Industry are made a May-Game, and the most serious Things
> in the World are described as so many several Scenes. (*Tale
> of a Tub*, p.317)

Wotton, of course, was not alone in being scandalised by the
book, but we must remember that Wotton's indignation on
behalf of religion will have been given edge by the ludicrous
version of himself he found in the accompanying *Battle of the
Books*. The devices he adopts in writing his *Observations* – the
very decision to write such a piece at all – are very much those of
a man who, having been cast as an object of satiric laughter,
wishes to assert his own identity, yet cannot choose to do so by
creating a satiric work for himself.

So Wotton, having at first taken care to draw the *Battle*'s other prime target, Richard Bentley, to his side – an attempt to recreate fellowship among those whom laughter has excluded from normal social fellowship – proceeds to dismiss the *Battle of the Books* as unworthy of notice, particularly when set against the serious moral damage of the *Tale*. For

> though Dr. *Bentley* and my self are coursely treated, yet I believe I may safely answer for us both, that we should not have taken any manner of notice of it, if upon this Occasion I had not been obliged to say something in answer to what has been seriously said against us. (*Tale of a Tub*, p.316)

He takes the opportunity, provided for him by the publication of both works together, of evading the personal attack upon himself – as Swift, describing, in the preface to the *Battle*, satire as 'a sort of Glass, wherein Beholders do generally discover every body's Face but their Own' (*Tale of a Tub*, p.215), predicted he would do – in favour of performing a valuable public service regarding the *Tale*. What concerns himself and Bentley, he observes, 'is much the innocentest part of the Book, tending chiefly to make Men laugh for half an Hour, after which it leaves no further Effects behind it'. He has 'no occasion to be concerned at any Man's Railery about it' (*Tale of a Tub*, p.316). Yet his anxiety about 'the rest of the Book which does not relate to us', but which 'is of so irreligious a nature' and 'is so crude a Banter upon all that is esteemed as Sacred among all Sects and Religions among Men' (*Tale of a Tub*, p.316–17), is itself one 'Effect' of the laughter he has been subjected to by the *Battle*, and his attempt to recruit 'all Sects and Religions among Men' to his party is one way of trying to counter the sense of exclusion that such laughter produces. He will, he says, take 'so fair an Opportunity' to 'be useful to many People who pretend they see no harm in it' – which, of course, means that most of these 'many People' will also have been engaged in laughing at Wotton – and to 'lay open the Mischief of the Ludicrous Allegory, and to shew what that drives at which has been so greedily brought up and read' (*Tale of a Tub*, p.317). To hold up the *Tale* as a blasphemous work, and to use of it such extreme language as Wotton employs, is to endeavour to deflect the reader's attention from the 'Wotton' of *Battle of the Books* and onto the apparently unperceived immorality of the *Tale*, and to turn, therefore, what had been laughter into the righteous indignation that will mean the expulsion of the *Battle* 'Wotton' and the grateful adoption of the real Wotton of the *Observations*. The 'horror' expressed in his work, then, is 'unqualified' in that for Wotton it must be convincing if he is to redeem himself from his portrait in *Battle of the Books*. His horror is not only the horror of a Christian faced with apparently deliberate infidelity, but the horror of a man desperate to prevent his own annihilation.

Significantly, Wotton concludes the *Observations* with another attempt to evade his possession in the creation of the satirist, and that is by questioning the originality of the satire. The danger a writer presents to his victim can be considerably reduced if it is proven that 'his *Wit* is *not his own*'. Several ideas in the *Tale* Wotton picks out as having been 'borrowed from a Letter written by the late Witty D. of *Buckingham*', and for the *Battle* itself Wotton has been 'assured' (another attempt to rally the confirmation of fellows to his side) that it 'is *Mutandis Mutandis* taken out of a *French* Book, entitled, *Combat des Livres*' (*Tale of a Tub*, pp.327–8). The final point of Swift's jest, however (a jest acknowledged, as Claude Rawson points out, in Swift's subsequent 'triumphant assimilation into the notes of Wotton's hostile exegesis'[72]), is that by casting around for literary models, by his itemizing from 'a' to 'z', repeatedly, charges relating to the *Tale*, by his 'discovery' of a design 'to pick Holes in the weak sides of Religion and Government' (*Tale of a Tub*, 'Preface' p.39), by his whole procedure in the *Observations*, Wotton has unwittingly rendered himself as the kind of '*TRUE CRITICK*' that Swift described in Section III of the *Tale*, giving Wotton as a heroic modern example (*Tale of a Tub*, p.94). The true critic is one 'from whom the Commonwealth of Learning has in all Ages' received 'immense benefits', who is 'a *Discoverer and Collector of Writers Faults*', and who becomes so great a 'Nuisance to Mankind' that 'as soon a he had finished his Task assigned' he 'should immediately deliver himself up to Ratsbane, or Hemp, or from some convenient *Altitude*' (*Tale of a Tub*, pp.94–5). Wotton, then, having proved in the *Observations* that he is indeed a true critic, should take the final step of returning himself to the state of non-existence where Swift's *Battle* placed him. And Swift's engulfing of

Wotton's work in his own notes, even more than the assimilation of the 'real' Partridge in the *Bickerstaff Papers*, represents a second and more decisive 'killing' of the real Wotton than the original rendering in the *Battle of the Books*.

The most notable instance, finally, of a victim's ability to 'kill' the satirist in return for his own treatment is that achieved by Cibber's *Letter from Mr. Cibber, to Mr. Pope*, published in July, 1742, between *The New Dunciad* and *The Dunciad, In Four Books* in which Cibber makes his appearance as hero.[73] While the effectiveness of the 'terrible *Tom Tit*' revelations undoubtedly had more to do with luck than with Cibber's skill in composing satiric rejoinders – a man who can ask Pope, as Cibber does in this *Letter*, whether he 'really' thinks him so guilty of Dulness 'as to deserve the Name of the Dull Fellow you make of me', and who follows this by declaring 'from my Heart solemnly . . . that I don't believe you *do* think so of me',[74] does not have a great deal of understanding of satire – the way Cibber goes about presenting his tale of Pope's adventure with the whore amply demonstrates that he was consciously trying to make Pope the satirist feel the same pain of exclusion as Cibber the victim. Citing Pope's line from the *Epistle to Dr. Arbuthnot*, 'And has not Colley too his Lord, and Whore', Cibber wishes to replace 'Colley' with 'Sawney', asking 'Why then may I not insist that *Colley* or *Sawney* in the Verse would make no Difference in the Satyr!' He will justify the amendation, and his motive, he says, is to have someone to keep him company in the face of society's laughter. Pope

> has so particularly picked me out of the Number to make an Example of: Why may I not take the same Liberty, and even single him out for another to keep me in countenance?[75]

What better companion than the satirist himself for one who has been satirically exposed to society's derision? But by proving Sawney and Colley, satirist and victim, interchangeable, Cibber will in fact have traded the victim's insecurity for the security of the satirist, have annexed, in Freud's terms, the role of the joke-maker so that he, Pope, is now forced to become the second person who is laughed at by the non-particiating onlooker. Cibber himself, of course, sees the matter largely in terms of just deserts, for 'when the Guilty are Accusers, it seems but just, to make use of any Truth, that may invalidate their Evidence'. He does, though, draw the reader to his side for endorsement of his role-reversal with Pope, and with a Pope, moreover, that Cibber's obvious lack of satiric artistry in the telling, his very guilelessness, forbids us to take as a rendered 'Pope'. Pope will be made an object when we laugh at him, but Cibber's Pope is told with all the naivety of an actual memory. The impression created by the *Letter* is that Cibber is too simple to have given us anything but the real man. With genuine self-assurance, then, he can ask:

> And now again, gentle Reader, let it be judged, whether the *Lord* and the *Whore* above-mentioned might not, with equal Justice, have been apply'd to sober *Sawney* the Satyrist, as to *Colley* the Criminal?[76]

Pope, Cibber claimed in his *Another Occasional Letter from Mr. Cibber to Mr. Pope*, published two years later, had been made 'as uneasy as a Rat in a hot Kettle for a Twelve-month together'[77] by his *Letter*. Certainly, as Norman Ault describes, 'numerous pamphlets, pictures, poems, and newspaper articles' were evoked by the publication, including

> the deployment of a pictorial attack on Pope, when a number of different caricatures of Cibber's 'rescue' of him began to be displayed for sale in the windows of the print shops.[78]

Pope, as always, claimed to be unaffected. Cibber, he observed to Hugh Bethel, had written him 'a very foolish and impudent Letter, which I have no cause to be sorry for, and perhaps next Winter I shall be thought to be glad of'.[79] Faced with the prospect of a further pamphlet (Cibber's *Another Occasional Letter*), he wrote to Warburton, he would welcome it as

> more to me than a dose of Hartshorn; and as a Stink revives one who has been oppressed with Perfumes, his Railing will cure me of a Course of Flatteries.[80]

Nonetheless, Cibber's *Letter* clearly achieves a most artlessly skilful turning of the laugh against the satirist to rank alongside Steele's discomfiting letter to Swift. That both Cibber and

Steele were to receive ample recompence for their successes, Cibber so conclusively in *The Dunciad, In Four Books* (and it is still uncertain how far Pope had been deliberately provoking Cibber to some rejoinder in preparation for his retributory elevation to *The Dunciad*), does not detract from the effectiveness of their psychological victories over the two major satirists of the age.

We have come a long way from the laughter that in Swift's hands enforces compassion for the *Beautiful Young Nymph Going to Bed*, for the satirist's normal business is not to make his reader face the responsibility for his own laughter, but rather to take his laughter as a ready means of endorsement as he laughs the deserved laugh against a figure whom the satire holds up as the deserving victim. That Swift was able to produce such responsibility, however, and that he was able, too, to be so piqued by Steele's letter, demonstrates how completely he understood the effect of the laughing act, and assures us that we shall find the satiric devices employed in his work controlled by a precise awareness of just what he was doing to his victims.

The easily given laugh of the non-participating onlooker is clearly of the utmost importance for both satirist and victim, for one is endorsed by it, while the other finds himself excluded. Yet, as Cibber's *Letter* demonstrates, such laughter can be fickle, and, given the proper nudge, can soon be switched from victim to satirist. The reader's desire for self-commendation, for the satisfaction of his ego, will overcome loyalty to one side, seeking out the easiest route to gratification. The most effective satire, therefore, will be that which anticipates the victim's reactions and provides, as happens with Partridge and Wotton, the means whereby those reactions can be engulfed by the original attack. The implication, though, is that those eighteenth-century writers who were uneasy with laughter, who saw it as the expression of man's fallen nature, were right, for laughter, as encouraged by the satiric techniques so far described, does seem to depend upon man as a pleasure-seeking, fickle, selfish and ultimately godless individual. Laughter, however, particularly for the satirist, should not be a solitary activity – indeed, is one of the most infectious activities enjoyed by man. What I shall turn to next is the laughter of society, not laughter as a collection of individuals who happen to be laughing, but to the laugh of the group.

3   Shewing the Teeth: Laughter in Society

The sound of laughter is produced by a deep inspiration followed by short, interrupted, spasmodic contractions of the chest, and especially of the diaphragm. . . . From the shaking of the body, the head nods to and fro. The lower jaw often quivers up and down, as is likewise the case with some species of baboons, when they are much pleased. During laughter the mouth is opened more or less widely, with the corners drawn much backwards, as well as a little upwards; and the upper lip is somewhat raised. The drawing back of the corners is best seen in moderate laughter, and especially in a broad smile. . . . Dr. Duchenne repeatedly insists that, under the emotion of joy, the mouth is acted on exclusively by the great zygomatic muscles, which serve to draw the corners backwards and upwards; but judging from the manner in which the upper teeth are always exposed during laughter and broad smiling, as well as from my own sensations, I cannot doubt that some of the muscles running to the upper lip are likewise brought into moderate action.

The human animal engaged in the act of laughing, as described here by Darwin in his 1872 work *The Expression of Emotions in Man and Animals*,[1] is a creature apparently remote from the thinking individual who endorses with his laugh the case levelled by Swift or Pope against the satiric victim. The 'great zygomatic muscles', the 'species of baboons', are details the satirist might use against the object of his attack, and yet they are clearly more applicable to the laugher than to those laughed at. Indeed, in *The Memoirs of Martinus Scriblerus* we find a comparable satiric description of laughter in which the satire is directed against laughers themselves. There are two cases among the 'Diseases of the Mind' which Martinus found 'extremely difficult'.

The second case was immoderate *Laughter*: When any of that risible species were brought to the Doctor, and when he consider'd what an infinity of Muscles these laughing Rascals threw into a convulsive motion at the same time; whether we regard the spasms of the Diaphragm and all the muscles of respiration, the horrible *rictus* of the mouth, the distortion of the lower jaw, the crisping of the nose, twinkling of the eyes, or sphaerical convexity of the cheeks, with the tremulous succussion of the whole human body; when he consider'd, I say, all this, he used to cry out, *Casus deplorabilis!* and give such Patients over.[2]

The machinery of laughter apparently reduces those who laugh to the level of automata, or at least to the state of an animal reacting in a predictable manner from instinct alone. To laugh, it would seem, is to give up that very claim to rationality to which satire's appeal is directed.

It is, however, in Darwin's territory, in those characteristics that man seems to share with animals, that the function of laughter in the group can be most usefully sought, for while the satirist may attempt to appeal to each individual reader as a rational judge, the expected accompaniment to such judgment will be the arousal of one of the most primal group activities. And laughter is one activity that Darwin finds most persistently paralleled in the behaviour of animals. The 'laughter of man and the tittering of monkeys' are both 'a rapidly repeated sound'.[3] Dogs, 'in their expression of fondness, have a slight eversion of the lips, and grin and sniff amidst their gambols, in a way that resembles laughter',[4] while a 'bark of joy' is often found to follow a 'grin'.[5] And of horses, too, he observes that

When pleased, as when some coveted food is brought to them in the stable, they raise and draw in their heads, prick their ears, and looking intently towards their friend, often whinny.[6]

The whole pattern of behaviour of both human and animal during intense pleasure, argues Darwin, can be spoken of in very similar terms.

Under a transport of Joy or of vivid Pleasure, there is a strong tendency to various purposeless movements, and to the utterance of various sounds. We see this in our young children, in their loud laughter, clapping of hands, and jumping for joy; in the bounding and barking of a dog when going out to walk with his master; and in the frisking of a horse when turned out into an open field. Joy quickens the circulation, and this stimulates the brain, which again reacts on the whole body.[7]

It is with monkeys, though, that the most striking parallels can be found. 'Young chimpanzees', says Darwin, 'make a kind of barking noise, when pleased by the return of any one to whom they are attached', which their keepers refer to as a laugh. When a young chimp is tickled, 'a more decided chuckling or laughing sound is uttered; though the laughter is sometimes noiseless'. In chimps, too, and in other monkeys, the 'corners of the mouth are then drawn backwards' and the lower eyelids are 'slightly wrinkled'. Their eyes 'sparkle and grow brighter'. Young Orangs, 'when tickled, likewise grin and make a chuckling sound', their eyes grow brighter, and once 'their laughter ceases, an expression may be detected passing over their faces, which, as Mr. Wallace remarked to me, may be called a smile'. Dr Duchenne's tame monkey, fed 'some choice delicacy', expressed a satisfaction 'partaking of the nature of an incipient smile, and resembling that often seen on the face of man'.[8] An Anubis baboon was insulted and then made friends with by his keeper. 'As the reconciliation was effected the baboon rapidly moved up and down his jaws and lips, and looked pleased. When we laugh heartily,' adds Darwin, 'a similar movement, or quiver, may be observed more or less distinctly in our jaws.'[9]

For Darwin, the evidence is conclusive, and modern writers in the field tend to agree with him, so much so that in 1973, writing in a centenary volume, Suzanne Chevalier-Skolnikoff could conclude that 'Darwin's work of 1872 is still the most encompassing work on the subject', and that

Darwin's central hypothesis – that the facial expressions of nonhuman primates and man are similar – has been strikingly confirmed, strongly supporting his theory that human facial expressions have evolved from those of man's nonhuman primate ancestors.[10]

The work of J. A. R. A. M. van Hooff in particular has
effected such confirmation. Van Hooff's observations of the
facial displays of the higher primates have led to his
distinguishing between two main kinds of monkey 'laughter' –
the 'grin-face' or 'silent bared-teeth display', and the 'play-face',
or 'relaxed open-mouth display'. Both, he argues, are important
precursors 'of the expressive movements of smiling and
laughter' in man.[11] The silent bared-teeth display is characterised by

> fully retracted mouth-corners and lips, so that an appreciable
> part of the gums is bared; closed or only slightly opened
> mouth; absence of vocalisation; inhibited body movements
> and eyes that are widely or normally open and can be directed
> straight or obliquely towards an interacting partner.[12]

A similar display, the 'vocalised bared-teeth display', characterised by 'screams, squeals, barks, geekers', is something the
higher primates share with most mammals, in many of whom,
like marsupials, rodents and other primitive carnivores, 'it is
often the only facial expression'. This display is produced when
the animal is 'subject to some threat or strong aversive
stimulation', or 'in a situation of defence' when 'the actor
manifests a strong or moderate tendency to flee'.[13] In the higher
primates the vocalised bared-teeth display may 'develop into a
signal of general frustration and excitement', whereas the silent
bared-teeth display, particularly among 'more advanced genera',
occurs in the course of a 'comparatively active social life' and is
often 'maintained for some time' in a 'ritualised version'. It is
primarily a gesture not of frustration but of submission and of
reassurance, or even 'a sign of attachment', and in some species is
mixed with the lip-smacking display which originally accompanied grooming – 'when swallowing the particles which have
been found' – and which itself therefore expresses reassurance and
attachment.[14] Such a mixture of gestures can be performed 'by
subordinate towards dominant group-members', or 'by dominant animals towards subordinates and between equals'. The
context, says van Hooff, 'suggests that it can serve as an
expression of attachment and as a reassurance in these species'.[15]
And he concludes this section of his work by arguing

that in the ascending scale of the primates leading to man, there is a progressive broadening of the meaning of the element of baring the teeth. Originally forming part of a mainly defensive or protective pattern of behaviour, this element becomes a signal of submission and non-hostility. In some species the latter aspect can become predominating, so that a reassuring and finally a friendly signal can develop. Correlated with this development is the tendency of *silent teeth-baring* to overlap functionally and, in some species also morphologically, with the *lip-smacking* display. At the end of the scale it has practically replaced *lip-smacking.* Our human *smile* appears to fit neatly at the end of this development.[16]

The relaxed open-mouth display, van Hooff's second important monkey expression, is 'characterised by a rather widely opened mouth, and lips that remain covering all or the greater part of the teeth'. It is 'often accompanied by quick and shallow rather staccato breathing' which in some species, like the chimpanzee, may be vocalised. 'The vocalisations then sound like "ahh ahh ahh".' This display is close to the 'aggressive *staring open-mouth* display', but can be distinguished 'by the free and easy nature of the eye and body movements and by the fact that the mouth-corners are not pulled forward'. In all the primates in which it occurs, says van Hooff, the relaxed open-mouth display signifies the same thing: it

> typically accompanies the boisterous mock-fighting and chasing involved in social play. It can be regarded as a ritualised intention movement of the *gnawing* which is a characteristic part of the play of many mammals, and may function as a metacommunicative signal that the ongoing behaviour is not meant seriously, but is to be interpreted instead as 'mock-fighting'. In the chimpanzee the *relaxed open-mouth* display can easily be elicited by tickling, and many authors were struck by its resemblance both in form and context with our laughter.[17]

Van Hooff had begun his paper by glancing briefly at various laughter theories: laughter 'might stem . . . from the savage shout of triumph and the cruel mockery over a conquered enemy'; its 'oldest form' might be 'to jest at other people we

despise or hate'; its function 'could be either to correct or to
repel abnormal and non-conforming individuals'; and 'Gloating
would be one of the early roots of the comic and the
ludicrous.'[18] Van Hooff's work, however, suggests that quite
the opposite is in fact the case, and that laughter, far from
deriving from aggressive tendencies, is, in the higher primates,
quite clearly associated with play. A second major researcher in
this field, J. S. Andrew, offers his strong agreement in a note to
van Hooff's paper, and states categorically that

> there is no evidence of association between typical laughter
> and attack behaviour. Claims that laughter has aggressive
> motivation rest on assertions that it is usual during jeering or
> mocking by a group. No accurate descriptions of such
> behaviour have been published.[19]

I do not wish to spend time here in the consideration of play,
which is treated at length in my next chapter. It is clear from van
Hooff's work, though (and both Andrew and Chevalier-
Skolnikoff[20] are in agreement here), that we may draw precise
conclusions from primate observation concerning the derivation
of smiling and laughing in man. To begin with, 'laughter and
smiling in the human species refer to a continuum of
intergrading signals' between 'two extreme forms, the *broad-
smile* on the one hand and the *wide-mouth laugh* on the other'.
These forms 'show formal, and most likely also functional,
resemblance with respectively the *silent bared-teeth* display and
the *relaxed open-mouth* display of the other primates'. The
agreement, says van Hooff, is obvious.

Laughter then fits neatly in the phylogenetic developmental
range of the *relaxed open-mouth* display, a metacommuni-
cative signal, designating the behaviour with which it is
associated as mock-aggression or play. Smiling fits well as the
final stage of the development of the *silent bared-teeth* display.
Originally reflecting an attitude of submission, this display
has come to represent non-hostility and finally has become
emancipated to an expression of social attachment or
friendliness, which is non-hostility *par excellence.*[21]

Laughter and smiling are 'social displays', they 'convey information with respect to the actor's relationship to its social fellows', and that relationship should be understood as unambiguously non-hostile, either mock-aggressive and playful, or reassuring and friendly.[22]

To turn, now, to the kind of laughter to be aroused by satire, it is clear that the laughter of the non-participating onlooker will be initiated at the expense of the satiric victim. But to laugh, of course, is a pleasurable activity, irrespective of what arouses it, and, as Bergson points out – an assertion which van Hooff's work must underline – 'Our laughter is always the laughter of a group.' The laugh, even the satiric laugh, is an end in itself, and the laugher, while he is perhaps expressing the hostility that is inevitably felt by the victim, is also enjoying the pleasure of laughing for its own sake, and, moreover, of laughing with those who laugh. He has joined, for the duration of his laughter, a higher society than his everyday vision has allowed him to perceive. He has become one of the group of those who laugh at this sort of thing. His pleasure in laughing is partly an expression of his pleasure at being a member of such a group, and of his fellow-feeling with its other members. Bergson, again, argues: 'However spontaneous it seems, laughter always implies a kind of secret freemasonry, or even complicity, with other laughers, real or imaginary.'[23] In this case, laughter should be seen far less as a denial, but rather as a spontaneous affirmation, though such an affirmation may have little direct relevance to the object or stimulus that originally inspired the laughter. Laughter, it seems, is not so much Janus-faced as two-dimensional. In one dimension it is to the victim or outsider or stranger a sign of his exclusion. From within, however, and quite separately, in the dimension that is the mentality of the laugher, the victim as an individual is so inconsiderable as to be irrelevant, for his laughter serves a much more important and expansive function than making a fellow creature uncomfortable. It affirms his membership of the 'secret freemasonry', of the group of people like him.

'If eating and drinking be natural,' says Shaftesbury, 'herding is so too.' Affection between the sexes becomes affection for and between offspring 'as kindred and companions', and

thus a clan or tribe is gradually formed; a public is recognised; and besides the pleasure found in social entertainment, language, and discourse, there is so apparent a necessity for continuing this good correspondency and union, that to have no sense or feeling of this kind, no love of country, community, or anything in common, would be the same as to be insensible even of the plainest means of self-preservation, and most necessary condition of self-enjoyment.[24]

Where the formation of a group is the direct consequence of such natural affection, the laugh may be expected to serve the fairly obvious social function of maintaining affective ties between members of the group. Laughter and smiling, as signals within a whole pattern of verbal and nonverbal communication, will reinforce the cohesive instincts of the individuals who make up the group: the group that laughs together stays together. And yet, while that formula is no doubt correct, the issue is more complicated. We should not hesitate to agree with Bergson when he argues that to understand laughter 'we must put it back into its natural environment, which is society, and above all must we determine the utility of its function, which is a social one'.[25] But we should also be aware (which is the concern of the satirist) that many groups do not deserve to stay together, or would be in some way better if freed from the limitations of understanding that group mentality imposes. In particular, no group can free itself from the limitation of exclusiveness – the fact that its very existence as a group depends upon the exclusion of some individuals or other groups of individuals. A religion, says Freud, 'even if it calls itself the religion of love, must be hard and unloving to those who do not belong to it', for 'cruelty and intolerance . . . are natural to every religion'.[26] Laughter and smiling, then, are non-aggressive, endorsements of group ties, but those ties are not necessarily worthy or desirable, especially in the eyes of the satirist.

In the opening sections of *Group Psychology* Freud cites the work of both Le Bon and McDougall, endorsing their unflattering conclusions on the characteristics of group mentality. This is what McDougall has to say of the psychological behaviour of the 'unorganized' group. It is

excessively emotional, impulsive, violent, fickle, inconsistent, irresolute and extreme in action, displaying only the coarser emotions and the less refined sentiments; extremely suggestible, careless in deliberation, hasty in judgment, incapable of any but the simpler and imperfect forms of reasoning; easily swayed and led, lacking in self-consciousness, devoid of self-respect and of sense of responsibility, and apt to be carried away by the consciousness of its own force, so that it tends to produce all the manifestations we have learnt to expect of any irresponsible and absolute power.[27]

And Le Bon, in general agreement, adds:

Inclined as it itself is to all extremes, a group can only be excited by an excessive stimulus. Anyone who wishes to produce an effect upon it needs no logical adjustment in his arguments; he must paint in the most forcible colours, he must exaggerate, and he must repeat the same thing again and again.[28]

If laughter serves to strengthen the ties of such groups then it is making them more resistant to change and their members less open to sympathetic identification with others outside the group, more inclined to overlook the shortcomings of group membership[29] and to see in the satiric glass every man's face but their own.

And few groups are ideal. Or rather, no 'real' group (to borrow Bergson's terms) can be so flexible as to extend membership to individuals who adopt more than a given degree of eccentricity. Bergson speaks of laughter as a social corrective of 'inelasticity' in individuals, but such inelasticity is, of course, defined by the group itself, and the definition will say as much about the rigidity of that group as it does about the individual. 'All groups', as Laing tells us, 'operate by means of phantasy', but the phantasy is experienced as 'reality'.[30] As group members, we hold a 'tenable position' within a phantasy system and, moreover, we 'never realize we are in' such a system.

We never even dream of extricating ourselves. We tolerate, punish, or treat as harmless, bad, or mad those who try to extricate themselves, and tell us that we should also.[31]

Even punishment of this kind, though, will strengthen the identity of the group, act as an opportunity to restate and reaffirm group values and assumptions, so much so that when an actual transgressor is not available a mock criminal or eccentric may be periodically chosen to fulfil the same function. A scapegoat, as Edward and Lillian Bloom put it,

> makes it possible for a community fragmented by shame and guilt to reintegrate itself. Society has always needed *pharmakoi*, ceremonial victims, upon whom man's aggregate sins are publicly and symbolically discharged. The scapegoat becomes the agent in whom is concentrated whatever threatens totemic well-being.[32]

We should add that not only will 'shame and guilt' be discharged with the scapegoat, but the remaining members of the group will be exempted from recognising shame and guilt as existing anywhere but on the person of the scapegoat, who can therefore be accepted as somehow responsible for the community's fragmentation. 'Comparably,' continue the Blooms, 'the butt of satire may be a convenient surrogate for expelling communal vice or folly.' The reader, 'in judging others guilty . . . can pretend that virtue accrues to him'.[33]

We have already seen, in chapter 1, Addison and Steele attacking the free-thinkers in a way which reasserts belief in the Christian religion, and in the virtue of those who uphold it. Laughter here is invited at that group of individuals who so usefully offer themselves as scapegoats, and in so doing serve to strengthen the ties between all right-thinking Christians. Robert Elliott (here quoting Hugh Dalziel Duncan) gives a more recent example of social cohesion through laughter at the expense of another group, here of outsiders who apparently desire integration into the larger group.

> Each newly arrived immigrant group in America became a butt of ridicule for older groups who had risen to power and who therefore were able to set standards of Americanization. The immigrant is always a challenge, even a threat, to established customs. He makes us realize that two (or more) evaluations of action are possible. Laughter helps to resolve this. As we ridicule the newcomer, we overcome confusion through the euphoria arising within us as we laugh.[34]

This 'euphoria', which may be equated with the joy of belonging to Bergson's 'secret freemasonry', not only overcomes the confusion of being challenged to admit an alternative 'phantasy system'. It also removes from the laugher any responsibility for examining and judging his own actions. His laughter confirms, here, his membership of a 'real' group, and that membership automatically defines him as 'virtuous'. His actions are therefore acceptable. If he were not 'virtuous' then he would no longer be allowed to remain a member. When what constitutes virtue, as what constitutes 'reality', is defined by the assumptions of the group mentality – as Freud says, every individual acting upon every other individual so that each one 'is ruled by those attitudes of the group mind which exhibit themselves in such forms as racial characteristics, class prejudices, public opinion, etc.'[35] – then every occasion for laughter makes group membership more secure and group 'phantasy' more 'real'. 'This accounts', says Bergson, 'for the comic being so frequently dependent on the manners or ideas, or, to put it bluntly, on the prejudices, of a society.'[36]

Even Shaftesbury, extolling that tendency in man to herd through an overwhelming natural affection between individuals, is prepared nevertheless to admit that man also tends to form, within the larger group, 'strong factions' for the furtherance of particular interests or from the 'want of exercise' among the 'associating spirits'.

Nothing is so delightful as to incorporate. Distinctions of many kinds are invented. Religious societies are formed. Orders are erected, and their interests espoused and served with the utmost zeal and passion. Founders and patrons of this sort are never wanting. Wonders are performed, in this wrong social spirit, by those members of separate societies. And the associating genius of man is never better proved than in those very societies, which are formed in opposition to the general one of mankind, and to the real interest of the State.

In short, concludes Shaftesbury, 'the very spirit of faction, for the greatest part, seems to be no other than the abuse or irregularity of that social love and common affection which is natural to mankind'.[37]

Man's tendency to group, and to form factions within larger groups – man's spirit, in other words, of disunity working permanently at odds with his equally strong spirit of unity – is, of course, prominently treated by the eighteenth-century satirists. *Tale of a Tub, Gulliver's Travels, The Dunciad, Rape of the Lock, The Beggar's Opera* – these are only the most obvious works by the most obvious writers in which group mentality, group cohesiveness and group limitations are of major concern. The ways in which these groups are satirically presented, though, especially in the work of Swift and Pope, repay some closer inspection, first in order to be more precise about the satirist's attitude towards groups, but also because of the need to be clear about the nature of the laughter aroused by the satire in that most important group of all, the satirist's readers.

The very reason for the existence of *A Tale of a Tub*, as we are assured by the writer of 'The Preface', is to protect the wider group, here the '*Commonwealth*' at large, against the under-mining operations of energetic individuals who, as the 'Wits of the present Age', are themselves described in terms of a group within a group. The members of this faction,

> being so very numerous and penetrating, it seems, the Grandees of *Church* and *State* begin to fall under horrible Apprehensions, lest these Gentlemen, during the intervals of a long Peace, should find leisure to pick Holes in the weak sides of Religion and Government. (*Tale of a Tub*, p.39)

Even the wits themselves, though, can be sub-divided again into smaller groups, as the 'nine thousand seven hundred forty and three Persons' assessed to qualify as such will be split 'into the several Schools' of the Academy which is eventually to divert them permanently 'from canvasing and reasoning upon . . . delicate Points' (*Tale of a Tub*, p.39) and where all wits will 'pursue those Studies to which their Genius most inclines them'. Each school, then, represents a sub-faction within the already dangerous faction of wits.

> There is first, a large *Pederastick* School, with *French* and *Italian* Masters. There is also, the *Spelling* School, *a very spacious Building*: The School of *Looking Glasses*: The School of *Swearing*: The School of *Criticks*: The School of

Salivation: The School of *Hobby-Horses*: The School of *Poetry*: The School of *Tops*: The School of *Spleen*: The School of *Gaming*: with many others too tedious to recount. (*Tale of a Tub*, pp.41–2)

Swift does not suggest – as he does later in 'The History of Martin' when '*Jack*'s friends fell out among themselves, split into a thousand partys, turn'd all things topsy turvy' (*Tale of a Tub*, p.306) – that so many smaller groupings of wits will necessarily breed animosity and hostility between the various factions. He does, however, imply that this will be the case by proceeding directly to explain how little one species of wit can be understood by another. A '*Modern* Piece of Wit', far from being universally welcomed and appreciated, is notable for its extreme isolation.

Somethings are extreamly witty *to day*, or *fasting*, or *in this place*, or *at eight o'clock*, or *over a Bottle*, or *spoke by Mr. Whatd'y'call'm*, or *in a Summer's Morning*: Any of which, by the smallest Transposal or Misapplication, is utterly annihilate. Thus, *Wit* has its Walks and Purlieus, out of which it may not stray the breadth of a Hair, upon peril of being lost. (*Tale of a Tub*, p.43)

What Swift is doing is so to sub-divide the wit faction that what appeared at first, 'like the Picture of *Hobbes*'s *Leviathan*' (*Tale of a Tub*, p.277), to be a group, emerges at last as a collection of separate individuals with nothing in common but their being a nuisance to themselves and others. So, in the *Tale* itself, the three brothers, who are not named until they begin to fall out, first Martin and Jack with Peter, and then Martin with Jack, divide and sub-divide over and over again, follower turning against follower, until we can perceive the prospect only of numbers of individual fanatics each at odds with every other.

Already, then, early in this early work of Swift's, we are being shown apparent unity within groups which becomes, on closer examination, an array rather of disunity as each individual blindly follows his own inclination and fights for his own limited ends. This display is underlined by Swift's turning next to 'the Multitude of Writers whereof the whole Multitude of Writers most reasonably complains'. Every member of the group of writers looks at the group of which he is apparently a member and endeavours, in his work, and especially in his prefaces 'wherein the Authors do at the very beginning address the gentle Reader concerning this enormous Grievance', to make some distinction between himself and the '*Rabble of Scriblers*' which constitutes the rest of the group (*Tale of a Tub*, p.45). And yet to the dispassionate observer he is just another writer complaining about writers, upon which Swift tells the reader 'a short Tale'.

> *A Mountebank in* Leicester-Fields, *had drawn a huge Assembly about him. Among the rest, a fat unweildy Fellow, half stifled in the Press, would be every fit crying out, Lord! what a filthy Crowd is here; Pray, good People, give way a little, Bless me! what a Devil has rak'd this Rabble together: . . . At last, a* Weaver *that stood next him could hold no longer: A Plague confound you* (said he) *for an over-grown Sloven; and who (in the Devil's Name) I wonder, helps to make up the Crowd half so much as your self? Don't you consider (with a Pox) that you take up more room with that Carkass than any five here?* (*Tale of a Tub*, p.46)

The weaver, Whartonesque though his language may be, is unusual in that, like the satirist himself, he has the vision to see the implications of group membership. He appreciates that belonging to a group is compatible with a proper self-consciousness – the ability to see oneself as one individual among many similar individuals – and that, in fact, the continuing cohesion of the group depends upon such self-consciousness in its members. What is not compatible with group membership, however, is selfishness.

A Tale of Tub is filled with examples of groups that are not groups, of individuals who have flocked together from motives of personal vanity, or through foolishness, or from fanaticism, none of which are states of mind which adapt the member to take proper account of anything other than self interest. We are also presented, however, with occasional and often inconspicuous examples of individuals who, like the weaver, are qualified by proper self-consciousness, by the capacity for unclouded observation and judgment, to be members of a group that will not immediately disintegrate into self-seeking factions.

The Bookseller, putting together his Dedication 'To The Right Honourable John Lord Sommers', has encountered many of the group of wits in his efforts to discover 'the Worthiest' to whom the author desired his work shoud be dedicated. Each wit distinguishes 'Himself to be the Person aimed at'. When an opportunity for self-elevation presents itself, all members of the group reveal themselves as governed solely by personal vanity. I went, says the Bookseller,

> to several other Wits of my Acquaintance, with no small Hazard and Weariness to my Person, from a prodigious Number of dark, winding Stairs; But I found them all in the same Story.

Fortunately, each wit, when pressed for a second choice, names Somers as the only possible alternative, whereupon the Bookseller, showing a degree of insight and of responsibility apparently unusual in his class – distiguishing himself, in other words, from the unscrupulousness normally found in the satirically presented behaviour of booksellers – is able to conclude in a manner that lifts him for a moment from the level of the fools and rogues of the *Tale* towards the large and humorous perspective of the satirist: 'I have somewhere heard, it is a Maxim, that those, to whom every Body allows the second Place, have an undoubted Title to the First' (*Tale of a Tub*, p.24).

Other groups – the tailor-worshippers, the Æolists, the philosopher-madmen – are invented, ridiculed and demolished as merely self-seeking individuals combining into factions, none of whom have the least capacity for self-criticism or proper self-consciousness. The superficial reader, says Swift, may laugh at such a show, but it will be laughter that bestows only the most physical of benefits: 'The *Superficial* Reader will be strangely provoked to *Laughter*; which clears the Breast and the Lungs, is Soverain against the *Spleen*, and the most innocent of all *Diureticks*.' The 'truly *Learned*' reader, however, will 'find sufficient Matter to employ his Speculations for the rest of his Life'. That Swift then proceeds to propose that

> every Prince in *Christendom* will take seven of the *deepest Scholars* in his Dominions, and shut them up close for *seven*

Years, in *seven* Chambers, with a Command to write *seven*
ample Commentaries on this comprehensive Discourse
(*Tale of a Tub*, p.185)

is, of course, a joke at which the 'truly Learned' reader is
expected to laugh. For Swift has already, during the course of
the 'Digression on Madness', dropped strong hints on how he
sees both the 'truly *Learned*' reader and the truly learned man,
and it is in terms quite contrary to the faction-forming
selfishness of the bulk of the creatures who occupy the *Tale*.

For, the Brain, in its natural Position and State of Serenity,
disposeth its Owner to pass his Life in the common Forms,
without any Thought of subduing Multitudes to his own
Power, his *Reasons* or his *Visions*; and the more he shapes his
Understanding by the Pattern of Human Learning, the less he
is inclined to form Parties after his particular Notions;
because that instructs him in his private Infirmities, as well as
in the stubborn Ignorance of the People.   (*Tale of a Tub*,
p.171)

To be truly learned is to be conscious of one's own inadequacies,
as it is to be aware, too, of mankind's inevitable limitations. No
man should be so certain that he is right that he will seek to
subdue multitudes or form parties in furtherance of his private
convictions. History and self-awareness should always counsel
otherwise. Such a reader, reflective and serene, is exactly the
reader who will be fitted to join the 'secret freemasonry' of those
who can laugh at *Tale of a Tub*, not the laugh of the superficial
reader, but the laugh of the '*Men of Wit and Tast*' (*Tale of a
Tub*, p.20). That is the only group Swift would have his readers
join. All other groups are no true groups, are in danger of falling
apart as soon as looked at, just as the *Tale* itself, as a tale, falls
apart under the variously pulling tensions of the author's
digressions, and of the digressions within the digressions, 'like a
Nest of Boxes' (*Tale of a Tub*, p.124). Only the truly learned
reader, whose brain is in a 'State of Serenity', will not be
himself discomposed by the discomposition of the *Tale*, and will
have the perspective necessary for creating a unity from such
apparent disunity. This is the reader who will have the right to

laugh at *Tale of a Tub*, and the right to belong, through his laughter, to the higher group that is mankind.

When Swift turns to writing directly political journalism, of course, in *The Examiner*, he readily looks again to such an ideal reader as the impartial onlooker who will weigh the account being presented to him and judge it as the production of a mind whose perspective is as unclouded as his own. Swift in *The Examiner* speaks as the man who himself belongs to the group of mankind, and who has always made it his practice, as he mentions in the opening sentence of his first paper, 'to converse in equal Freedom with the deserving Men of both Parties' (*Prose Writings*, III, 3). This direct method, quite unlike the organization of *Tale of a Tub*, continues into the third of his papers, which explains how 'we are unhappily divided into two Parties, both which pretend a mighty Zeal for our Religion and Government'. The essay begins by pointing to the want of such a paper as *The Examiner* will ideally be, and by assuring Swift's impartial readers, both through what he says and through the frank, unequivocal way in which he says it, that this writer, like the reader himself, is above party and concerned only for the general good of all mankind.

> It must be avowed, that for some Years past, there have been few Things more wanted in *England*, than such a Paper as this ought to be; and such as I will endeavour to make it, as long as it shall be found of any Use, without entring into the Violences of either Party. Considering the many grievous Misrepresentations of Persons and Things, it is highly requisite, at this Juncture, that the People throughout the Kingdom, should, if possible, be set right in their Opinions by some impartial Hand; which hath never been yet attempted: Those who have hitherto undertaken it, being upon every Account the least qualified of all Human-kind for such a Work. (*Prose Writings*, III, 13)

And yet, of course, what Swift is doing in *The Examiner* is equating this wider, impartial group with the particular political group – the Harley-St. John administration – whose cause he wishes to espouse, while the principal opponents of that group, and therefore of the wider group whose only interest is the interest of mankind, are cast as self-seeking members of a mere faction. The Whigs, in fact, in *The Examiner* show many of the characteristics of McDougall's 'unorganized' group – violent, extreme in action, careless in deliberation, hasty in judgment, deficient in reasoning, easily swayed and led, and tending to produce all the manifestations of absolute power. The Whigs are a collection of self-seeking individuals brought together by interest, though once assembled showing all the worst signs of mob mentality. The Tories, on the other hand, emerge as that group of individuals who stay individuals through proper self-consciousness and, therefore, are able to maintain a clear view of the greater good of mankind. A 'real' group, in fact, is being equated with Bergson's 'imaginary' group of those who judge and, because *The Examiner* is also a satiric work, of those who rightly laugh. That no Whig will be expected to laugh at anything in *The Examiner* should prove Swift's case, for the man who cannot laugh can have no spirit of unity with his fellows and no proper detachment from the self-seeking of everyday life. Such a man can enjoy 'secret freemasonry' only with himself.

What the Whigs do laugh at, on the contrary, as we learn in *Examiner* 35, is 'National Faith': 'Union in Discipline and Doctrine, the offensive Sin of Schism, the Notion of a Church and a Hierarchy, they laugh at as Foppery, Cant and *Priestcraft*' (*Prose Writings*, III, 123). Nor should the Whigs be properly considered as a party, but rather as 'a *Faction*, raised and strengthened by Incidents and Intrigues'. They have few uniting motives, and even if they could achieve their ends they would not be able to stay together as a genuine group.

I do not take the Heads, Advocates, and Followers of the *Whigs*, to make up, strictly speaking, a *National Party*; being patched up of heterogeneous, inconsistent Parts, whom nothing served to unite but the common Interest of sharing in the Spoil and Plunder of the People; the present Dread of their Adversaries, by whom they apprehended to be called to an Account, and that general Conspiracy, of endeavouring to overturn the Church and State; which, however, if they could have compassed, they would certainly have fallen out among themselves, and broke in Pieces, as *their Predecessors* did, after they destroyed the Monarchy and Religion. (*Prose Writings*, III, 122)

The envisaged breaking in the Whig ranks, we may take it, is a warning of the breaking into pieces of the nation should a Whig administration be again returned.[38]

Party and faction, moreover, at the more personal level of the capacity for clear thinking of their members – and by party and faction Swift always makes it abundantly plain that he means Whig – will inevitably stand between a man and genuine knowledge of himself. Marlborough, attacked as Marcus Crassus, is guilty, says *The Examiner*, of avarice. This is a fact known by his entire army. '*One Minute's Reflection*' (*Prose Writings*, III, 83) would be enough for Crassus to effect a cure upon himself, for '*No Man of true Valour and true Understanding, upon whom this Vice hath stolen unawares, when he is convinced he is guilty, will suffer it to remain in his Breast an Hour*' (*Prose Writings*, III, 85). And yet Crassus is prevented from such reflection, and from such a conviction therefore, because he is a creature of party. As a leading Whig, he will not be told the truth by his own group – will indeed be praised as a '*God*' – while the truth told by others will pass unrecognised because of the blinkered vision imposed by party. This will always be the case with such prominent men of faction.

> Encompassed with a Crowd of depending Flatterers, they are many degrees Blinder to their own Faults than the common Infirmities of Human Nature can plead in their Excuse; Advice dares not be offered, or is wholly lost, or returned with Hatred: And whatever appears in Publick against their prevailing Vice, goes for nothing; being either not applied, or passing only for Libel and Slander, proceeding from the Malice and Envy of a Party. (*Prose Writings*, III, 82–3)

In quitting this vice, says Swift, Crassus would become '*a truly Great Man*', not only insofar as he had rid himself of his prevailing vice, but also, we should understand, because he had succeeded in liberating himself from party vision and, like the '*truly Learned*' reader of *A Tale of a Tub*, conscious of 'his private Infirmities', had thereby shown himself qualified for membership of the higher group of mankind.

When he leaves named individuals, too, and turns to those who make up the multitude of the led – 'the insignificant Brood of Followers' – Swift is still concerned to show how party membership entirely prejudices individual thinking and at the same time blinds a person to his own faults and partiality – takes away, in fact, the individual's need to be responsible for his own behaviour and motives.

> *Parties* do not only split a Nation, but every Individual among them, leaving each but half their Strength, and Wit, and Honesty, and good Nature; but one Eye and Ear, for their Sight and Hearing, and equally lopping the rest of the Senses.

No member of a party need ever exercise his personal judgment, for his party membership automatically defines what is right and wrong: 'Where *Parties* are pretty equal in a State, no Man can perceive one bad Quality in his own, or good one in his Adversaries.' When called upon for a judgment, even in the least political matters, the party member cannot think for himself but must hang upon known political facts: 'I asked a Gentleman t'other Day, how he liked such a Lady? but he would not give me his Opinion, 'till I had answered him whether she were a *Whig* or *Tory*.' Nor can the most trivial choices in items of dress or public nicety be made independently, but must be decided according to party considerations.

> . . . the Women among us have got the distinguishing Marks of Party in their Muffs, their Fans, and their Furbelows. The *Whig* Ladies put on their Patches in a different Manner from the *Tories*. They have made *Schisms* in the *Play-House*, and each have their particular Sides at the *Opera*. (*Prose Writings*, III, 102)

If party concerns define for the individual what he should himself be and do, they also define what, for him, his opponents should be and do. So, in *Examiner* 33, Swift explains how 'The *Papists* since the Reformation' have used 'all Arts to palliate the Absurdities of their Tenets' and to load 'the Reformers with a thousand Calumnies; the Consequence of which hath been only a more various, wide, and inveterate Separation'. In the same way, he continues, 'A *Whig* forms an Image of a *Tory*, just after the Thing he most abhors; and that Image serveth to represent the whole Body' (*Prose Writings*, III, 111). Moreover, we should add, the very existence of the 'Image' in such a form, like the existence of the scapegoat, itself strengthens the group that has cast out the abhorred qualities, and reinforces the group's own adopted definition of virtue. Much better, says Swift, were the 'Apologies of the ancient Fathers' which have 'done greatest Service to the Christian Religion'. This has been

> because they removed those Misrepresentations which had done it most Injury. The Methods these Writers took, was openly and freely to discover every Point of their Faith; to detect the Falshood of their Accusers; and to charge nothing upon their Adversaries but what they were sure to make good.
> (*Prose Writings*, III, 110–11)

So, following their example, Swift outlines both the Tory principle of '*Passive Obedience as charged by the* WHIGS' and '*Passive Obedience, as professed and practised by the* TORIES' (*Prose Writings*, III, 112–13). Indeed, this is the essence of Swift's own claims for the stance and function of *The Examiner*. His declared impartiality will, after the example of the Fathers, be to the end of explaining what is factually true, of stripping away falsehood, and of pointing out only what is equally true of his political opponents.

His more general aim, though, in *The Examiner* as elsewhere, is to lead his reader away from prejudice and into seeing clearly. For this it is essential that the reader sees the limitations of group membership when that group is a political party – that Swift so exclusively sees the political party as the Whigs and the higher group as the Tories is a concession to be made to the circumstances of the commissioning and writing of *The Examiner* papers. The whole context and content of political debate, he claims in *Examiner* 15, reinforce prejudice and the party mentality. Party writers, 'like a couple of Make-bates', will

> inflame small Quarrels by a thousand Stories, and by keeping Friends at Distance, hinder them from coming to a good Understanding, as they certainly would, if they were suffered to meet and debate between themselves. (*Prose Writings*, III, 15)

The thinking of the nation, far from being modelled on the example of the 'reasonable honest Man of either Side', is 'misled on both Sides, by mad, ridiculous Extreams, at a wide Distance on each Side from the Truth' (*Prose Writings*, III, 14). If one of the tasks of *The Examiner* will be 'to remove these Misapprehensions among us' (*Prose Writings*, III, 16) by examining the productions of the party presses, he will nevertheless, in so doing, also bring the reader to examine his own assumptions in the act of reading. In paper 38, Swift explains how writing is interpreted not necessarily as the writer intends but according to the assumptions and prejudices of the readers.

> For, suppose I should write the Character of an Honest, a Religious, and a Learned Man, and send the first to *Newgate*, the second to the *Grecian Coffee-House*, and the last to *White*'s; would they not all pass for *Satyrs*, and justly enough among the Companies to whom they were sent? (*Prose Writings*, III, 119)[39]

Swift's whole art as a satirist works to ensure that the understanding of his writing is governed not by the reader's predisposed mentality, be it predisposed by his membership of the Whigs, of the group at White's or of any 'real' group, but by his reading with only his basic human disposition of reason and honesty.

Laughter is not a prominent feature of *The Examiner*, nor might laughter be expected as a frequent response to reading the papers, certainly not in the way that one might laugh at Swift's more comic works. What we do come away from *The Examiner* with, though, is a clear understanding of how Swift perceived party groups as responsible for undermining the moral integrity of the nation, both public and personal. For what he has to say about the role of laughter within groups – and here it is the social group in which he is primarily interested – we must look to his *Polite Conversation*.

There is, indeed, a great deal of laughter in the *Complete Collection of Genteel and Ingenious Conversation, According to the Most Polite Mode and Method Now Used At Court, and in the Best Companies of England* and, as Swift, writing as 'Simon Wagstaff', points out in his introduction, there would have been much more.

I did therefore once intend, for the Ease of the Learner, to set down in all Parts of the following Dialogues, certain Marks, Asterisks, or Nota Bene's,(in *English*, Mark-well's) after most Questions, and every Reply or Answer; directing exactly the Moment when one, two, or all the Company are to laugh. But, having duly considered that this Expedient would too much enlarge the Bulk of the Volume, and consequently the Price; and likewise, that something ought to be left for ingenious Readers to find out: I have determined to leave the whole Affair, although of great Importance, to their own Discretion.

(*Polite Conversation*, p.23)

(With this in mind, of course, those occasions of laughter which Swift does remark in the dialogues will be ones the 'ingenious Readers' should on no account miss.) Not content, however, with merely attesting to the frequency of laughter 'in the Best Companies', Swift also uses his introduction to explain why the laugh is so necessary in society. In that the whole intention of gathering in company is that 'the Ball of Discourse' be 'kept up' and not allowed to fall and drop 'to nothing, like a Fire without Fuel', a most useful social talent is his who 'can fill the Gap with laughing or commending what hath been said' (*Polite Conversation*, p.21). The association of laughter with emptiness, however, should make us wary: is Swift not already approaching the territory of the madman, laughing at nothing? Or is he not, at least, in the commendation of 'what hath been said', giving a hint of man as a mechanical idiot, repeating only what others say, endorsing everything equally and therefore endorsing nothing, as the laughing madman endorses everything and nothing? Such a suspicion is confirmed five paragraphs later when Swift specifically refers to the mechanical nature of the human body in laughter: 'There is a natural involuntary Distortion of the Muscles, which is the anatomical Cause of Laughter.' He proceeds immediately to the social cause, but this slight reminder of the mechanical is enough to make the reader see what follows as also bearing a mechanical interpretation.

But there is another Cause of Laughter which Decency requires, and is the undoubted Mark of a good Taste, as well as of a polite obliging Behaviour; neither is this to be acquired without much Observation, long Practice, and a sound Judgment. (*Polite Conversation*, p.23)

We are being encouraged to see 'Decency', 'good Taste' and 'obliging Behaviour' as being as mechanically produced as 'involuntary Distortion of the Muscles' – or at least the kind of decency and good taste that will be associated with this kind of laughter. When 'long Practice', too, is found to be necessary for the attainment of what should be a spontaneous expression, and 'sound Judgment' is made to refer merely to the social nicety of when to laugh, then we rightly question the capacity for individual thought of any participant in polite social grouping, and wonder how far the 'ingenious' reader will be instructively employed in filling in for himself the laughter of such a company.

Swift's view of 'society' in *Polite Conversation*, and of what engagement in it does to the mentality of its members, is as devastating as his view of party and faction in *The Examiner*. To become a successful member of this society, for example, it is essential that all individual spontaneity be banished, for no eventuality can be left to chance but must be prepared for and practised with much 'Time and much Application'. He or she who 'would aspire to be compleatly Witty, Smart, Humorous, and Polite' must not only 'by hard Labour be able to retain in his Memory every single Sentence contained in this Work'. It is also necessary that 'the true Management of every Feature, and of almost every Limb' be understood and mastered. This is because

there is hardly a polite Sentence in the following Dialogues, which doth not absolutely require some peculiar graceful Motion in the Eyes, or Nose, or Mouth, or Forehead, or Chin; or suitable Toss of the Head, with certain Offices assigned to each Hand; and in Ladies, the whole Exercise of the Fan, fitted to the Energy of every Word they deliver: By no Means omitting the various Turns and Cadencies of the Voice, the Twistings, and Movements, and different Postures of the Body; the several Kinds and Gradations of Laughter, which the Ladies must daily practise by the Looking-Glass, and consult upon them with their Waiting-Maids. (*Polite Converation*, p.24)

The member of this kind of society resembles more Bergson's 'jointed puppet', one whose inelasticity demands our laughter, than a thinking individual capable of any 'effort of soul'. Even terms that would otherwise carry suggestions of a higher capacity are rendered mechanical and ridiculous by their immediate context, as 'graceful' is by 'Nose' and 'Chin' and 'Energy' by 'the whole Exercise of the Fan'. Thought is nowhere. Learning by rote, and by long and private practice, is everything. Moreover, 'daily practise by the Looking-Glass' will be also a covert encouragement to personal vanity, to that 'secret freemasonry' only with the self, rather than a means to self-understanding or proper self-consciousness. The willingness to look at oneself should not be mistaken for a readiness for self-criticism.

Such useful knowledge as his book contains, says 'Wagstaff', should also form the basis of society's system of education, in that 'some expert Gentlewomen, gone to Decay' should 'set up publick Schools, wherein young Girls of Quality or great Fortunes, might first be taught to repeat this following System of Conversation', and in particular be instructed 'in every Species and Degree of Laughing, in the proper Seasons at their own Wit, or that of the Company' (*Polite Conversation*, p.25). As laughing at the wit of others of the company – all trained by the same system of group instruction – will be virtually the same as laughing at one's own, the laugh in this society has come to be an expression of man's capacity not for generosity or affection, but for complacency. But when laughing has itself been learned at a looking-glass, then the implications became damning: what has been laughed at is the self laughing, and in particular the self taking the opportunity to admire the self, laughing; and yet what has been laughed at is also nothing, a mere reflection, and that reflection, too, in its mindless act of learning and in its readiness to laugh at nothing, is of a person who is no person, but rather a set of conditioned mechanical responses. Transferred to the social circle, the laugh does nothing different: individuals, all ready with the same polite conversation, laugh only at themselves, at nothing. And this is man in society: an idiot before a looking-glass, laughing. '*Colonel Atwit.* How's that, *Tom*? say that again. Why, If I am a Dog, shake Hands Brother. [*Here a great, loud and long Laugh.*]' (*Polite Conversation*, p.170).

A kind of fellow-feeling, therefore, is produced by the laughter of the group under observation in *Polite Conversation*, and the illusion is created that society exists to some good end, be it only the end of justifying the charade its members will continue to play. But the fellow-feeling is not one that we should consider worthy, for it binds members of an unworthy group. Like Wharton, they have no capacity for individual choice in their speech, relaying only what they have learnt, and that, notwithstanding it has 'received the Stamp and Approbation of at least one hundred Years' (*Polite Conversation*, p.24), is for that reason a sign of their inadequacy for shaping their own responses to life. In fact, according to one of the definitions 'Wagstaff' gives of 'the Circle of Politeness' – 'whereof I take the present Limits, to extend no further than *London*, and ten miles round, although others are pleased to confine it within the Bills of Mortality' (*Polite Conversation*, p.36) – polite society should itself be equated not with life but with death. There is, we should understand, nothing of life in this society to respond to, for its members, like the drunkards of *Tatler* 241, are themselves nothings and so not properly alive. Well, in that case, may 'the Circle of Politeness' by measured by 'the Bills of Mortality'.

It would even be wrong, though, to see the group which is polite society as a proper group, just as the Whigs in *The Examiner* should not be considered a proper group. As soon as one examines closely, one perceives the existence of smaller groups, distinguishable perhaps by their language, and rendered exclusive by it, as 'Pedants' are

> who affect to talk in a Language not to be understood; and, whenever a polite Person offers accidentally to use any of their Jargon-Terms, have the Presumption to laugh at *us* for pronouncing those Words in a genteeler Manner. (*Polite Conversation*, p.25)

Here the emphasized '*us*' and the 'genteeler Manner' indicate that it is not just the 'Pedants' who see themselves as an exclusive group. Or there are those words – 'Cant-Words' – introduced by and distinguishing particularly elite groups, like those attached to 'The Honourable Colonel *James Graham*, my old Friend and Companion' whose 'Set of Words and Phrases' were current among 'Courts and Politicians', or the 'single

Words' like '*Bite*' and '*Bamboozle*' invented by 'the late D——
of R——, and E—— of E——'. Even one's adoption of these
terms, though, while for a time marking one as part of a
fashionable group, will soon have the contrary effect and
distinguish the speaker as being hopelessly out of date and
therefore in no group at all, for

> a great Variety of new Terms . . . are annually changed, and
> those of the last Season sunk in Oblivion. Of these, I was once
> favoured with a compleat List, by the Right Honourable the
> Lord and Lady *H*——, with which I made a considerable
> Figure, one Summer, in the Country, but returning up to
> Town in Winter, and venturing to produce them again, I was
> partly hooted, and partly not understood.
>
> (*Polite Conversation*, pp.26–7)

Where this society's true lack of unity is seen most clearly,
however, is at the card-table, where 'Wagstaff' has 'sate by many
hundred Times with the utmost Vigilance, and my Table-Book
ready, without being able in eight Hours, to gather Matter for
one single Phrase in my Book'. The reason, it seems, is that 'the
Turbulence and Jostling of Passions' of 'Play' involves 'the
Mind being wholly taken up' and there being therefore 'no Time
allowed for Digressions or Tryals of Wit'. What is happening, in
fact, is that the members of this group are more properly alive in
a state of competition that when in a state of apparent unity.
Wit, repetition of stock phrases, laughter, poise, these are all
forgotten when people who are normally nothings become for a
while individuals relying upon themselves alone for the personal
satisfaction of winning at cards. The group breaks down. At the
heart of polite society there is no unity at all but only self-
seeking, the clashing of Hobbesian man – and woman – in the
battle for superiority.

> *Quadrille* in particular, bears some Resemblance to a State of
> Nature, which we are told, is a State of War, wherein every
> Woman is against every Woman: The Unions short,
> inconstant, and soon broke; the League made this Minute,
> without knowing the Allye; and dissolved in the next. Thus,
> at the Game of *Quadrille*, Female Brains are always employed
> in Stratagem, or their Hands in Action.
>
> (*Polite Conversation*, p.35)

If this is society at heart, then we may even look back and question the harmony of polite conversation, where the response and the laugh are so vital to maintaining the illusion. That the group will fall into a vacancy and see the emptiness of its social milieu is obviously one danger of letting conversation flag. But a second and, we assume, equally pressing reason for members to keep up 'the Ball of Discourse' will be each person's anxiety not to be an object of another's triumph. Society itself, under the veneer of polite conversation, becomes a battle-ground. All the while one is providing one's share of the repartee, laughing one's share of the laughs, then the group is maintained, no one is excluded. As soon as one fails, then a new group is formed to the exclusion of that individual. It is crucial, therefore, to keep talking and laughing, for talk and laughter avert hostility and cover the fear of it – as in Sheridan's *The Critic* Sir Fretful Plagiary must respond only with increasingly strained laughter while Sneer repeats to him increasingly sharp criticisms of his latest play.[40] Laughter here, far from binding, gives only the illusion of harmony. Beneath it, each individual secretly hides his or her own fear of and readiness for attack. This is laughter not as affection and reassurance, not as an expression of social cohesion – not, in fact, properly laughter at all – but rather as a socialised version of the snarl, the 'vocalised bared-teeth display' which indicates aversion, defence, and general frustration and excitement. In animals, it is a response to the threat from without, to the approaching enemy. Only in humans, the humans of societies like that in *Polite Conversation*, is it made to other members of the group that is no group at all, to the enemy who is laughing at you as a friend, which is exactly what you are doing to him. As Colonel Atwit in the 'Third Conversation' testily responds to the laugh of Miss Notable at the damage incurred to his snuff-box, 'What, Miss, you can't laugh, but you must shew your Teeth' (*Polite Conversation*, p.172).

That we laugh at Swift's introduction and at the puppets in his dialogues is a measure of the distinction to be made between their laughter and ours. Our laughter is a sign of our picking up the intention of Swift the satirist, of our appreciating the irony of his remarks as 'Simon Wagstaff', and an indication therefore of our sophistication as readers, of how far we are 'truly *Learned*'. And that places us in an entirely different dimension to 'Wagstaff' and the characters of *Polite Conversation*. Where we laugh in understanding, and as part of the 'imaginary' group of those who, like us, also understand, they laugh because they have learnt to, and because not to laugh would leave them open to laughter. Where we appreciate Swift's book as part of the educating process that has fitted us to laugh at such things, 'Wagstaff' proposes the book only as 'a Pocket Companion' by which 'all Gentlemen and Ladies' should 'prepare themselves for every Kind of Conversation, that can probably happen' (*Polite Conversation*, p.26), and declares:

> I cannot find what use there could be of Books, except in the Hands of those who are to make Learning their Trade; which is below the Dignity of Persons born to Titles or Estates.
>
> (*Polite Conversation*, p.25)

The reader, in fact, realises through his laughter that the 'Best Company' he could be in is the company of the man who has written the work he is engaged in reading.

Grouping and group mentality, then, are demonstrably of major significance in Swift's satire, and we frequently find, too, that the groups within the works are to be measured against the 'imaginary' group that is being created in the mind of the reader. This group is itself defined in response to the satirically rendered group, and that response is made most precisely when it is identified by the reader's laughter. Such satiric intention, however, is not confined to Swift. One of the best-known satires of the early eighteenth century, *The Rape of the Lock*, works in exactly the same way, and in fact shares a great deal with *Polite Conversation* in terms of assessment of society and in the devices adopted to reveal that assessment. In *Rape of the Lock*, too, there is a group whose apparent unity is found to be superficial. When we first meet the 'Fair Nymphs, and well-drest Youths' (*Rape of the Lock*, II, 5) they are united in the admiration of the only 'Nymph' who has so far been distinguished as an individual, Belinda. Her demeanour, moreover, serves further to unite them.

> Favours to none, to all she Smiles extends,
> Oft she rejects, but never once offends.
> Bright as the Sun, her Eyes the Gazers strike,
> And, like the Sun, they shine on all alike.
>
> (*Rape of the Lock*, II, 11–14)

In the next canto these 'Heroes and Nymphs' are described as united in a different activity, the truly polite conversation, in which the absent are automatically excluded from the group, and dangerous gaps in the discourse are filled by the traditional social adhesives.

> In various Talk th' instructive hours they past,
> Who gave the *Ball*, or paid the *Visit* last:
> One speaks the Glory of the *British Queen*,
> And one describes a charming *Indian Screen*;
> A third interprets Motions, Looks, and Eyes;
> At ev'ry Word a Reputation dies.
> *Snuff*, or the *Fan*, supply each Pause of Chat,
> With singing, laughing, ogling, and all that.
>
> (*Rape of the Lock*, III, 11–18)

Our first sight of this social group, however, in canto II, is carefully placed by Pope's distinguishing of two of its apparently prominent members, Belinda and the Baron, who are, of course, to be the principal combatants of the action and who thereby are to expose the real disunity of this group that is no group. We see Belinda before her looking-glass, engaged in that 'secret freemasonry' with herself that is the preserve only of those least fitted for genuine group membership.

> A heav'nly Image in the Glass appears,
> To that she bends, to that her Eyes she rears;
> Th' inferior Priestess, at her Altar's side,
> Trembling, begins the sacred Rites of Pride.
>
> (*Rape of the Lock*, I, 125–8)

'Like the Sun' she may be among her admirers in canto II, but like the sun she is also quite alone, and may find company only in the unreal image of her own reflected glory. Like Swift's Corinna her appearance is owing to artificial means, but unlike Corinna the reader is allowed to watch the 'gath'ring up herself', for this is work not of necessity but of vanity and the reader is expected not to recoil in sympathetic horror but to look on and criticise as Belinda observes the emergence of her own public face and of the perfectly practised social accomplishments,

'Repairs her Smiles, awakens ev'ry Grace, / And calls forth all the Wonders of her Face' (*Rape of the Lock*, I, '141–2). As she works and adores, she smiles in recognition of the self she is becoming, smiles in affection and reassurance to herself, and in the same display smiles the practised mechanical gesture of social intercourse – the public smile which, while equally false to all on whom it is bestowed, will no doubt be made real by Belinda's genuine inner satisfaction at receiving once again her due of group and personal admiration.

Equally distinguished, and equally in communion with himself alone, is the Baron, though here the emphasis is on the self-gratifying action to be taken in apparent defiance of the requirements of group membership. The Baron is not witnessed before his looking-glass, but the sacrificial pyre is similarly described as an 'Altar' (*Rape of the Lock*, II, 37), and the materials used in its construction make it equally a version of himself, for on the 'three Garters, half a Pair of Gloves; / And all the Trophies of his former Loves', and on the 'tender *Billet-doux*' (*Rape of the Lock*, II, 39–41) used to light them, he and we are able to read an image of the Baron, the man he is, the glories he has known, elevated to the level of an offering to the god of love, just as Theobald and Cibber offer to Dulness versions of themselves in the attempted burning of their own works in *The Dunciad*. The Baron, no more than Belinda, is able to enter into genuine communion with his kind. He can only relate to images of himself. Even love, the power to which he raises the altar, is clearly thought of in terms of self-gratification, for his love for Belinda is not even a sexual desire – which at least is some kind of communion – but a desire to possess the locks, which 'He saw, he wish'd, and to the Prize aspir'd: / Resolv'd to win' (*Rape of the Lock*, II, 30–1).

That this social group is no group, then, is made clear by the displayed selfishness of Belinda and the Baron. Their division will split the group into the disorganised rabble of canto V. First, though, as in *Polite Conversation*, the true values of the group – and these, of course, are values with which the Baron's intentions are not at all at odds – are displayed in the play at cards.

Belinda now, whom Thirst of Fame invites,
Burns to encounter two adventrous Knights,

At *Ombre* singly to decide their Doom;
And swells her Breast with Conquests yet to come.
(*Rape of the Lock*, III, 25-8)

In the fates of the cards, too, we seen the degeneration into disunity that will shortly, and inevitably, overcome the group itself.

With like Confusion different Nations fly,
Of various Habit and of various Dye,
The pierc'd Battalions dis-united fall,
In Heaps on Heaps; one Fate o'erwhelms them all.
(*Rape of the Lock*, III, 83-6)

But it is with Belinda's cry of victory – 'The Nymph exulting fills with Shouts the Sky, / The Walls, the Woods, and long Canals reply' (*Rape of the Lock*, III, 99-100) – that we hear Swift's 'State of War' most unashamedly affirmed. Her shouts of joy are the celebration of triumphant selfishness, the apparent opposite but true counterpart of her 'Smiles' of canto I, for her animal freedom from social restraint in exultantly shouting allows the expression of the self-satisfied vanity that her smiling revealed at the same time as it rendered it fitting in social display. She is making a cry quite unlike the normal sounds of polite society, a kind of laugh remote from the laughing that helps to 'supply each Pause of Chat', and yet it is one for which each member of the group would also wish to have occasion. Belinda, in expressing her exultation, expresses too the selfishness at the heart of each member of her group and, therefore, demonstrates at the same time that group's irredeemably deep disunity.

The second line of Belinda's triumphant couplet, however, brings with it a different perspective, and one that prepares us for the authorial 'Oh thoughtless Mortals!' lines (*Rape of the Lock*, III, 101-4) that immediately follow. For the walls, the woods and the long canals lift our attention from the limited scope of Belinda's personal ambition and gratification, from the social battleground of the card table, and even from the mock epic heroics in which the cards are engaged. Instead we see on the visual perspective of an English landscape set out before us the moral perspective we shall be expected to take of these 'trivial Things' – a perspective, needless to say, that Pope has already begun to establish through the propriety of his own couplets and through the arousing of our laughter. Such a perspective, too, is found in the words of the only character who does genuinely stand alone in that her moral values are out of keeping with the values of all other members of the group and who, of course, therefore speaks unheeded, 'grave *Clarissa*'. While she is alone *in* the poem, however, Clarissa does have a part in a much wider group than the 'Fair Nymphs, and well-drest Youths' of Belinda's circle, for Clarissa shows by her words that she is in harmony with the satirist himself, sees from his moral perspective and speaks for the qualities he would value: that if one is to be distinguished from the generality of mankind it should be for inner as the proper accompaniment of outer beauty – 'Behold the first in Virtue, as in Face' (*Rape of the Lock*, V, 18) that humankind has a duty to learn, both 'earthly' things 'of Use' (*Rape of the Lock*, V, 22) and the transience of earthly things where 'frail Beauty must decay' (*Rape of the Lock*, V, 25); and, chiefly, that the quality best fitted for the conditions of this life is good humour.

> What then remains, but well our Pow'r to use,
> And keep good Humour still whate'er we lose?
> And trust me, Dear! good Humour can prevail,
> When Airs, and Flights, and Screams, and Scolding fail.
> (Rape of the Lock, V, 29–32)

Clarissa's 'good Humour' is neither Belinda's smile of vanity nor her laugh of triumph. It is that moral perspective which knows what is to be expected of life on earth, what we can accomplish, and which, above all, in the fellow feeling of its stating by Clarissa, is expressed in affectionate reassurance to other members of the group of mankind. And what more fitting endorsement of this perspective than that the reader, following Pope's opening advice in the dedicatory letter 'To Mrs. Arabella Fermor', should laugh?

Pope told Arabella Fermor that *Rape of the Lock* 'was intended only to divert a few young Ladies, who have good Sense and good Humour enough, to laugh not only at their Sex's little unguarded Follies, but at their own'. Our laughter will equally express our consciousness of the limitations of our kind, and at the same time will be a mark of our capacity to learn, to become members of the higher group. In particular we see, treated as we already are by Pope as the higher group (just as the 'few young Ladies' are drawn out of the many as a group noted for their 'good sense and good Humour'), the limitations of vision suffered by each group in the poem, or by individuals who distinguish themselves in some unworthy or foolish way. This is clearest at the end of the poem, when Pope's 'quick Poetic Eyes' watch the final fate of the lock as it shoots 'A sudden Star . . . thro' liquid Air' (*Rape of the Lock*, V, 124, 127). Of the groups in the poem, only the unearthly sylphs are able to 'behold it kindling as it flies' (*Rape of the Lock*, V, 131). The human groups, labouring under the scope of their limited vision, interpret the new figure in the heavens each according to their own passions and ambitions.

> This the *Beau-monde* shall from the *Mall* survey,
> And hail with Musick its propitious Ray.
> This, the blest Lover shall for *Venus* take,
> And send up Vows from *Rosamonda*'s Lake.
> This *Partridge* soon shall view in cloudless Skies,
> When next he looks thro' *Galilæo*'s Eyes;
> And hence th' Egregious Wizard shall foredoom
> The fate of *Louis*, and the Fall of *Rome*.
> (*Rape of the Lock*, V, 133–40)

Only the readers, of all human groups, see what has happened in the night sky, and, moreover, only the readers see the other groups seeing. Their certainty, the vision they take for 'cloudless', is placed by our vision which Pope has assured us is, for the duration of the poem at least, genuinely cloudless. And we see, too, not 'the Fall of *Rome*', but, more accurately, and more humanely, that 'those fair Suns shall sett, as sett they must, / And all those Tresses shall be laid in Dust' (*Rape of the Lock*, V, 147–8). Our response to the poem, our laughter, like our laughter at *Tale of a Tub*, is part of the process of our becoming the 'truly *Learned*' readers, the far-sighted and humanely sympathetic members of the higher group to which Pope is already treating us as belonging.

Freud, referring once again to McDougall, cites that author's 'principal conditions' for an 'unorganized' group to become an 'organized' one. These are conditions 'for raising collective mental life to a higher level', and include requirements 'that there should be some degree of continuity of existence in the group'; that the individual member should 'develop an emotional relation to the group as a whole'; that 'the group should possess traditions, customs and habits, and especially such as determine the relations of its members to one another'; and that 'the group should have a definite structure, expressed in the specialization and differentiation of the functions of its constituents'.[41] One only has to look at a work like *Essay on Man*, or at *Windsor Forest*, to realise how far Pope's thoughts were in harmony with this last of McDougall's conditions. But, more broadly, it would seem that one of satire's prominent functions is to endeavour to organize the unorganized group. Works like *Tale of a Tub*, with its recommendation to the reader that 'he shapes his Understanding by the Pattern of Human Learning'; *The Examiner*'s attack on all faction as dangerous to the well-being of mankind, and as impeding the individual's knowledge of himself and his proper relations with other people; techniques of rendering for our laughter social groups like those in *Polite Conversation* and *Rape of the Lock*, and of making that laughter at the same time endorse a moral perspective – McDougall's conditions, his emphasis on perspective, on the individual's relations with the group as a whole, and on tradition, these can only be brought closer to fulfilment by such writing.

Yet Freud draws back from full agreement with McDougall. Or rather, he wishes to state the conditions 'in another way'.

> The problem consists in how to procure for the group precisely those features which were characteristic of the individual and which are extinguished in him by the formation of the group. For the individual, outside the primitive group, possessed his own continuity, his self-consciousness, his traditions and customs, his own particular functions and position. . . . Owing to his entry into an 'unorganized' group he had lost this distinctiveness for a time.

We should, concludes Freud, 'recognize that the aim is to equip the group with the attributes of the individual'.[42] Satire, with the obligation it places upon the individual to judge; with the techniques at its disposal whereby we are encouraged, by a writer like Swift, to see all faces in the glass including our own; and with its offer to the reader of arousing his laughter, addresses itself to the individual, and yet refuses to let him forget, through these very factors, that he is an individual who is also one of his kind, one of the 'secret freemasonry' of those who laugh, and of the higher group of mankind. As we laugh we clarify and restate the values of that higher group, and thereby reinforce our membership of it. Satire, by organizing our laughter as individuals, also organizes our moral and group life.

4 The Playground of the Mind

The major topic still to be treated in this exploration of the nature and uses of satiric laughter is the problem of the reader's judgment. There can be no denying that satire obliges us to exercise our critical and moral judgment in some way, but why should the making of such judgments be enabled or even clarified for us as readers by the fact that the work we are reading makes us laugh? Is there some perceivable logical process whereby the act of laughing produces, too, the act of judgment? Or is it rather that the mental state created by genuine laughing is such that the required judgment is nodded through, is made almost by default? As Freud observes in the remarks quoted earlier, jokes 'bribe the hearer . . . into taking sides with us without any very close investigation' and laughter, far from producing clarity of judgment, in fact 'upsets the critical judgment which would otherwise have examined the dispute'.[1] What this chapter and the concluding one will endeavour to explain is why such upsetting should take place and what kind of judgment does in fact proceed as a consequence of the laughter produced by satire.

It is Bergson who points the way (and we find Freud citing with approval what Bergson has to say[2]).

> Perhaps we ought even to carry simplification still farther, and, going back to our earliest recollections, try to discover, in the games that amused us as children, the first faint traces of the combinations that make us laugh as grown-up persons.[3]

Much of this chapter will be concerned with the subject of play, the play of children and the play that is literature. And yet our laughter does not quite appear with our capacity for play, even defining play at its broadest. As van Hooff writes, laughter 'appears early in childhood' and only 'later on' is it 'especially characteristic of children's play'.[4] We should look to the very beginnings of infant smiling and laughter if we are to give the laughter of play its proper due.

Freud, in a footnote to *Jokes and their Relation to the Unconscious*, attempts to locate the first smile. It appears, he says,

> in an infant at the breast when it is satisfied and satiated and lets go of the breast as it falls asleep. Here it is a genuine expression of the emotions, for it corresponds to a decision to take no more nourishment, and represents as it were an 'enough' or rather a 'more than enough'.[5]

Freud's 'decision' is perhaps a little firmly stated. Charlesworth and Kreutzer in their paper 'Facial Expressions of Infants and Children' are more cautious in their phrasing, and are in only partial agreement with him as they summarize observation on infant smiling.

> During the first week or two of life, smiling seems to be closely related to internal events occurring mostly during irregular sleep or drowsiness, and seldom or never occurring during regular sleep or when the infant is alert and attentive.

Smiling at this period, they argue, is 'reflexive and void of any accompanying emotional state'. They do add, though, a reassuring note: 'Spoilsports are wont to point out to pleased parents that early smiles occur merely as reactions to gastro-intestinal disturbances; however, there is no evidence to substantiate this.'[6]

The question of when smiling begins, however, and of what constitutes proper smiling is *almost* indistinguishable from identical questions concerning the origins of play. Darwin spends some time in logging infant smiles, both in *The Expression of Emotions in Man and Animals*[7] and in his paper 'A Biographical Sketch of an Infant'.[8] A little more recently, J. Y. T. Greig devoted a section of his book, *The Psychology of Laughter and Comedy*, to a summary of the evidence and opinion advanced by 1923, the time of his writing.[9] Both agree in placing genuine smiling quite late in post-natal development,

Darwin observing one of his children, 'being at the time in a happy frame of mind', to smile at forty-five days.[10] But just as smiles of a kind can be observed considerably earlier than this (and Greig cites cases of infants who reportedly smiled on the tenth, sixth and even fifth days 'of their eager young lives'[11]), so it is argued that play originates with the infant's first relationship with the breast. Piaget asks:

> When does play begin? The question arises at the *first stage*, that of purely reflex adaptations. For an interpretation of play like that of K. Groos, for whom play is pre-exercise of essential instincts, the origin of play must be found in this initial stage since sucking gives rise to exercises in the void, apart from meals.[12]

Greig, too, had argued of the smile that it 'begins with the behaviour of the feeding instinct. It is a kind of preparation to suck.'[13] Yet, as Piaget continues, 'it seems very difficult to consider reflex exercises as real games when they merely continue the pleasure of feeding-time and consolidate the functioning of the hereditary set-up'.[14] Infants, too, spend considerable time while still in the womb practising sucking. To locate the origins of play this early would mean that for the baby, as Piaget says, 'everything . . . except feeding and emotions like fear and anger, is play'. While such reflex exercises are later reproduced 'merely for pleasure' and are then 'accompanied by smiles and even laughter', we expect both play and laughter to correspond to a decision or, in Piaget's words, to 'have an external aim'.[15] Such a decision, and such an aim, will bring us from the non-social to the beginnings of the social in the development of the infant.

According to Charlesworth and Kreutzer, 'the smile for the infant does not seem to be social until sometime during the second to fourth month'. Various kinds of stimuli have been used to elicit smiling between birth and six months, including 'tickling, shaking, and patting' and recourse to 'squeaking sounds' or 'a human face or Halloween mask viewed only from the front (a profile face was ineffective)'. A one-month old infant, however, may smile at a person or, equally, at 'a simple pattern of dots or angles'. Since, say Charlesworth and Kreutzer, the human face has dot- and angle-like features and moves into the infant's visual field in most experiments, it is possible that the elicited reaction is determined more by nonsocial factors including novelty, surprise, or simply stimulus change.

While there has probably been insufficient demonstration of 'a true age change in the susceptibility of smiling to inanimate, as differentiated from animate objects', it has nevertheless been argued that smiling tends 'to be directed more frequently to inanimate objects during the first 4 months' after which it shifts 'toward the animate'.[16]

Van Hooff, approaching this topic from his observations of higher primates, distinguishes the 'unusual shape' of 'the first expression to be generally interpreted as a social smile', describing it with the term *round-mouth smile*. The 'croissant' smile, on the other hand, 'appears in social settings only at an age of 4 to 5 months' at about the time when 'the human infant starts to differentiate between familiar and strange faces and smiling becomes selective'. The 'open-mouth' smile remains, he argues, in 'true laughter' and in the human 'play-face'. These, then, are the questions with which van Hooff concludes his paper and which draw together his propositions concerning facial expressions in higher primates and the development of infant laughter and smiling:

> Is the early *round-mouth smile* comparable to the *relaxed open-mouth face*, and is it the manifestation of a relaxed attitude when vital needs are fulfilled in which 'playful' interaction is appreciated? Does the *croissant smile* bear more an affinity to the *silent bared-teeth* display, and is it perhaps more a greeting display, in which the infant greets with relief the recognised familiar?[17]

The distinction is a significant one, and is underlined by two further comments. One is from Charlesworth and Kreutzer, who point out that psychologists today 'view the smile as an important communication mechanism for controlling parent-infant behavior, a view which is currently shared by those interested in applying ethology to human behavior'.[18] The other concerns essential prerequisites to the infant's ability to engage in play proper - his ability to manipulate and his awareness of contingency. This is J. Watson reporting his observations in his paper, 'Smiling, Cooing and "The Game" '.

> It is not likely to be a coincidence that the average normal infant is expected to show peak vigorous smiling to a human face at about the third or fourth month, which is also the time he is expected to show active instrumental behaviour. If the proposal made here is correct, both developments arise from an infant's initial experience of a clear contingency.[19]

Social smiling and play, it would seem, do in a real sense begin at roughly the same time – indeed Watson's hypothesis is that faces elicit smiling only when the infant is able to perceive the reappearing face in a pattern of repeated stimuli that is itself regarded as play (the beginnings of peek-a-boo). By the crucial 'third or fourth month' the infant is capable of recognising those patterns of stimuli, including the reappearing human face, which develop into play. By the fourth or fifth month, as van Hooff suggested, his *croissant smile* indicates that his perception of the human face now includes actual recognition of the face and implies, therefore, the greeting that is relief in this renewal of the familiar. 'The Game' and the greeting, play and relief, are merging in the smile. Satire depends for its effectiveness upon this combining, early in infanthood, in the single response of smiling both our capacity for playfulness and our need for social recognition and approval.

That the mother, with whom the infant most frequently experiences the relief of greeting, acts too as the predominant stimulus to social play must make for strong reinforcement of this blurring of reactions, of 'play-face' and 'croissant smile'. Indeed, when we move from smiling to laughter as aroused by such activities as tickling, it is often found that the response, especially in the older infant (six months and onwards) is 'contingent upon who does the tickling'.[20] As Jerome Bruner suggests, 'the capers most likely to produce laughter when performed by the mother are the ones most likely to produce tears when performed by a stranger'.[21] Laughter, there is general agreement, 'appears developmentally later than smiling' and, say Charlesworth and Kreutzer, 'occurs more frequently to tactile social stimulation than to most forms of nontactile–social stimulation (a person smiling, for example)'. With time, they add, 'social stimulation becomes more effective'.[22] The role of the mother in all forms of social stimulation, it is clear, will be crucial. (It is noted, for example, that institutionalised infants reach 'their peak smiling frequency approximately 4 weeks later than children reared in families'.[23]) In fact, of games such as peek-a-boo, one of the earliest of nontactile-social stimulations, the role of the mother is a nicely balanced one, for at the introduction of such a game she is breaking new ground (and ground where we should remember those fears of non-existence described in Chapter 2). At the onset of the game, say Bruner and Sherwood,

> it is also very important for mother to keep the child's activation level at an appropriate intensity, and one is struck by the skill of mothers in knowing how to keep the child in an anticipatory mood, neither too sure of outcome nor too upset by a wide range of possibilities.[24]

The pleasure of a game like peek-a-boo must depend almost entirely upon the exact coincidence of play and greeting. The pattern of repeated disappearance and reappearance, with appropriate variations in timing and exact placing of the reappearing face, which is distinguished as one of the infant's earliest perceived play patterns, coincides with the fact that it is the mother's (or, if one is reading Darwin or Greig, the father's) face that is the object of play. Each smile-laugh of pleasure at the unexpected expected reappearance, then, is also a smile-laugh of greeting at the expected return of the face of reassurance and recognition. As Bruner says, one role of the adult in play is that she or he '*introduces* the novel, inducts the young into new, challenging, and frightening situations'.[25] The child's own readiness to instigate peek-a-boo, to hide his own face in the expectation of being discovered, is a measure of this game's effectiveness in bringing the infant close to the terrors of non-existence in a pleasurable and just controlled context. What is also effected, however, is a means to satisfy the child's instinct for mimicry. Mimicry, as Freud argues, 'is the child's best art and the driving motive of most of his games. A child's ambition aims far less at excelling among his equals than at mimicking the grown-ups.'[26] As soon as the infant covers his face, or merely his eyes, to be discovered peeping out by the mother or father, then he has undergone an important change of role. He is now an agent in his own play, can disappear and reappear for the adult, and can arouse adult laughter for doing so. This is the great leveller. If, as Freud says, children receive great pleasure 'when a grown-up lets himself down to their level, renounces his oppressive superiority and plays with them as an equal',[27] how much greater pleasure will an infant receive when his own initiation of play succeeds in raising him to the adult level. The laugh of the adult, responding to the infant's peek-a-boo, is a double reassurance, not only the normal assurance of greeting, but an assurance that the play brought into being by the child is approved by the loved parent.

Not all play laughter, however, will be laughter shared by the parent, and nor, in that case, will the play be fully endorsed by the parent. This will be particularly so as the child develops from the total dependence of infanthood. The universally practised rough-and-tumble play is interesting here. Blurton Jones observes of this popular form of play that it 'has been persistently ignored by psychologists', but that

> The existence of laughter and the play-face as characteristic signals associated with this behaviour suggest that it is an important piece of social behaviour that may involve important non-verbal communication.

The effect of such play 'on peers', however,

> is usually greater than its effect on mothers, which suggests that it has no function specifically concerned with mother-infant interaction distinct from the one concerned with interaction with peers and other adults (there are many species in which the mother will not play with her infant).[28]

Blurton Jones' observations of children's facial expressions during rough-and-tumble play suggest that greeting and reassurance do not enter into the expression of this mock aggression. It is 'laughing and open-mouthed smiles' which are associated with 'running and jumping, hitting at others, wrestling and chasing' – findings which, he says, 'provide independent support for some of the conclusions of van Hooff'.[29] Such signals, as van Hooff has suggested, may well indicate 'that the ongoing behaviour is not meant seriously', but is rather to be interpreted as 'mock-fighting'.[30]

While rough-and-tumble play, though, is play to which the mother will at best be indifferent, it does appear to serve an important function among peers. Blurton Jones, in a separate paper on 'Rough-and-tumble Play among Nursery School Children', observes its close relation to 'real hostile behaviour': 'Some children respond as if it were hostile', 'Sometimes play fleeing becomes real fleeing' and 'Some motor patterns are similar.' Moreover, many adults cannot distinguish between rough and tumble and real hostility. Nevertheless, he concludes,

> Most of the time, despite these similarities, the players neither respond as if their playmates were hostile nor show any indication of their own motivation being hostile (i.e. of the causes of rough and tumble being at all related to the causes of fighting).

In fact, there is if anything a strengthening of the peer group by the mutual laughter and play of rough and tumble.

> Short-term effects of this play are eventual exhaustion, continuing to stay with the playmates, seeking them out another time to play with. If anything, its short-term effect is to gain friends rather than to lose them.[31]

Clearly, the child's ability to engage in a form of play which may be frowned upon by the parent, but which makes for the coherence of a group which excludes the parent, is a significant step away from the mother- or father-dominated structure of play and laughter. Simone de Beauvoir tells how, as a child, she did not mind when her parents would lock away for safe keeping her nicest toys: 'I was flattered to possess objects which could amuse grown-ups.' But her favourite activities were the pretend games with her sister which had to be played without adult knowledge.

> But other scenarios, the ones we liked best, required secret performances. They were, on the surface, perfectly innocent; but in sublimating the adventure of our childhood or anticipating the future, they drew upon something secret and

intimate within us which would not bear the searching light of adult gazes.[32]

Play and performance in front of, or even, as Greig suggests, *for* 'a loving and loved spectator',[33] are replaced by the need for play in the company of one or more fellows, away from the approval or disapproval of adults. Play may still be based upon the mimicry of those adults from whom the child now wishes to be hidden, but the mimicry is adopted not in order to be sure of the parent's approval and greeting. Rather, such mimicry represents the liberating of the child's imagination, of his capacity to be whoever he chooses. It is not that there are no rules in secret play, but that here the rules need not be governed by the known conventions of the adult world, the child's assumptions of what the adult will approve. (Another way of looking at this is to remember the child's pleasure at the adult's renouncing 'his oppressive superiority' and consenting to play 'as an equal'.) In deliberately seeking out occasions for unobserved games, the child is beginning to take responsibility for the structure and assumptions of his own play.

In some cases, of course, as with Freud's 'disappearing boy', we may conclude that the taking of such responsibility is premature. The dread of non-existence compels the child to compensate by the invention of a private game before the normal playing of observed and approved games has prepared him. The kind of insecurity we have seen Laing discussing in *Self and Others* and *The Divided Self* would be one likely consequence of this child's dilemma. But many forms of private play do, nevertheless, occur relatively early in childhood and for these the presence of adults, while no obstacle, is also quite unnecessary. Play involving the acquisition of manipulative skills would be one wide-ranging kind, as would, later, the child's earliest attempts at drawing.[34] But the most significant of these unobserved observed kinds of play, and from our point of view the most interesting, is the child's play that involves his acquisition of language.

Freud, again, testifies to the importance of play from the earliest stages of language acquisition.

During the period in which a child is learning how to handle the vocabulary of his mother-tongue, it gives him obvious pleasure to 'experiment with it in play', to use Groos's words. And he puts words together without regard to the condition that they should make sense, in order to obtain from them the pleasurable effect of rhythm or rhyme.[35]

Ruth Weir, writing about the language play of her 2½-year-old son, summarizes first the apparently international agreement among previous observers of the recurrence of play patterns in their subjects' linguistic behaviour.

> We often encounter reference to linguistic play in the literature on child language. Thus Chao says: 'There is occasional intentional playing with language. . . . The resulting syllables are usually not expected to make sense.' Or Kaper talks of the use of words for pleasure by the young child. Ohnesorg also confirms the play with words, as do Jespersen and Stern and Stern. The latter two, however, go further when they mention the child's predilection for rhythm, rhyme, and alliteration. Scupin and Scupin discuss 'Klangassoziationen', association based on recurring sounds. in our recordings, a great deal of play with the sounds of words and with the words themselves is found.[36]

Language, as Bruner, Jolly and Sylva point out, 'increases the range of play',[37] but also, we should add, the child's capacity for play increases the range of his language, both in terms of the sounds and patterns it is possible to express and of the content – including unacknowledged and, later, acknowledged nonsense – which language can be made to embody. Ruth Weir draws attention not only to the child's pleasure in repetition and repetition with single item variation – 'What colour / What colour blanket / What colour mop / What colour glass'[38] – and in word coinage, but to his early capacity to arrange the forms of language, 'the syntactic constructions and sentence types', with considerable freedom.[39] The forms of language, more than any other kind of play, apparently bring about an imaginative release in the child, which release at the same time allows the playful exploitation of those forms to the limit of their capacity to give pleasure. And such playfulness, while clearly dependent upon the child's proximity to spoken language, and so ultimately upon Freud's 'mimickry', seems quite independent of parental approval or disapproval, at least in its early stages. (Ruth Weir's son, like many others, was recorded in his cot before going to sleep at night. It would seem unlikely, though, that privacy was necessary for his experiments with language.) Only with a parent's negative response to the child's early language will come any sign of censorship or neglect of linguistic items as a consequence of adult reaction. Bruner and Sherwood cite the case of 'Sandy' whose mother would never let him be an 'agent' in the game of peek-a-boo, with the result that the game was increasingly rarely played.

> They are an instructive failure and the disappearance of the game is reminiscent of the failures reported by Nelson that occur when mother attempts to correct the child's linguistic usage or insists upon an interpretation of the child's utterance that does not accord with his own. Under the circumstances, the lexical items in question disappear from the child's lexicon, just as peekaboo disappears from the game repertory of this pair.[40]

Rules, however, are also learnt without positive parental action. And, as Bruner and Sherwood observe of peek-a-boo, 'What the child appears to be learning is not only the basic rules of the game, but the range of variation that is possible within the rule set.' It is, they add, 'this emphasis upon patterned variation within a constraining rule set that seems crucial to the mastery of competence and generativeness'.[41] One way of looking at such rules is Freud's, who immediately follows the last quotation from *Jokes and their Relation to the Unconscious* by remarking of the pleasure to be derived from the child's play with the sounds of words:

> Little by little he is forbidden this enjoyment, till all that remains permitted to him are significant combinations of words. But when he is older attempts still emerge at disregarding the restrictions that have been learnt on the use of words. Words are disfigured by particular little additions being made to them, their forms are altered by certain manipulations, . . . or a private language may even be constructed for use among playmates.[42]

Such 'enjoyment' that is 'forbidden', of course, is central to Freud's exploration of the relation of jokes and laughter to the unconscious. And yet, as in any game, the child's learning of the rules seems if anything to increase his pleasure: the very act of discovering and practising them can itself be pleasureable. Moreover, as we shall see shortly, the ability to recognise nonsense once the appropriate rules are acquired, is also a source of considerable pleasure to the child.

Ruth Weir, again, observes her son performing 'an exercise in noun substitution' (the 'What colour' example cited earlier).

> The first line is merely the frame of the pattern, the full pattern occurring in the second line, with lines three and four repeating the frame with different substitution items of the same form class as in the original pattern sequence. The items are selected phonologically, that is, on the basis of sound. . . . However, the primary function of this paragraph is pattern practice, sound play being relegated only to the selections of items within the form class to be substituted.[43]

This 'paradigmatic selection', so vital to the child's mastery of language rules, is crucial, too, in 'the language patterns of children's games, nursery rhymes, and sayings', where the play and practice of the child are 'formalized' into approved patterns of sense and nonsense.[44] For himself, though, the experimenting child 'finds great joy in practising his discovery that linguistic units can be combined freely up to a point, but subject to rules which he is exploring'.[45] Such play, as Bruner, Jolly and Sylva remark, 'is directed at the very nature of grammar. The child pushes its rules to the limit. . . .'[46]

While such play can proceed perfectly well without parental interference, approval is, nevertheless, an important part of the process of language development. This is not just to the extent, remarked upon already, that adult reaction can cause a lexical item to 'disappear from the child's lexicon'. Approval, in fact, is at the heart of language play, again, of course, learnt by mimicry, but no less real for that. The approval, though, is the child's approval either of the content or the performance of what he is saying.

One two three four
One two
One two three four
One two three
Anthony counting
Good boy you
One two three.

Ruth Weir comments on this example:

> Here the child even informs us what he is doing, he commends himself for the activity and counts once more for good measure. He not only produces the speech event, but discusses it as well, as if he were citing someone else.[47]

Just as in secret play the child is later able to exercise responsibility on his own behalf, based upon the adult role but imaginatively independent of it, so here we see the child as an independent user of a language which he can take responsibility for making perform a variety of functions. As such, he is also entitled and ready to act *in loco parentis* over himself, dispensing approval both for his own activity and for his linguistic skill in one and the same commendation. This is from Ruth Weir's concluding paragraphs.

> In these linguistic sessions the child does not assume only the role of the student, however, for he is the other participant in the language learning situation, the model, as well. It is really inaccurate to call these soliloquies monologues, because outside of the fact that they are produced while the child is physically isolated, he becomes his own interlocutor and produces the equivalent of a dialogue spoken by a single person. He can switch roles in this interchange readily – he asks a question and provides the answer, he performs a linguistic task and commends himself on the accomplishment, he produces a linguistic event and explicitly corrects himself.[48]

The play that is the complex process of acquiring language, then, includes the play which involves the child's adopting the role of approving adult over himself as learning child, and his increasing skill in the manipulation of language not only makes for more effective statements of approval for linguistic tasks more successfully performed. His skill actually gives him the right to sit in judgment over himself. (The most obvious literary exploitation, of course, of the patterns of the child's play with language is *Tristram Shandy*, where Sterne experiments liberally with the forms and sounds of English, but incorporates too this 'equivalent of a dialogue spoken by a single person' in which the narrator adds the roles of questioner and approver to his main function of getting the story told.)

A distinction betwen unacknowledged and acknowledged nonsense should be made. A child's own capacity to recognise nonsense and yet still to take pleasure in it marks an interesting stage not only in the development of language and linguistic responsibility but in the development, too, of the child's sense of what may legitimately be laughed at. Unacknowledged nonsense is a source of pleasure largely, it would seem, because of the sounds which the child has complete freedom to combine at will. As he begins to take charge of the forms and content of his own language, however, his functions as corrector and approver, while also making for pleasure in the exercises, nevertheless pull against and limit his freedom to bring together sounds for their own sake. At the point where words regularly begin to make sense, one vast range of phonetic and grammatical possibilities must be excluded because the language being learnt has no forms for them. But a further range of combinations, while grammatically possible, nevertheless demands exclusion because they do not correspond with the child's increasing knowledge of how things are. This range, if adopted, would be nonsense. The stage of recognising nonsense is important because the child apparently needs stronger approval than his own for admitting what makes no sense as something allowable in speech simply on the grounds of the pleasure – and here, for the first time in our discussion of language acquisition, pleasure means laughter – it can produce.

Kornie Chukovsky, worrying over the attraction of 'rhymed topsy-turvies' for children, generation after generation, and in particular at their role in 'proper psychological development', relates a story of his own 2-year-old daughter that will no doubt strike a familiar chord in the memories of most parents. (The extract is long, but demands quoting in full to appreciate the mood which Chukovsky describes.) For his daughter, he begins, as for many other children of similar age, it was a source of great emotional and mental activity, although in itself seemingly insignificant, that a rooster cries cock-a-doodle-doo, a dog barks, a cat miaows.

These simple bits of knowledge were great conquests of her mind. Indelibly and forever did she ascribe to the rooster the 'kukareku', to the cat the 'miaow', to the dog the 'bow-wow', and showing off justifiably her extensive erudition, she demonstrated it incessantly. These facts brought simultaneously clarity, order, and proportion to a world of living creatures as fascinating to her as to every other tot.

But, somehow, one day in the twenty-third month of her existence, my daughter came to me, looking mischievous and embarrassed at the same time – as if she were up to some intrigue. I had never before seen such a complex expression on her little face.

She cried to me even when she was still at some distance from where I sat:

'Daddy, 'oggie – miaow!' – that is, she reported to me the sensational and, to her, obviously incorrect news that a doggie, instead of barking, miaows. And she burst out into somewhat encouraging, somewhat artificial laughter, inviting me, too, to laugh at this invention.

But I was inclined to realism.

'No,' said I, 'the doggie bow-wows.'

''Oggie – miaow!' she repeated, laughing, and at the same time watched my facial expression which, she hoped, would show her how she should regard this erratic innovation which seemed to scare her a little.

I decided to join in her game and said:

'And the rooster miaows!'

Thus I sanctioned her intellectual effrontery. Never did even the most ingenious epigram of Piron evoke such appreciative laughter in knowledgeable adults as did this modest joke of mine, based on the interchange of two elementary notions. This was the first joke that my daughter became aware of – in the twenty-third month of her life. She realized that not only was it not dangerous to topsy-turvy the world according to one's whim, but, on the contrary, it was even amusing to do so, provided that together with a false conception about reality there remained the correct one.[49]

The incident is an instructive success. We see the child's uncertainty, not in approaching her father with her 'news', though we must suppose that to be a possibility in another relationship, but in the very nature of the 'news' itself. She will have broken new ground before, but perhaps without being aware that she was doing so, and perhaps, too, will have been led through play with either parent to the exploration of the new. Now her own play has brought her to something which has the potential to scare her, and which must therefore be rendered safe by securing for it parental approval. It is important, however, to pick up Chukovsky's insistence that his daughter knew what she was doing – that she had been accustomed to practise hard and long the proper sounds of animals, and that this was, 'to her, obviously incorrect news'.

Here, though, the use of laughter becomes especially interesting. The child is clearly aware that as well as being wrong, and perhaps dangerously so, her 'news' could become a source of immense pleasure to her, provided that it can be afforded some kind of legitimacy. For the expression of this she looks to her father for the customary signal of reassurance and play: she invites him to laugh, and does so by her own 'somewhat encouraging, somewhat artificial laughter', by attempting, in fact, to produce his mimicry of her. That he does so, not by merely accepting the invitation to mimic her 'artificial laughter', but by the deeper mimicry of joining in her game, produces in her the genuine and 'appreciative laughter' of knowing that her experiment has been approved, and of immense relief in that knowledge. The point of danger to which her playfulness has brought her has been rendered safe by the child's ability to present that discovery to her father, to find a correspondence between her own and his playfulness. Not only has the discovery itself been legitimised. The enjoyment of that sort of pleasure has been shared and made acceptable. The child as self-approver is able henceforth to approve herself in the pursuit of such enjoyment. The 'news' itself, its being rendered safe, the amusement derived from such 'news', the anticipation of future amusement from similar sources, the pleasure of the adult coming down to her level, the shared joke with her father, the relief of renewed parental acceptance – all these emotions find their proper and pleasurable expression in the child's 'appreciative laughter'. We feel that a corner has been turned.

To recall Laingian terms for a moment, the child's ontological insecurity – or rather the threat of insecurity if her uncertainty in the face of this and similar discoveries is permitted to accumulate to the stage where her 'experiences' seem habitually to be 'utterly lacking in any unquestionable self-validating certainties'[50] – has been steadied at a crucial point (as it must be at a series of points through childhood) by contact with and reassurance from one whose 'presence in the world' is as 'a real, alive, whole, and, in a temporal sense, a continuous person'[51]: the ontologically secure adult. And we can see, too, in Chukovsky's exchange, how the child's reaffirmed security from someone she still regards as unshakeably secure, as the standard for being real, alive and whole against her own recurring uncertainty, strengthens her confidence in the father as well as in herself. The approver, the model for her mimicry, holds his place more firmly for his 'knowledgeable' approval. In affirming her play he has reaffirmed his authority and certainty in his daughter's world in a way that his disapproval (or failure to understand, which amounts to the same thing) would not have done. A series of crises in which ontological security is expressed as disapproval means that authority is increasingly regarded as beyond and other than the child. Such a child therefore finds self-approval increasingly difficult and ontological insecurity gradually confirmed. When authority corresponds with the child's sense of expectation, her or his self-approval, temporarily suspended, is strengthened in the relief that identifies, once again, its own existence in relation to the model. Renewed self-confidence is also renewed confidence in the approver, a growing security in that which is secure and, now, that much more achievable by the child herself. And again, when the subject of approval is play and amusement, laughter is a proper celebration of that renewed confidence.

One final quotation on the subject of language acquisition will bring us, at last, to literature. Courtney B. Cazden, in a paper presented to the second Lucy Sprague Mitchell Memorial Conference in New York in 1973, speaks of meta-linguistic awareness, 'the ability to make language forms opaque and attend to them in and for themselves'.[52] Referring to the child's capacity for play with language for its own sake, Cazden makes the obvious but vital connection between the playing child and the poet.

Children may shift more easily than adults between using language forms transparently in inter-personal communication, and treating them as opaque objects in play. In other words, when the child's intention is to communicate, he – like the adult – can 'hear through' his language to that end; but it is hypothesized that the child can also intend to play with the elements of language for the very delight of self-expression and mastery, and does so more easily than the adult unless the latter is a poet.[53]

The idea, of course, that creative literature, and poetry in particular, has close associations with play is far from new. Johan Huizinga's *Homo Ludens* was first published in 1939, the same year that the twentieth century's most massive work of literary play, *Finnegans Wake*, also appeared. For Huizinga, 'the function of the poet still remains fixed in the play-sphere where it was born', and poetry itself 'proceeds within the play-ground of the mind'.[54] All poetry, in fact, 'is born of play'; specifically,

the sacred play of worship, the festive play of courtship, the martial play of the contest, the disputatious play of braggadocio, mockery, and invective, the nimble play of wit and readiness.[55]

Enumerating 'the characteristics we deemed proper to play', Huizinga describes it as 'an activity which proceeds within certain limits of time and space, in a visible order, according to rules freely accepted, and outside the sphere of necessity or material utility'. The 'play-mood', moreover, 'is one of rapture and enthusiasm'.[56] Such a definition, he adds, 'might serve as a definition of poetry':

The rhythmical or symmetrical arrangement of language, the hitting of the mark by rhyme or assonance, the deliberate disguising of the sense, the artificial and artful construction of phrases – all might be so many utterances of the play-spirit. To call poetry, as Paul Valéry has done, a playing with words and language is no metaphor: it is the precise and literal truth.[57]

While not wishing to quarrel with Huizinga's general assertions, we can be rather more precise in examining certain areas of identity between poetry and play, and in particular concerning the manipulation of a relationship between writer and reader, what Huizinga calls the writer's aim to 'enchant' the reader, to 'hold him spellbound'. Huizinga ascribes this enchanting to the writer's ability to 'create a tension', and suggests that the writer requires, therefore, 'some human or emotional situation potent enough to convey this tension to others'. Such situations 'rise either from conflict, or love, or both together'.[58] And yet tensions of this kind are exclusively those deriving from the content of the imaginative work, important enough in due course, but secondary to the tension which first and foremost derives from the poet's play with his reader's expectations of language and its forms (an aspect which Huizinga also includes as part of the enchanting 'play-element' of poetry). It is here, above all, that our knowledge of children's play, of language acquisition and of the relation this process bears to the development of self-responsibility, to the emergence of ontological security, can focus our attention on the 'play-element' in literature and on the function of laughter for the satirist.

It is Dryden who asserts the pre-eminence of poetic form for the expression of a 'repartee' which otherwise is wanting in nothing. A thought may in itself be excellent, but cannot be perfect until properly expressed, and for Dryden such proper expression must be in rhyme.

> When a poet has found the repartee, the last perfection he can add to it, is to put it into verse. However good the thought may be; however apt the words in which 'tis couched, yet he finds himself at a little unrest while rhyme is wanting: he cannot leave it till that comes naturally, and then is at ease, and sits down contented.[59]

The play with language one can appreciate in verse, however, while often more pronounced than in prose, can equally be perceived as a moving factor in a sentence by Swift or in a couplet by Pope. Huizinga's 'rhythmical or symmetrical arrangement of language', his 'hitting of the mark', the 'deliberate disguising' and 'artful construction', are as much the art of the prose satirist as they are of the poet. The 'ease' and contentment of the reader in the hands of the satirist – the manipulation by the joke-maker of the non-participating onlooker – and the nature of that 'ease', the relief of his 'unrest', will be of major concern in any successful work of satire.

The very business of satire is to attack authority, or assumed authority, of some kind. The business of the satirist is to set himself in the reader's eyes in place of the authority attacked. Our respect for authority, from our earliest childhood, our need for approval, makes it difficult for us to turn aside from one kind of authority – be it church, state, laureate or the certainty of our own mortality – without the reassurance of an attractively presented alternative to take its place. This role, clearly, falls to the satirist. And yet the authority he presents will be of quite a different kind from the authority he attacks, for he is also the joke-maker, the arouser of laughter. As such, he is responsible both for initiating the play that is the satiric work, and at the same time for sanctioning it. He sanctions his own play but, more significantly, also sanctions our enjoyment of it. His authority, then, corresponds to that of the ontologically secure adult who has steadied our childhood insecurity, the parent who has approved our play by joining it. The satirist, if he is successfully to draw the reader to his side, must present his attack as our own imagination at play legitimised by the satirist's own playfulness.

In the second book of *The Dunciad*, for example, a chain of play is constructed depending for much of its satiric impact upon the child's relations with kinds of authority, including the self-approving process by which the child should properly be taking increasing responsibility for authorising his or her own thoughts and actions. Most obviously, Pope gives us prominent figures in the world of letters – and especially those whose normal activities make them dictators of public taste: critics, booksellers, the Gazetteers, the laureate himself – engaging in a kind of play which, while dignified in its ancestry, could not be authorised by even the most liberal of parents. But immediately the links in the chain cease to be obvious: the 'high heroic Games' (*Dunciad*, II, 18)[60] upon which the dunces' sports are modelled are impeccably respectable, sanctioned by the authority of antiquity; and yet that sanction must be withdrawn when it becomes apparent how degenerate are the competitions in which these contemporary cultural authorities, like uncorrected children, intend to engage.

For Dulness herself, though, the play of her children has a distinct and crucial function. She has, after all, gathered together under her motherhood a 'motley mixture' (*Dunciad*, II, 21) drawn from several branches of public life. As a group, they are no true group at all, but are united only by the single characteristic of being 'true Dunces' (*Dunciad*, II, 25). This very feature, however, is likely to render them less, not more, united, for as dunces their habitual motivating factors are 'Glory, and gain' (*Dunciad*, II, 33), those strong self-interested forces which we have already seen as destructive of unorganized human groups. The sons of Dulness are those who would normally expect to pray upon one another for their livelihood. What the goddess undertakes in order to organize her 'endless band' (*Dunciad*, II, 19) is a ritualisation of their normal aggressive behaviour into the mock aggression of competition. Such parentally sanctioned and rewarded rough-and-tumble play – including Blurton Jones's running, jumping and chasing – effectively transforms a collection of self-seeking individuals into a group precisely by encouraging self-interest. As the ready agonists enter combat, the spectators, as one, 'follow with their eyes' (*Dunciad*, II, 185) Curll's stream, hail as victor 'sonorous Blackmore's strain' (*Dunciad*, II, 267, 259), admire Oldmixon's judgment 'Who but to sink the deeper, rose the higher' (*Dunciad*, II, 289–90), and look, sigh and call 'in vain' for 'Smedley lost' (*Dunciad*, II, 293–4). Finally, the sons of Dulness, like Blurton Jones's exhausted playmates, are irresistibly lulled to sleep together under the eyes of their approving mother. She, far from dull in this instance, has successfully organized her children into a durable group, though not, of course, one that Pope would have us approve. Indeed, the very organizing through play undertaken by the mighty mother must be seen, too, in the context of the much subtler and much more authoritative organizing of play that is going on under the hands of the mighty father, the satirist himself. Dulness's skills are impressive, creating from thin air the 'Poet's form' (*Dunciad*, II, 35), the many and glittering prizes for the games, and inventing appropriate sports for the gaining of them. The dunces, moreover, and Theobald/Cibber himself in particular, despairing in Book I in lonely isolation – imagining himself unwitnessed, in Laingian terms, and therefore ready to make real his felt non-being by the suicidal act of destroying the self that is his literary achievement – are reassured in their true selves, blossom into happy and secure individuals 'under the loving eye of the mother'.[61]

Pope's own sense of play here, which the nice reader might initially doubt, is redeemed (and with it the reader's own) with the realisation that the sordid play we are being invited to witness is the visual equivalent of the habitual behaviour of the morally depraved adult. The approval or disapproval of play, as in the Chukovsky incident, is a serious business, albeit a business often expressed through enjoyment and laughter. Pope's play with the dunces here demands our approval for the serious moral condemnation it conveys. Where the poet is truly playing, and touching our own self-approved sense of play, is not in presenting the slapstick of the games, but at the deeper level where a moral state can legitimately be portrayed in visual terms. Serious and damaging analysis of character and moti-vation – indeed, of a whole sphere of social activity – is expressed not in terms of straightforward condemnation but playfully. While we disapprove of the dunces' play, we have no choice but to endorse and enjoy the play of Pope which has framed it, for our childhood delight in play has been aroused in the same spectacle that calls upon our learned capacity for increasingly confident approval or disapproval.

At the same time, of course, the authority of the satirist is also approving, and encouraging us to approve, our own playfulness. By presenting us with morally sound reasons for laughter, Pope is endorsing the more private places of childhood. The 'games that amused us as children', in Bergson's phrase, are not always accessible to memory, or approved of when recalled. To witness the fascination of the dunces and of their mother/goddess with things faecal is to indulge a distantly self-censored source of pleasure (another of Freud's 'forbidden' enjoyments) and at the same time to receive the satisfaction of self-approval for having left such pleasures safely in the half-forgotten past. We endorse ourselves against the regressive activities of the dunce, while we are able to relish their enjoyment of what we, before we became self-responsible, might also have enjoyed. As Freud observes, 'Tendentious jokes . . . are able to release pleasure even from sources that have undergone repression.'[62] That the poem's figure of authority, the mother/goddess Dulness, not only permits but initiates the play, underlines for us our own genuine authority. The satirist, then, has presented a spectacle and characters for moral condemnation, but he has also given us safe grounds for self-approval. Such subtle flattery is a powerful source of Huizinga's enchantment, and to be encouraged to laugh by such means might well make us question the basis for the judgments we are apparently, as mature and rational readers, being invited to make.

Huizinga, however, finds 'tension', not flattery, to be necessary for enchantment by the literary work, and offers 'conflict' as one powerful source of such tension. There is indeed conflict in the second book of *The Dunciad*, and it is conflict which, as contest, can itself be included under the heading of play.[63] And yet the contest that is the sport of the dunces is no source of tension: it is immaterial to the reader whether Curll or Osborne send the 'salient spout' (*Dunciad*, II, 162) the higher, or who of the several contenders most widely 'pollutes around / The stream' (*Dunciad*, II, 279–80). Nor does the less apparent contest, that between Pope and his victims, create the work's tension, not because we are disinterested but because the conclusion is not in doubt. The tension, rather, created by Pope, which is the basis of his satiric authority, and which does 'enchant' the reader by touching his deep-seated instincts for play, is in his handling of the couplet.

So many characteristics of play – and particularly those characteristics which comprise the expected unexpected – are also found to be features of the couplet that the conclusion is inescapable: the couplet, before all other poetic arrangements, depends for its effect upon the reader's own infant and childhood experience of play. At the very beginnings of play proper, as Watson observed, is the infant's ability to notice repetition: without this there would be no play.[64] And, as Huizinga remarks, 'In nearly all the higher forms of play the elements of repetition and alternation (as in the *refrain*) are like the warp and woof of a fabric.'[65] Freud, in *Beyond the Pleasure Principle*, speaks of the 'compulsion to repeat' which 'really does exist in the mind', and he relates to this compulsion 'the impulse which leads children to play'.[66] For Freud, too, the pleasure derived from certain kinds of jokes depends upon unexpected repetition, for 'their common characteristic' is 'the fact that in each of them something familiar is rediscovered, where we might instead have expected something new'.[67] If tickling, which, as Darwin suggests, is a kind of play in which 'the precise point to be touched must not be known',[68] is the expected unexpected (and, as Darwin adds, 'something unexpected – a novel or incongruous idea which breaks through an habitual train of thought – appears to be a strong element in the ludicrous'), then Freud's group of jokes plays with the listener's anticipations to produce the unexpected expected. Both kinds should be seen as examples of Huizinga's 'repetition and alternation', and both, too, are significant features of the play that finds its form in the satiric couplet.

It is Bergson, though, who most precisely draws such features of play towards our experience of the laughable. 'The farther we proceed in this investigation into the methods of comedy,' he remarks, 'the more clearly we see the part played by childhood's memories.'[69] This may be with reference to a particular game or toy, like the Jack-in-the-box, to which Bergson relates our pleasure in repetition of words: *'In a comic repetition of words we generally find two terms: a repressed feeling which goes off like a spring, and an idea that delights in repressing the feeling anew.'*[70] But more generally his point is that such memories refer 'less to any special game than to the mechanical device of which that game is a particular instance'. What is of importance, then,

> and is retained in the mind, what passes by imperceptible stages from the games of a child to those of a man, is the mental diagram, the skeleton outline of the combination, or, if you like, the abstract formula of which these games are particular illustrations.

And the example Bergson then chooses is of peculiar relevance to the couplet: what he calls *'The Snow-ball'*. The snow-ball effect is what happens when the first of a line of toy soldiers is pushed against the second, or when a house of cards is touched into a process of destruction which, 'gathering momentum as it goes on, rushes headlong to the final collapse'. These instances, concludes Bergson,

> are all different, but they suggest the same abstract vision, that of an effect which grows by arithmetical progression, so

that the cause, insignificant at the outset, culminates by a necessary evolution in a result as important as it is unexpected.[71]

(As 'dire', we might add, as the 'Offence' which 'springs' from apparently insignificant 'am'rous Causes' in *Rape of the Lock*, and of which Pope's own couplets are the appropriately cumulative form for him to sing in warning of such 'mighty Contests'.)

It is hardly necessary to labour the point. That the couplet in Pope's hands depends for its effects upon the authority given by skilful manipulation of what the reader expects against what he does not expect, of repetition against variation, of the familiar against the new, has been a commonplace of Pope criticism since Tillotson. In fact Tillotson, whose *On the Poetry of Pope* was first published in 1938, one year before *Homo Ludens*, testifies eloquently to the enchanting qualities correctness in the couplet has upon the reader. This, first, is in terms of the trust established between satirist (in our discussion, the leader of play) and reader (who is looking to have his own spirit of playfulness endorsed, and rewarded with the bribe of laughter).

> The value of correctness in or out of the heroic couplet lies first of all in the effect it has on the reader's attitude. When a reader finds that his poet considers himself responsible for every syllable . . . then his alertness is intensified, his curiosity aroused, his trust increased. Here, he sees, is a poet who will set him in a motion which will only change as a dance changes, not as a walk on ice changes. Correctness elicits and does not abuse the reader's confidence.

And yet, says Tillotson, the reader is not content simply to be led by the poet through known ways, but wishes, in Darwin's phrase, to enjoy, too, the 'something unexpected' which is necessary for both physical and mental tickling. The poet's authority, like Chukovsky's, like the approving parent's, must be tested to be reaffirmed.

> The reader will, however, soon tire if nothing happens to show how strong his confidence is. Once he can trust his poet, he looks to have the steadfastness of his trust proved and deepened by variety of experience.

This is where Pope's understanding and practised mastery of the couplet is crucial and rewarding.

> Pope satisfies this expectation in a thousand ways. Pope's practice is to provide expectation rather than surprise. But the expectation is expectation *of* surprise. The reader of Pope anticipates perfect responsibility syllable by syllable, and awaits the changes which will show that the responsibility is being put to advantage.

And Tillotson concludes this section of his argument by himself anticipating the word Huizinga will use to describe the effect of poetic tension upon the reader: 'The thousand surprises come and they enchant all the more because, as certainly as rime in a known stanza, they have been subconsciously anticipated.'[72]

The perpetually recurring tension, then, which is resolved in order to be revived, is in the very form and language of Pope's verse. As he moves towards his expected victory over the dunces, he moves, too, across a series of infinitely subtle, infinitely varied victories over the constraints of linguistic and poetic form, over expectations constantly raised and constantly satisfied in expected unexpected ways. If, as readers, we are willing to grant to him the right to direct our play and to lead our judgment, claiming as he does so our laughter as the expression of our compliance, it is as one adept in language, who can play better with words and conquer more wittily the limitations of form, that we acknowledge his authority. Pope's security in the handling of language, the assurance his verse gives of his being 'real, alive, whole, and, in a temporal sense, a continuous person' to the last syllable of each and every couplet, steadies our own lingering insecurities in the face of linguistic novelty and of the responsibilities our attraction to word and thought play inevitably imposes. Like Chukovsky's daughter, we wish for sanction for 'intellectual effrontery'. Pope leads us to the effrontery and provides the sanction at one and the same time. When we laugh at a couplet by Pope, we laugh not only at the wit of the attack upon the victim or of the liberties taken with language, but we laugh too with relief to be again reassured that such liberties can be taken and got away with. And yet the rules remain. Poetic limitation has been pleasurably stretched, made to incorporate new possibilities, but, as each rhyme recurs, the form is reaffirmed. The world is threatened with topsy-turvy, but finally ends with its feet on the ground. That it does so endorses both the topsy-turvy and the way things are. The 'Mighty Mother' legitimises the sports of her children, but leads them ultimately only to the oblivion of sleep. Pope the father, through his own example, affirms the validity of inventive play as he provides the basis for poetic and satiric authority.

At the very opening of Book I of *The Dunciad*, in fact, we find Pope drawing an unmistakable distinction between two kinds of inventive play with ideas and language – his own and that of the sons of Dulness. Against the assurance of Pope's 'Proposition' and 'Invocation', and the contract such authority sets up between poet and reader, and against his citing, too, of the legitimate and creative play of Swift –

> O Thou! whatever title please thine ear,
> Dean, Drapier, Bickerstaff, or Gulliver!
> Whether thou chuse Cervantes' serious air,
> Or laugh and shake in Rab'lais' easy chair, . . .
>
> (*Dunciad*, I, 19–22)

– we are invited to place, first, that age 'e'er mortals writ or read' (*Dunciad*, I, 9), that age, therefore, before such a contract as we are now enjoying was possible, and then a whole range of illegitimate and non-creative invention based upon what some mortals have done since they could write and read, since, in other words, they had their full learned possession of language and its literary forms. Creativity – the relationship between parent and created child, between writer and created work, and between form, language and reader – is under analysis in this opening section of the poem, and all the instances put forward can only be judged as wanting – as miscreation, the inventive spirit run wild – against the finished creation of the Popeian couplets. Dulness herself is born in the 'dotage' of her parents, 'Chaos and eternal Night' (*Dunciad*, I, 12–13), and the line which summarizes her characteristics – 'Laborious, heavy, busy, bold, and blind' (*Dunciad*, I, 15) – is itself born of and itself reflects the sightless fumbling (the ugly alliteration disguising the lack of contentual relationship between business, boldness and blindness) of her mother and father. This is the primal creative act of the poem and, unlike the similarly primal act at

the start of *Tristram Shandy* which is interrupted by time, it is
an act which sets the pattern of creativity throughout time to
come, from the bronzing of Cibber's 'brainless brothers'
(*Dunciad*, I, 32), to escaped 'Monsters' and newly-sprung
'Miscellanies' (*Dunciad*, I, 38–9), and finally to the hatching of 'a
new Saturnian age of Lead' (*Dunciad*, I, 28). From this pattern,
too, the creativity that is literature takes its first form,
applauded by Dulness, which is also the 'self-applause' with
which she approves 'her wild creation' (*Dunciad*, I, 82).

> Here she beholds the Chaos dark and deep,
> Where nameless Somethings in their causes sleep,
> 'Till genial Jacob, or a warm Third day,
> Call forth each mass, a Poem, or a Play:
> How hints, like spawn, scarce quick in embryo lie,
> How new-born nonsense first is taught to cry,
> Maggots half-formed in rhyme exactly meet,
> And learn to crawl upon poetic feet.
>   (*Dunciad*, I, 55–62)

These mockery children, born of a travesty of literary creation,
nevertheless begin their development to a kind of formal
maturity – such embraces as are possible between 'Tragedy and
Comedy', the 'jumbled race' begot by 'Farce and Epic'
(*Dunciad*, I, 69–70) – under the kindly eye of their mother. In
the person of Cibber in particular, surrounded as he is by 'much
Embryo, much Abortion', and by 'Much future Ode, and
abdicated Play' (*Dunciad*, I, 121–2), we find the concentration of
mock creativity. The 'twisted Birth-day Ode' with which he
fittingly 'completes' his sacrificial 'spire' (*Dunciad*, I, 162) is
fully in keeping with all those twisted births and twisted literary
productions we have already seen in this opening book of the
poem. And it is he, of course, who is hailed, in a new birth day,
by Dulness as her very own son, fit to rule 'the promis'd land'
(*Dunciad*, I, 291–2).

What is happening is that the poet has been engaging our own
sense of creativity by the skilful depiction of its antithesis.
Normal healthy development of the child, of the literary work, of
the reader under the hand of the writer, is stood on its head in
the productions of Dulness and of the dunces (works which, of
course, are unlikely to be read much by anyone), and that very

overturning of the norms, held as it is within the strict form of the couplet, defines for us both true creativity and the true relationship between parent and child, writer and reader. Our laughter at anti-creativity, then, is an act which places us firmly with the creativity of the satirist. Our willingness to enjoy his inventive play, constrained within the literary and linguistic forms that both define and are genuine order, distances us from the anti-play of the dunces, and from the non-form which defines and is their chaos. Poetic order, the natural development of the child, and proper play, are presented as one and the same thing, and are greeted by the reader with his approving and approved laughter.

Significantly, Dryden, affirming in the *Discourse on Satire* the superiority of the English heroic, allows two particular images to dominate his argument: space and play. He would, he says, 'prefer the verse of ten syllables' to verse of eight:

> For this sort of number is more roomy. The thought can turn itself with greater ease in a larger compass. When the rhyme comes too thick upon us, it straitens the expression; we are thinking of the close, when we should be employed in adorning the thought. It makes a poet giddy with turning in a sphere too narrow for his imagination. He loses many beauties without gaining one advantage. . . . 'tis as in a tennis court, when the strokes of greater force are given, when we strike out and play at length.[73]

Dryden is describing from the poet's point of view the formal space necessary for proper poetic play – limitation without unnecessary constriction. In particular, rhyme is the predominant feature of poetry which is selected for a correspondence in play terms: we need the full length of the court if our rhyme is to land with sufficient impact. Huizinga, too, in his chapter on 'Nature and Significance of Play as a Cultural Phenomenon', speaks of the special space necessary for proper play.

> We found that one of the most important characteristics of play was its spacial separation from ordinary life. A closed space is marked out for it, either materially or ideally, hedged off from the everyday surroundings. Inside this space the play proceeds, inside it the rules obtain.[74]

To suggest that the couplet is the playground of the poetic mind is to see in this particular form a concentration of features which can be perceived, too, in all other forms of literary expression, from the sonnet to the prose sentence. Huizinga, however, sees the eighteenth century as an age especially 'full of play-elements and playfulness'.[75] The couplet, I suggest, is the closed space in which the rules obtain, but obtain in order to make play more enjoyable because more daring, the expected unexpected more surprisingly achievable. And the couplet, too, is that place 'hedged off' from the real world of everyday judgments in which the reader can receive his bribe of laughter, find his own lost playfulness endorsed by a reliable and secure satiric authority who, in return, requires only his reader's moral affirmation for an attack which he would not have examined in the cold spaces of critical daylight.

This buying-off of the reader, though, while true of much satiric poetry and prose, does not hold good for a certain kind of satire. Swift's poems on his own death are such an exception, and are so for two main reasons. First, the subject itself is one which preys, albeit benignly, on our most deep-seated childhood fears, and second there is an enormous variance between this subject and the easy tone of tolerant acceptance made possible by Swift's form – not, here, suggestive of Dryden's poetic giddiness, but rather expressing and making available to the reader the calm of Swift's own sanity.

In choosing to write satiric poems such as *The Life and Genuine Character of Doctor Swift* and *Verses on the Death of Dr. Swift*, Swift is confronting an area of mental life which would normally be regarded as beyond play. To explore the slow degeneration of oneself to the state of non-existence and to try to picture the world carrying on as if nothing had happened – the circles of 'female Friends' continuing uninterrupted at cards (*Verses*, 225–42), Lintot still pushing whatever seems likely to sell (*Verses*, 253–98) – is to approach those regions of childhood where the dread of not being threatens whenever the mother leaves the room or the light is put out. And yet Swift cheerfully invites his readers to join him in the game of 'let's pretend': 'Suppose me dead', he suggests in the *Verses* (l.299), and, in *The Life and Genuine Character*, 'To make these *Truths* the better known, / Let me suppose the *Case* my *own*' (ll.66–7). The way he reports his death in each poem is nothing if not playful. In *The*

Life and Genuine Character the play takes the form of poetic rendering of common speech and even a joke characteristically expressed in what Dryden had dismissively referred to as 'a burlesque rhyme'[76]:

> The Day will come, when't shall be said,
> "D'ye hear the *News* – ? the *Dean* is dead – !
> "*Poor Man*! he went, all on a sudden – !"
> H'as dropp'd, and *giv'n the Crow a Pudden*!   (ll.68–71)

In *Verses on the Death of Dr. Swift*, he refrains from jokes at the exact point of his own death, but, more even than in *The Life and Genuine Character*, Swift is clearly making play with the possibilities of the poetic form, here especially in respect of change of pace from the last lingerings of life to the sudden speed of the spreading news (picking up the 'Prognosticks' which 'run too fast' of a few lines earlier) and of the subsequent gossip and outrage.

> "Behold the fatal Day arrive!
> "How is the Dean? He's just alive.
> "Now the departing Prayer is read:
> "He hardly breathes. The Dean is dead.
> "Before the Passing-Bell begun,
> "The News thro' half the Town has run.
> "O, may we all for Death prepare!
> "What has he left? And who's his Heir?
> "I know no more than what the News is,
> " 'Tis all bequeath'd to publick Uses.
> "To publick Use! A perfect Whim!
> "What had the Publick done for him!"   (ll.147–58)

And earlier, in anticipation, we have already seen Swift using with cheerful acceptance the most terrifying rhyme in the English language: 'The Time is not remote, when I / Must by the Course of Nature dye' (ll.73–4). One section of his acquaintance even hears of the death while engaged in play, and Swift makes it clear that the activity of playing governs the whole public and private behaviour of these 'Friends', from their habitual playing of 'Parts' to their lip-service to the Dean's 'Soul', a matter of aside when considered against the serious business of play conveyed in the rhyme word *'Vole'*.

> My female Friends, whose tender Hearts
> Have better learn'd to act their Parts.
> Receive the News in *doleful Dumps*,
> "The Dean is dead, (*and what is Trumps?*)
> "Then Lord have Mercy on his Soul.
> "(Ladies I'll venture for the *Vole*.) . . ." (ll.226–30)

As the lines progress, we see the play at cards gradually moving out of parentheses to infiltrate the conversation itself, the ostensible topic of which has been Swift's death. So, 'Lady *Club* wou'd take it ill' if attendance at Swift's funeral should rob her of her party for *'Quadrill'*. Even the declaration that the Dean was 'lov'd' is followed in the same line by the more immediate leading of an appropriately inappropriate *'Heart'*. With underhanded irony, Swift has the ladies, in their final line, express the wish that 'he's in a better Place' (ll.237–8, 239, 242).

In these poems, though, we find Swift laying open not only his own mortality but every care or affection he might be supposed to hold dear: his desire for a bishopric (*Verses*, ll.-195–6 and 298); the promised *'Medals'* over which, apparently, 'the *Dean* was bit' (*Life*, ll.90–2 and *Verses*, ll.184–8); his achievements for his country, like 'the *Drapier's Letters'* which he 'shou'd have left . . . for his *Betters*' (*Life*, ll. 95–8). Even his fears over the loyalty of 'those I love' are exposed and imagined true, for 'Poor POPE will grieve a Month; and GAY / A Week; and ARBUTHNOT a Day' (*Verses*, ll. 205–8). The reader, too, along with Swift, is stripped of any flattering illusions he might hold as to selflessness or merit in human nature, for both poems, of course, are written in apparent illustration of the maxim of 'Wise *Rochefoucault*' (*Life*, l.1): while 'we *outwardly* may Grieve' at our friends' *'Disasters'* we are often secretly *'Laughing in our Sleeve'* (*Life*, ll.7–10) – as clear a restatement of Hobbes' views on laughter as any to be written eighty years after the publication of *Leviathan*. Swift is apparently looking, and inviting us to look, into the satiric glass and to see not our own faces but our own nothingness, the nothingness we shall leave behind when we cease to be.

L. S. Vygotsky, writing about 'Play and its Role in the Mental Development of the Child', refers to 'two sisters, aged five and seven' who, as reported by James Sully, agreed with each other: 'Let's play sisters.'[77] Swift, surely, is similarly inviting us to play at what is in fact true. We shall all 'by the Course of Nature dye' and shall all, too, be sooner or later forgotten. What makes Swift's poems so remarkable, however, is the tone in which he explores this grimly true pretence. Often, of course, Swift's casual surface thinly hides nicely aimed barbs, such as the carefully piled adjectives in praise of Lady Suffolk and the Queen:

> KIND Lady *Suffolk* in the Spleen,
> Runs laughing up to tell the Queen.
> The Queen, so Gracious, Mild, and Good,
> Cries, "Is he gone? 'Tis time he shou'd.
> "He's dead you say; why let him rot;
> "I'm glad the Medals were forgot...."   (*Verses*, ll.179–84)

But the tone does have its effect even here. The frequency of the rhyme allows less room for rhythmic variation than the full Popeian couplet, while the reduced space for striking out and playing at length affords less weight to the sentiments and consequently less serious moral and satiric authority. The impression is that Swift is neither embittered, as Pope is in parts of the *Epistle of Dr. Arbuthnot*, though his sentiments would afford him ample material for bitterness, nor is he adopting the preaching tone of the *Moral Essays*. He is, on the contrary, resigned to the common fate of mankind, and happy to watch as life, in his imagined absence, proceeds in its haphazard way.

> SUPPOSE me dead; and then suppose
> A Club assembled at the *Rose*;
> Where from Discourse of this and that,
> I grow the Subject of their Chat.   (*Verses*, ll.299–302)

What is happening in these poems is that Swift, more genuinely than Pope, is filling the role of parent to his readers. Like Freud's disappearing boy, we are being invited to find playful means of coming to terms with the dread of non-existence. Pope's satiric stance makes use of the reader to endorse without properly judging: we cannot resist the offer of play, the bribe of easy laughter. Steadying though the experience may be of laughing with Pope's authority, and of judging ourselves right to do so, nonetheless we are being tricked. Pope's authority is first and foremost poetic, and only secondarily and consequently moral. Swift, in these death poems, is truly the parent who, through play, brings 'the young, so to speak, to the edge of terror' and 'inducts' them 'into new, challenging, and frightening situations'.[78] And yet the terror is never allowed to dominate: we approach the terrifying without terror, for Swift's own exemplary sanity takes us, too, calmly to face our own non-being. Swift safely draws the line, as sensitive mothers do, between what is play or 'Let's pretend' and what is actual and threatening. As Bruner and Sherwood observe, 'one of the objectives of play in general is to give the child opportunity to explore the boundary between the "real" and the "make-believe" '.[79] We explore with Swift more securely and so more profitably than would be possible through our own play: indeed, to play thus with Swift increases the likelihood that our future play in these areas will lead us independently to profit rather than to terror. Swift's poems of self-negation, therefore, are also, in a way in which Pope's poetry is not, poems of genuine self-effacement, for the reader is being asked to respond not to the satirist putting his own case, but to him standing in for the reader. When we affirm, then, when we laugh, it is the signal not of our endorsement of this or that political or personal attack striking home, but of our having been successfully brought close to the unthinkable for ourselves. The sound of this laughter is not the chink of the coins of bribery, but the celebration of childhood play properly transferred to the adult world.

In his paper on 'Humour', Freud first describes the humorist's attitude towards others as the adult's towards the child, 'when he recognizes and smiles at the triviality of interests and sufferings which seem so great to it'. The humorist, it seems, 'would acquire his superiority by assuming the role of the grown-up and identifying himself to some extent with his father, and reducing other people to being children'.[80] This is some help (but only some) in explaining the satirist's attitude towards his readers, whether he intends to gain their support for his satiric attack, or whether, like Swift, he is bringing them closer to subjects of threatening novelty. What is more interesting, though, is the way Freud develops his argument to include the relations between ego and super-ego.

> Genetically the super-ego is the heir to the parental agency. It often keeps the ego in strict dependence and still really treats it as the parents, or the father, once treated the child, in its early years. We obtain a dynamic explanation of the humorous attitude, therefore, if we assume that it consists in the humorist's having withdrawn the psychical accent from his ego and having transposed it on to his super-ego. To the super-ego, thus inflated, the ego can appear tiny and all its interests trivial.[81]

This is more helpful, for we may include under 'humorist' not only the satirist himself, the man who initiates humour, but also the reader who responds with his laughter. Within the laugher the 'psychical accent' is 'transposed' to the super-ego which then says, in Freud's words, to the ego: 'Look! here is the world, which seems so dangerous! It is nothing but a game for children – just worth making a jest about!' And finally, says Freud, shifting his emphasis slightly from the triviality of the ego's 'interests', 'if the super-ego tries, by means of humour, to console the ego and protect it from suffering, this does not contradict its origin in the parental agency'.[82]

Our response to the satirist, then, if it is at one stage to look to him as the steadying adult, is also effective in distinguishing the child within us from the adult within us, the part of ourselves which recalls the terrors of childhood and the bliss of maternal reassurance, and the faculty which has learnt ways of accepting those terrors and of giving such reassurance. That which makes us laugh, more than anything else, makes us perform our own affirmation and our own consolation. The literature of play, as play itself, helps to make us 'master of the situation'.[83] It helps us to create for ourselves an order we should otherwise lack.

For Huizinga, too, play 'creates order, *is* order', and as such it 'has a tendency to be beautiful'. It may be, he goes on to explain,

> that this aesthetic factor is identified with the impulse to create orderly form, which animates play in all its aspects. The words we use to denote the elements of play belong for the most

part to aesthetics, terms with which we try to describe the effects of beauty: tension, poise, balance, contrast, variation, solution, resolution, etc. Play casts a spell over us; it is 'enchanting', 'captivating'. It is invested with the noblest qualities we are capable of perceiving in things: rhythm and harmony.[84]

The terms Huizinga adopts, of course, are particularly appropriate to the traditional effects of poetry, in which the very form itself, as Shaftesbury testifies, is supposed to create that harmony which will bring an inner order to the minds and hearts of its readers. Poets, 'men of harmony', says Shaftesbury, deal in a 'moral magic': the 'very passion which inspires them is itself the love of numbers, decency and proportion'. And Shaftesbury himself adopts 'enchantment' to describe the effects of poetry upon the reader.

> For this is the effect, and this is the beauty of their art; "in vocal measures of syllables and sounds to express the harmony and numbers of an inward kind, and represent the beauties of a human soul by proper foils and contrarieties, which serve as graces in this limning, and render this music of the passions more powerful and enchanting."[85]

With satire, and with satiric poetry especially, we should expect to experience the harmony of form coinciding with the harmony of a psychological steadying, and to express our experience through laughter. Humour, as Carlyle says, is the '*sport* of sensibility', the 'playful teasing fondness of a mother to her child'.[86] We are predisposed, it seems, from our earliest childhood, as from our instinctive yearnings towards harmony, 'decency and proportion' – from our natural spirit of play of which satire is the poetic expression – to side with the satirist. The moment he can make us laugh, we are his, and what is more, the world is ours. As Carlyle again observes, true humour is

> the bloom and perfume, the purest effluence of a deep, fine, and loving nature; a nature in harmony with itself, reconciled to the world and its stintedness and contradiction, nay finding in this very contradiction new elements of beauty as well as goodness.[87]

We have, perhaps, after all, come a long way from Hobbes.

5   Glory, Jest and Riddle

It was Shaftesbury's Ethiopian in Paris, laughing first at 'ridiculous mummers' and then at 'a man of sobriety and sense', whose example raised the prospect of increasingly broad frames of laughter in which each laugher is himself sooner or later the justifiable object of someone else's laugh. A change in circumstances or a shift in perspective can render the grounds for laughing ridiculous, and what had at one moment been taken as an expansively godlike vision becomes as laughably blinkered as any other human pretence to wisdom. The purpose of this chapter is to discuss the final frame, the broadest circle of laughers, and to ask how far satirists like Swift and Pope expect and create an ideal laugher for their work, and just what is being judged and affirmed by such laughter.

We have witnessed a series of created readers within the work of both Swift and Pope – the 'Wise and Learned' who 'laugh at and despise' the pretended science of almanack-making, the 'truly *Learned*' reader of *Tale of a Tub*, and those readers of 'cloudless' and humane vision created by *Rape of the Lock* – who, it is suggested, rightly belong to Bergson's 'secret freemasonry' of people capable of laughing at this sort of thing and of feeling, too, the companionship of others who laugh with equal clear-sightedness. One particularly clear example, though, of the kind of satiric reader Swift has in mind comes with the creation of the 'One quite indiff'rent' whose judgment provides the long concluding section to *Verses on the Death of Dr. Swift*, and by examining the qualities given to the clear-sightedness of indifference we shall be able to understand something of what Swift saw as valuable in the proper reading of satire.

The function of the speech of the 'One quite indiff'rent', of course, is primarily to draw Swift's own 'Character' with impartiality. But as he speaks we realise that he is not only creating a protrait of Swift but of himself, what as a reader of works and of men he notices and values. His reading is being

presented to us by Swift as a model of the right reading of
Swift's satires and Swift's character, and it is one which should
be distinguished, too, from the self-interested readings we
encounter elsewhere in the poem – from the Queen and 'Sir
Robert' as well as from Lintot and lesser nameless speakers – and
from the false 'Indifference clad in Wisdom's Guise' which
observes only 'I'm sorry; but we all must dye' (*Verses*, ll.212–13).
Swift's comment here is (and he isolates a significantly positive
quality in making it, one we have already seen at work behind *A
Beautiful Young Nymph Going to Bed*):

> For how can stony Bowels melt,
> In those who never Pity felt;
> When *We* are lash'd, *They* kiss the Rod;
> Resigning to the Will of God.
>
> (*Verses*, ll.215–18)

This apparent glimpse of divine vision through the comforting
example of the suffering of others is not what Swift would have
us understand by indifference or impartiality. The very fullness,
as well as the balance, of the final speech excludes such
abbreviated drawing of lessons as a true reading of any man's life
or work. Genuine impartiality, on the contrary, is able to
perceive and approve the workings of pity in another's actions,
as Swift is moved to 'Pity' by 'True genuine Dulness' (*Verses*,
l.473) and by those who meant to wound him (*Verses*, l. 364),
and to positive aid by his feelings for friends and acquaintance:
he

> "Without regarding private Ends,
> "Spent all his Credit for his Friends:
> "And only chose the Wise and Good;
> "No Flatt'rers; no Allies in Blood;
> "But succour'd Virtue in Distress,
> "And seldom fail'd of good Success;
> "As Numbers in their Hearts must own,
> "Who, but for him, had been unknown."
>
> (*Verses*, ll.331–8)

Such exercise of human sympathy is returned not merely in the
privacy of the 'Hearts' of its recipients. A 'grateful People stand

his Friends' (*Verses*, l.430) over the *Drapier's Letters* affair, and 'not a Traytor cou'd be found, / To sell him for Six Hundred Pound' (*Verses*, ll.357–8).

To be impartial it is necessary to appreciate that Swift's satire, as much as Swift the man, is moved not by the desire to lash but by that sympathy with humankind which seeks to amend, for Swift's 'Satyr points at no Defect, / But what all Mortals may correct' (*Verses*, ll.467–8). To laugh at this kind of satire is to express one's conviction less of the folly than of the correctibility of mankind. And again we have found other kinds of laughter in the poem against which to assess our own and that of Swift and the 'One quite indiff'rent' – the laughter of those who 'jibe' at 'a Hump or crooked Nose' (*Verses*, ll.470–1), of those who 'will bear' Swift's 'Jokes' for the sake of his wine (*Verses*, l.94), and of 'KIND Lady *Suffolk*' who 'Runs laughing up to tell the Queen' of Swift's death (*Verses*, ll.179–80). The laughter Swift would have us laugh is laughter not of malice or of narrow self-interest but laughter which expresses an awareness of a proper perspective on human affairs, of the correction along with the folly, and of self-disinterest along with the inevitable self-interest without which nothing will be found laughable at all. When Swift 'laugh'd to hear an Idiot quote, / A Verse from *Horace*, learn'd by Rote' (*Verses*, ll.477–8), his laughter has the perspective of his understanding of Horace's works and their untouchable status by which to place the single foolish act of a single fool. When Swift tells his 'Hundred pleasant Stories, / With all the Turns of *Whigs* and *Tories*' (*Verses*, ll.479–80) he is laughing with the perspective of one who, having been long and deeply involved in party matters, is now able (at least for the duration of the story) to feel himself at a distance from what once passionately held him. His being 'chearful to his dying Day' (*Verses*, l.481) demonstrates the same perspective on his own approaching demise – awareness of the inevitable end accompanied by good-humoured acceptance of the common lot of mankind. That Swift's actual 'dying Day' was to be another fourteen years in coming is, of course, immaterial: Swift is not writing a biographical poem, but is presenting rather his view of the proper attitude towards satire and satirists through the precisely put view of an ideally impartial reader. And it is in the final lines of the poem that we find that reader's own sense of a more divine perspective on

human affairs – 'That Kingdom he hath left his Debtor, / I wish
it soon may have a Better' (*Verses*, ll.487–8) – for the benevolence of his wish on behalf of mankind is balanced by the
expectation that it may never have a 'Better', and certainly not
'soon'.

Interest and disinterest, then, pity and a sense of perspective,
these seem, from this poem, to be the major qualities Swift
would attribute to the ideal satirist and would wish, by means of
satire itself, to foster in the ideal and 'indiff'rent' reader.

It is in the work of Shaftesbury that we find expressed the
coincidence that is possible between what man sees and what
God sees, provided that the man is an artist. As René Wellek
puts it:

> In Shaftesbury beauty is form, proportion, eternal
> harmony. We can learn to percieve it correctly. But this
> beauty is not necessarily physical proportion and form. The
> higher stages of beauty reveal an "inward form," "interior
> numbers," a secret invisible measure and harmony, a design or
> "idea" which at times is conceived as residing in the mind of
> the artist, in his inner vision, and at times is conceived of as a
> reflection of the light of God.[1]

The perspective, too, which Shaftesbury attributes to poets is
one which approaches the benevolent perspective of God
himself rather than being confined by self-interest or by one
particular time and place. This is what he has to say in the
second section of '*Sensus Communis*', a section which opens by
asserting the legitimacy of ridiculing folly and of recommending
'wisdom and virtue . . . in a way of pleasantry and mirth'[2]: the
'very passion which inspires' poets, he says,

> is itself the love of numbers, decency and proportion; and
> this too, not in a narrow sense, or after a selfish way (for who
> of them composes for himself?), but in a friendly social view,
> for the pleasure and good of others, even down to posterity
> and future ages.[3]

Shaftesbury's good artist, like Swift's ideal satirist, combines
good intentions towards mankind with a sense of perspective in
a way which brings him closer to the 'light of God' than is

possible for the normal man. When that artist is a satirist, whose business is to produce laughter, we should bear in mind two observations. One is Shaftesbury's, reflecting upon the humourousness of 'our Saviour's style' which is

> not more vehement and majestic in his gravest animadversions or declamatory discourses than it is sharp, humorous, and witty in his repartees, reflections, fabulous narrations, or parables, similes, comparisons, and other methods of milder censure and reproof, his exhortations to his disciples, his particular designation of their manners, the pleasant images under which he often couches his morals and prudential rules; even his miracles themselves (especially the first he ever wrought) carry with them a certain festivity, alacrity, and good humour so remarkable that I should look upon it as impossible not to be moved in a pleasant manner at their recital.[4]

Christ's being here made to sound, both in manner and intention, like the kind of satirist of whom not only Shaftesbury but Addison, Steele, Hutcheson and a whole host of contemporary theorists would approve, is one extreme view of the divine benevolence possible to laughter-makers. Against this, however, and in chilling warning to the satirist, should be set what Hobbes finds in Bedlam.

> If some man in Bedlam should entertain you with sober discourse; and you desire in taking leave, to know what he were, that you might another time requite his civility; and he should tell you, he were God the Father; I think you need expect no extravagant action for argument of his madness.

The madman, whose behaviour is ruled by 'too much appearing passion' – 'some of them raging, others loving, others laughing, all extravagantly' – is found inwardly to be governed by the conviction that he either is, or is especially favoured by, God himself. Certain that they have received inspiration, such men 'presently admire themselves, as being in the special grace of God Almighty, who hath revealed the same to them supernaturally, by his Spirit'.[5] And here is the other extreme view of the laughter-maker: he is convinced of his being blessed with the truth, may even present a lucid and plausible discourse, but inwardly he is only a poor madman whose judgment is so distorted that he makes 'so singular a truth' from an 'untruth'[6] and thinks himself God Almighty as he laughs in his isolation at nothing at all.

It is the nature of artistic creativity that is in question here. Cibber, who 'wrote and flounder'd on, in mere despair' (*Dunciad*, I, 120), Shadwell, the 'writer' of *Tale of a Tub*, are terrifying figures as well as figures of fun to the extent that they might just embody the true artistic qualities: they are madmen trying desperately to keep at bay the knowledge of their own insanity. Pope's superior literary skills enable him to emerge triumphant from *The Dunciad*, and to set Cibber, like Mr Burns at the end of Conrad's *The Shadow-Line*, as a fearful warning, 'like a frightful and elaborate scarecrow set up on the poop of a death-stricken ship, to keep the seabirds from the corpses'.[7] Our laughter signifies his victory. And yet that very poetic endeavour of which his victory is made may itself, when viewed with the eye of God, constitute the irrefutable evidence of Pope's own over-weening madness, and be, therefore, a proper object for the laughter of heaven.

> Oh sons of earth! attempt ye still to rise,
> By mountains pil'd on mountains, to the skies?
> Heav'n still with laughter the vain toil surveys,
> And buries madmen in the heaps they raise.
>
> (*Essay on Man*, IV, 73–6)

The poet may seek to come close to heavenly vision, and seek the expression of his privilege through his skill in poetic form, but how is he, a son of earth, to know whether his aspirations are not just the puny piling of line upon line until the whole unnatural heap topples under its own absurdity? Here, more completely than the trick accomplished by Cibber's *Letter*, is the laugher laughed at, and the laughter both defines him as a madman and at the same time obliterates him and his attempts at artistic creation.

J. S. Cunningham in an article, 'On Earth as it Laughs in Heaven: Mirth and the "Frigorifick Wisdom"', speaks of 'godly derision' as opening up 'the distances between earth and heaven' except that 'we might feel at one with heaven in finding man derisory'. And he goes on to distinguish, as indeed Swift does in *Verses on the Death of Dr. Swift*, between the qualities of a godlike perspective and a human sympathy within the single laugh. It is often convenient, says Cunningham,

> to conceive of an ideal laughter as the integration of two kinds of mirthful response to life: one, the lofty scrutiny whose long perspective clarifies and penetrates and tends to belittle; the other, the felt conceiving of what is laughable, a vision intimately in touch with what it contemplates.

It is Johnson who provides one of 'the most articulate expressions of a blending of the two' with his

> invocation of the laughter of Democritus in *The Vanity of Human Wishes*. This exemplary comedian laughs with his whole being, and by evoking laughter he brings home invigoratingly a sense of life which might otherwise merely depress us with the conviction of our folly.[8]

Such 'ideal laughter', too, bears strong relation to Freud's discussion of 'Humour' cited at the end of the last chapter, for Cunningham's 'long perspective' should correspond to the psychically accentuated super-ego to which 'the ego can appear tiny and all its interests trivial', while the 'vision intimately in touch with what it contemplates' is also the super-ego's trying, 'by means of humour, to console the ego and protect it from suffering'.[9]

What is of particular significance, though, is the role and status of the satiric artist. Ideally a Democritus, he in practice will move between the state of a god and the condition of a man, sure of himself at neither pole and yet expecting to blend the vision of both in the arousal of the ideal laugh. As a god he is entitled to judge mankind, in terms both of the absurdity of specific vices and follies, and of the long vista on human affairs which renders the specific transgression negligible. As such he is himself open to condemnation by a laughing heaven for his own arrogant folly, for being in reality only a madman laughing to himself. As man, however, he must sympathise with the weakness of his own kind, feel their frailties as his own, and weep behind his laughter that they are no better. The 'Dilemma' is

expressed by Pope in the *Epistle to Dr. Arbuthnot*. His reaction
on being pestered for judgments on literary works is also his
very human reaction to the task of judging as a satirist: 'Seiz'd
and ty'd down to judge, how wretched I! / Who can't be silent,
and who will not lye' (*Arbuthnot*, ll.33–4). The dilemma is eased
when exemplary fools are to be exposed.

> You think this cruel? take it for a rule,
> No creature smarts so little as a Fool.
> Let Peals of Laughter, *Codrus*! round thee break,
> Thou unconcern'd canst hear the mighty Crack.
> Pit, Box and Gall'ry in convulsions hurl'd,
> Thou stand'st unshook amidst a bursting World.
>   (*Arbuthnot*, ll.83–8)

Pope's sense of common humanity, however, prevents him from
taking the proper relief of laughter when faced with the poor
efforts of ordinary scribblers.

> To laugh, were want of Goodness and of Grace,
> And to be grave, exceeds all Pow'r of Face.
> I sit with sad Civility, I read
> With honest anguish, and an aking head....
>   (*Arbuthnot*, ll.35–8)

The poem thus fluctuates between satiric detachment,
judgment, the godlike perspective on the one side, and pity for
frail mankind, deserving and vulnerable, on the other. He
laments, as man, unintended reactions to his satire occasioned
through misunderstanding or misinterpretation.

> Curst be the Verse, how well soe'er it flow
> That tends to make one worthy Man my foe,
> Give Virtue scandal, Innocence a fear,
> Or from the soft-eye'd Virgin steal a tear!
>   (*Arbuthnot*, ll.283–6)

But such effects strongly resemble those he attributes to the
'babling blockheads' (*Arbuthnot*, l.304) whom he does attack,
who 'hurts a harmless neighbour's peace, / Insults fal'n Worth,
or Beauty in distress' (*Arbuthnot*, ll.287–8). Forced to sit in

judgment, he cannot, however, be completely sure that he will be properly applied. The 'honest anguish' of the satirist's calling apparently includes the fear of giving pain where it is not intended.

This side of Pope's dilemma is allowed to dominate as the poem ends. The portrait of the poet's father is a portrait, too, of a nature spared both the corruptions of his age and the curse of sitting in judgment over them.

> Stranger to Civil and Religious Rage,
> The good Man walk'd innoxious thro' his Age.
> No Courts he saw, no Suits would ever try,
> Nor dar'd an Oath, nor hazarded a Lye:
> Un-learn'd, he knew no Schoolman's subtle Art,
> No Language but the Language of the Heart.
>
> (*Arbuthnot*, ll.394–9)

The innocence of the father is the innocence both of one who never experienced corruption and of a man who knew, like a child, no subtlety in the use of language. The honesty of his feelings was apparent in all he spoke. For the satirist, who will be misinterpreted and misapplied, who speaks the language of the fallen world, and who is himself deeply knowledgeable of the corruption he exposes, such innocence will be a pattern of the truly worthy man. Against such a pattern he must judge not primarily the victims of his satire but himself. Hence the uncertainty behind the wish expressed in the final lines of this passage: 'Oh grant me thus to live, and thus to die! / Who sprung from Kings shall know less joy than I' (*Arbuthnot*, ll.404–5). Pope, we know from the rest of this poem, has not been granted 'thus to live'. How far will the corruption of his calling also cause to be withheld from him heaven's grace 'thus to die'? How 'worthy' a man, in fact, is the satirist himself when judged in terms not of his capacity to see as heaven sees but, alongside the example of his father, of his human ability to feel as man should feel?

The temptation, for the satirist engaged in the practice of his calling, is always away from the 'felt conceiving of what is laughable', from the humane sympathy, and towards the 'lofty scrutiny' which 'clarifies and penetrates and tends to belittle', which looks down with divine detachment and almost casual interest: 'Pretty! in Amber to observe the forms / Of hairs, or straws, or dirt, or grubs, or worms' (*Arbuthnot*, ll.169–70). In much the same way, as Cunningham observes, Pope has Jove watching the gods themselves meeting in conflict over the fate of Troy. '*Jove*, as his Sport, the dreadful Scene decries, / And views contending Gods with careless Eyes' (*Iliad*, XXI, 454–5).[10] And when Pope is brought to remark, as he does in the second *Epilogue to the Satires*,

> Yes, I am proud; I must be proud to see
> Men not afraid of God, afraid of me:
> Safe from the Bar, the Pulpit, and the Throne,
> Yet touch'd and sham'd by *Ridicule* alone
> (*Epilogue to the Satires, Dialogue II*, ll.208–11)

he is expressing an essential characteristic of the satirist's fate. The artist who deals in judgment, in exposing his own kind through laughter, inevitably finds himself arrogating the role of a god, and in doing so also finds himself sacrificing his capacity for fellow-feeling. Such distortion of feeling, the detached perceiving in human nature of only the corrupt and the vicious, is even more bleakly stated in Swift's poem, 'The Day of Judgement'. The poet is 'oppress'd' with 'a Whirl of Thought' which gives rise to 'An horrid Vision' which 'seiz'd my Head' ('Day of Judgement', ll.1–3). Like Pope's 'honest anguish' and 'aking head', we assume that this mental tribulation is a direct consequence of the dilemma of satiric judgment. Here, though, common humanity is nowhere. Jove's judgment on mankind is pronounced unlaughingly, contemptuously, and yet concluding with the admission that it has all been only a joke.

> "Offending Race of Human Kind,
> By nature, Reason, Learning, blind;
> You who thro' Frailty step'd aside,
> And you who never fell – *thro' Pride*;
> You who in different Sects have shamm'd,
> And come to see each other damn'd;
> (So some Folks told you, but they knew
> No more of Jove's Designs than you)
> The World's mad Business now is o'er,
> And I resent these Pranks no more.

I to such Blockheads set my Wit!
I damn such Fools! – Go, go, you're bit."
('Day of Judgement', ll.11–22)[10]

The *Epistle to Arbuthnot* does contain one section, however, which, expressing neither the extreme of human feeling of the lines on Pope's father nor the extreme of lofty judgment of the Codrus and Sporus passages or of Swift's 'Day of Judgement', is concerned rather to integrate these two capacities into something closer to Cunningham's 'ideal laughter', to what Cunningham also refers to as 'the laughter of heaven . . . thoroughly humanized'.[11] This is the section on Atticus, which Pope introduces in a way which itself points to the satirist's duty to feel as a man while judging as a god.

A man's true merit 'tis not hard to find,
But each man's secret standard in his mind,
That Casting-weight Pride adds to Emptiness,
This, who can gratify? for who can *guess*?
(*Arbuthnot*, ll.175–8)

Pope is conceiving of the possibility of entering, as Blake was to put it in Orleans' speech in *The French Revolution*, 'into the infinite labyrinth of another's brain / Ere thou measure the circle that he shall run',[12] and while the following couplets firmly deny this possibility, turning it rather to contemptuous satiric use, nevertheless this is how he proceeds to deal with Addison, especially in comparison with the other portraits in the poem. Bufo and Sporus are portrayed in strong visual terms.

Proud as *Apollo* on his forked hill,
Sate full-blown *Bufo*, puff'd by ev'ry quill.
(*Arbuthnot*, ll.231–2)

Yet let me flap this Bug with gilded wings,
This painted Child of Dirt that stinks and stings.
(*Arbuthnot*, ll.309–10)

The language used is designed to convey inner corruption solely in terms of external absurdity or revulsion, as Sporus has

A Cherub's face, a Reptile all the rest;
Beauty that shocks you, Parts that none will trust,
Wit that can creep, and Pride that licks the dust.
(*Arbuthnot*, ll.331-3)

For Atticus, as Bloom and Bloom remark, 'Pope's language is measured, as line by sardonically balanced line he builds the case against a secretive, reticent man accused of arrogance and self-esteem'.[13]

The very grammatical arrangement of the portrait's opening – 'and were there One' – already suggests, in the tentative nature of its enquiry, the secrecy which is characteristic of the man. This unreadiness of the poet actually to admit that there is such a one is a major influence on the tone of the passage. Pope's holding back from a firm knowledge enables him to match Atticus's reticence with his own. The subject's character, as much as the characters of Bufo or Sporus, is allowed to set the tone for the portrait. And yet Pope's analysis of Addison's character is far from uncertain, though framed in a structure which is itself expressive of uncertainty. The very nature of the man is one in which arrogance is so equally matched by timorousness that his state of mind is a perpetual uneasiness, and one which finds expression not in the showy antics of a Bufo or a Sporus, but in a quiet self-absorption that could easily pass for cultivated contentedness. Within the smooth veneer of the 'sardonically balanced' lines, though, Atticus is at war with himself: he is 'too fond to rule alone' and yet will bear 'no brother near the throne' (*Arbuthnot*, ll.197-8); he is 'scornful' yet 'jealous' (*Arbuthnot*, ll.199); he will 'Damn' but only with 'faint praise' (*Arbuthnot*, l.201); and is 'Willing to wound' yet 'afraid to strike' (*Arbuthnot*, l.203). This precise clarity about the nature of the shortcomings means that Pope's hesitancy about the existence of 'One' such as Atticus is itself balanced by a sureness of diagnosis which relieves the poet of the suspicion of a secretiveness equal to his subject's. The satirist, rather than himself trying 'without sneering' to 'teach the rest to sneer' (*Arbuthnot*, l.202), is giving a delicate and properly open poetic expression to reticent arrogance. The impression is that Atticus has indeed been understood in terms of the 'secret standard in his mind' and judged accordingly and damningly. And Pope's last lines of the section, finishing the uncertainty of the opening (but not, indeed, resolving it) draw attention to the complete satiric response this exemplary satiric portrait should draw: 'Who but must laugh, if such a man there be? / Who would not weep, if *Atticus* were he!' (*Arbuthnot*, l.213–4). For a rare moment, we are invited to laugh as gods and yet to weep as men, for we can be simultaneously amused by the absurdity of such a spectacle, a man torn between two opposing sides of his own nature, and touched to tears of pity for the wasted talents of the known individual whose birthright, 'to write, converse, and live with ease' (*Arbuthnot*, l.196), he has himself turned from a blessing to a curse.

If Atticus has been rendered as a satiric victim, the presentation is nevertheless of a victim who is understood as he is judged. If he has been held up for our laughter, it is at least laughter which also entertains the possibility of tears. For the satirist to write thus, to invite from his reader the complete satiric response, one which draws upon the full scope of the ideal laugh, is to assume a relationship which goes far beyond that of joke-maker and non-participating onlooker. The trust we are able to place in such a writer is wider than the trust in his ability to amuse us, or even in his artistic integrity. We trust his moral perspective, that he will use our laughter wisely, and that the judgment on human affairs to which he leads us will, even after many intricacies, be a judgment in some way affirmative of our own kind. Such intricacies and such affirmation are what we find in the work of Swift.

One of Lemuel Gulliver's most conspicuous gullibilities as a writer is the ease with which he assumes he will be able to convey the moral lessons of his *Travels into Several Remote Nations of the World* to his readers. His own dedication to the truth, he suggests in his final chapter, has been throughout of paramount importance in the performance of his task.

> Thus, gentle Reader, I have given thee a faithful History of my Travels for Sixteen Years, and above Seven Months; wherein I have not been so studious of Ornament as of Truth. I could perhaps like others have astonished thee with strange improbable Tales; but I rather chose to relate plain Matter of Fact in the simplest Manner and Style; because my principal Design was to inform, and not to amuse thee. (*Prose Writings*, XI, 291)

For

> a Traveller's chief Aim should be to make Men wiser and
> better, and to improve their Minds by the bad, as well as good
> Example of what they deliver concerning foreign Places.
>
> (*Prose Writings*, XI, 291)

Such an aim, he continues, will render his work quite exempt
from possible misunderstanding and completely immune to
criticism, 'For what Objections can be made against a Writer
who relates only plain Facts that happened in such distant
Countries' (*Prose Writings*, XI, 292). Gulliver writes 'without
any View towards Profit or Praise' but 'for the noblest End, to
inform and instruct Mankind' (*Prose Writings*, XI, 293). He has
no doubt, therefore, that all he has put down will necessarily be
taken exactly as it was meant.

> I never suffer a Word to pass that may look like Reflection, or
> possibly give the least Offence even to those who are most
> ready to take it. So that, I hope, I may with Justice pronounce
> myself an Author perfectly blameless; against whom the
> Tribes of Answerers, Considerers, Observers, Reflecters,
> Detecters, Remarkers, will never be able to find Matter for
> exercising their Talents. (*Prose Writings*, XI, 293)

Against this confident expectation we may judge Gulliver's
bitterness in the added introductory letter 'From Capt.
Gulliver, to his Cousin Sympson', in which Gulliver, who had
'firmly counted upon' innumerable 'Reformations' in mankind –
'as indeed they were plainly deducible from the Precepts
delivered in my Book' (*Prose Writings*, XI, 7) – is now seen to be
far wiser after the event.

> I do in the next Place complain of my own great Want of
> Judgment, in being prevailed upon by the Intreaties and false
> Reasonings of you and some others, very much against mine
> own Opinion, to suffer my Travels to be published. Pray
> bring to you Mind how often I desired you to consider, when
> you insisted on the Motive of *publick Good*; that the *Yahoos*
> were a Species of Animals utterly incapable of Amendment by
> Precepts or Examples. (*Prose Writings*, XI, 6)

He has, in short, been disappointed in every expectation of the effect of his plainly factual book,

> for instead of seeing a full Stop put to all Abuses and Corruptions, at least in this little Island, as I had Reason to expect; Behold, after above six Months Warning, I cannot learn that my Book hath produced one single Effect according to mine Intentions. (*Prose Writings*, XI, 6)

Had Gulliver framed his expectations of easy communication with his readers with his own experiences in mind, he would have been less surprised. Very early in his narrative he draws attention to his 'great Facility' in learning languages owing, he says, to 'the Strength of my Memory' (*Prose Writings*, XI, 20), but, while he does eventually master every language he encounters during his travels, he does nevertheless at the beginning of each part lay considerable stress on the difficulty he experiences communicating with his hosts. In Lilliput he is subjected to 'a long Speech' made by someone 'who seemed to be a Person of Quality', of which Gulliver 'understood not one Syllable', though he is able to 'observe many Periods of Threatnings, and others of Promises, Pity, and Kindness' (*Prose Writings*, XI, 23). Gulliver himself has to resort to the visual means of sign language in order to communicate his wants, being aware, as he does so, of how he is infringing his own standards of civilized behaviour.

> I answered in a few Words, but in the most submissive Manner, lifting up my left Hand and both mine Eyes to the Sun, as calling him for a Witness; and being almost famished with Hunger, having not eaten a Morsel for some Hours before I left the Ship, I found the Demands of Nature so strong upon me, that I could not forbear shewing my Impatience (perhaps against the strict Rules of Decency) by putting my Finger frequently on my Mouth, to signify that I wanted Food. (*Prose Writings*, XI, 23)

At the visit of the emperor, 'His Imperial Majesty spoke often to me, and I returned Answers, but neither of us could understand a Syllable' (*Prose Writings*, XI, 31). Nor does Gulliver's proficiency in a range of European languages help him.

There were several of his Priests and Lawyers present (as I conjectured by their Habits) who were commanded to address themselves to me, and I spoke to them in as many Languages as I had the least Smattering of, which were *High* and *Low Dutch*, *Latin*, *French*, *Spanish*, *Italian*, and *Lingua Franca*; but all to no purpose. (*Prose Writings*, XI, 31)

Finally it is decided that 'six of his Majesty's greatest Scholars should be employed to instruct me in their Language' and 'in about three Weeks' Gulliver and the emperor are able 'to converse together in some Sort' (*Prose Writings*, XI, 33).

The difficulties in understanding the Brobdingnagians are increased, if anything, by the discomfort of hearing them speak. The farmer, he relates,

spoke often to me, but the Sound of his Voice pierced my Ears like that of a Water-Mill; yet his Words were articulate enough. I answered as loud as I could in several Languages; and he often laid his Ear within two Yards of me, but all in vain, for we were wholly unintelligible to each other. (*Prose Writings*, XI, 89)

Again Gulliver resorts to signs and gestures to communicate his most basic bodily needs (*Prose Writings*, XI, 93–4) until given rudimentary instruction by Glumdalclitch, who

was likewise my School-Mistress to teach me the Language: When I pointed to any thing, she told me the Name of it in her own Tongue, so that in a few Days I was able to call for whatever I had a mind to. (*Prose Writings*, XI, 95)

The same pattern is followed with the voyages to Laputa and to the Houyhnhnms. Difficulty in communication is followed by the most fundamental stage in language acquisition, learning the names of things and especially (appropriately enough for one reduced to the communication level of a young child) of food. At his first meal on Laputa, Gulliver

made bold to ask the Names of several Things in their Language; and those noble Persons, by the Assistance of their *Flappers*, delighted to give me Answers, hoping to raise my

Admiration of their great Abilities, if I could be brought to converse with them. I was soon able to call for Bread, and Drink, or whatever else I wanted. (*Prose Writings*, XI, 161)

Similarly, among the Houyhnhnms Gulliver is taught by his 'Master' at the first meal 'the Names for Oats, Milk, Fire, Water, and some others; which I could readily pronounce after him; having from my Youth a great Facility in learning Languages' (*Prose Writings*, XI, 232).

By the time we reach the fourth voyage, however, the subjects of language and communication have been so much emphasized that the suspicion must arise that they are not the mere incidental details of a traveller's narration that Gulliver would have us believe and clearly believes himself. The Houyhnhnm master, more than any previous instructor, takes enormous interest in the process of language acquisition in order to be told Gulliver's story – to be, in fact, himself exposed to a traveller's tale as we are in reading, though it is what is supposedly familiar to us that will be new and incredible to him.

The Curiosity and Impatience of my Master were so great, that he spent many Hours of his Leisure to instruct me. He was convinced (as he afterwards told me) that I must be a *Yahoo*, but my Teachableness, Civility and Cleanliness astonished him;... My Master was eager to learn from whence I came; how I acquired those Appearances of Reason, which I discovered in all my Actions; and to know my Story from my own Mouth, which he hoped he should soon do by the great Proficiency I made in learning and pronouncing their Words and Sentences. To help my Memory, I formed all I learned into the *English* Alphabet, and writ the words down with the Translations. This last, after some time, I ventured to do in my Master's Presence. It cost me much Trouble to explain to him what I was doing; for the Inhabitants have not the least Idea of Books or Literature. (*Prose Writings*, XI, 234–5)

Language and the process of acquiring it are here being associated with an incapacity to comprehend the existence of the literature we as readers are actually engaged in reading. Our entire experience of Gulliver's world is being rendered in a medium, and apprehended through an activity, of which the Houyhnhnm master (already established as a worthy and serious figure) has no comprehension and can scarecely be brought to credit. In the light of what we have already seen in Part III of Swift's apparent delight in emphasising the impediments to communication and the shortcomings of language – the example of the Dutchman whose loading of 'Curses and injurious Terms' upon Gulliver is circumscribed only by the limitations of what 'his Language could afford' (*Prose Writings*, XI, 155); the example of the Laputans themselves who need the constant attention of their '*Flappers*' to make good any communication at all (*Prose Writings*, XI, 159-60); the professors of the 'School of Languages' with their schemes for improving 'that of their own Country' by 'cutting Polysyllables into one, and leaving out Verbs and Participles' or by 'entirely abolishing all Words whatsoever' and replacing them with the '*Things*' themselves (*Prose Writings*, XI, 185); or the '*Struldbruggs*' whose 'Memory will not serve to carry them from the Beginning of a Sentence to the End' and who find themselves linguistically isolated in a country of which the language 'is always upon the Flux' (*Prose Writings*, XI, 185) – we should by now be reading this work of literature with strong suspicions not only about the status of all literature but about the adequacy of the reading act and of language itself as means for communicating or expressing any kind of 'Truth', let alone for the conveying of instruction to mankind. Swift, in other words, has contrived that our very reading of *Gulliver's Travels* should make us distrustful of what and how we read. Only magicians, if Gulliver's address to his first Houyhnhnms is to be credited, are able to understand exactly what is meant to be conveyed through language: 'Gentlemen, if you be Conjurers, as I have good Cause to believe, you can understand any Language' (*Prose Writings*, XI, 226). For the rest of us, we must endeavour to find a different way of coming to the 'Truth', or at least of acquiring the language that is collected together as *Gulliver's Travels*.

In chapter VI of his narration, Gulliver describes the 'Manner of Writing' of the Lilliputians which is, he says,

> very peculiar; being neither from the Left to the Right, like the *Europeans*; nor from the Right to the Left, like the *Arabians*; nor from up to down, like the *Chinese*; nor from down to up,

like the *Cascagians*; but aslant from one Corner of the Paper to
the other, like Ladies in *England*.   (*Prose Writings*, XI, 57)

In the context of the many comments Gulliver makes on his
own writing of his travels, of his reasons for doing so and of the
difficulties involved, this observation is relevant enough. While
Gulliver does not write 'aslant', there are, nevertheless, tensions
in his work which make it advisable for us to be prepared to read
'aslant'. But in terms of what Swift is doing in the *Travels*, the
joke is entirely appropriate. Not only are we led from the
familiar '*Europeans*' to the increasingly remote and unlikely and
thence to the quite unexpected 'Ladies in *England*', but we are
shown, as clearly as anywhere, that Gulliver is not in control of
his own material (the joke, after all, is not his). Or rather, we are
shown that the hand that moves is not Gulliver's, and that the
material is not to be controlled by conventional ways of writing
and reading. In order to catch sight of the hand of the artist
behind the words on the page we shall need to train ourselves to
look 'aslant' at every turn in the book.

The tensions under which Gulliver writes are those which are
common to any man telling of his own experience – that as a
writer he must be in control of material of which as a man he has
had only partial control while living. From Tristram Shandy to
Charles Arrowby in Iris Murdoch's *The Sea, The Sea*, first
person narrators have bent and sometimes cracked under the
pressure of the events they were called upon to live as they told
them. As a writer Gulliver is required to know both what has
happened, from start to finish, and the self to whom it
happened. The work on which he engages himself purports to be
a narration of finished events, just as the narrator who begins
chapter I – 'My Father had a small Estate in *Nottinghamshire*; I
was the Third of five Sons' (*Prose Writings*, XI, 19) – writes with
the assurance of one who will maintain a sufficient artistic
detachment from the events of his own life. Such a writer, while
not seeking necessarily to arouse laughter, would nevertheless
seem well placed to combine the godlike with the human, having
at the time of writing the advantage both of a 'lofty scrutiny'
which will clarify, and yet, because it is his own life, of being
'intimately in touch' with what he contemplates. Such a work
should produce between writer and reader the ideal relationship
in which one shares with the other the 'integration' of heavenly

perspective and non-heavenly feeling, the god-like made human, the human made godlike. At such a work, as at *Middlemarch* or *War and Peace*, we might not laugh, but the tears of our weeping should have behind them the awareness that laughter is also possible.

Gulliver, of course, far from maintaining such an ideal attitude towards his material, is apparently profoundly affected not only by the details of what he has to tell us as he tells it but, like Robinson Crusoe, by the very fact of having something to tell at all. He regrets, at the opening of Part II, that he has 'been contemned by Nature and Fortune to an active and restless Life' (*Prose Writings*, XI, 83) – and complains, after returning from that voyage, of the 'evil Destiny' which 'so ordered' that his wife 'had not Power to hinder me' from going to sea any more (*Prose Writings*, XI, 149); and at the outset of the 'Voyage to Laputa' he speaks ruefully of 'the Thirst I had of seeing the World, notwithstanding my past Misfortunes' (*Prose Writings*, XI, 153–4). Entering a Houyhnhnm house for the first time, he even 'feared my Brain was disturbed by my Sufferings and Misfortunes' (*Prose Writings*, XI, 229). And yet, as he laments the gaining of the experience that has given the book its existence, and that therefore forms the basis of his relationship with the 'gentle Reader' (*Prose Writings*, XI, 94), he also makes claim to unusual understanding of human nature as a consequence of his travels, of these very 'Sufferings and Misfortunes'.

> But I must freely confess, that the many Virtues of these excellent Quadrupeds placed in opposite View to human Corruptions, had so far opened mine Eyes, and enlarged my Understanding, that I began to view the Actions and Passions of Man in a very different Light; and to think the Honour of my own Kind not worth managing; which, besides, it was impossible for me to do before a Person of so astute a Judgment as my Master, who daily convinced me of a thousand Faults in my self, whereof I have had not the least Perception before, and which with us would never be numbered even among human Infirmities. (*Prose Writings*, XI, 258)

What Gulliver now sees is the huge gap between himself and his kind, or rather between the Houyhnhnm nature he is capable of understanding and therefore of aspiring to emulate, and his own irredeemably human nature, the nature which he shares with his readers. Swift is having Gulliver increasingly distance himself from the human, and yet the perspective he is acquiring is far from a godlike 'lofty scrutiny', for what Gulliver sees through his 'opened Eyes' is, by the end of his account, thoroughly distorted by those two eminently human passions, anger and frustration.

> But, when I behold a Lump of Deformity, and Diseases both in Body and Mind, smitten with *Pride*, it immediately breaks all the Measure of my Patience; neither shall I ever be able to comprehend how such an Animal and such a Vice could tally together. (*Prose Writings*, XI, 296)

Far from writing in any spirit of affirmation appropriate to the common humanity of his readers, Gulliver has reached such an extreme and isolated position in relation to mankind that, like Codrus, he 'unconcern'd' renders himself entirely laughable, both to us as readers and to the various people he meets towards the end of his travels – the Portuguese seamen's 'laughing at my strange Tone in speaking, which resembled the Neighing of a Horse' (*Prose Writings*, XI, 285); his stealing out from his cabin and attempting 'to leap into the Sea, and swim for my Life, rather than continue among *Yahoos*', in consequence of which he is 'chained to my Cabbin' like the madman for which the crew clearly take him (*Prose Writings*, XI, 286–7); and his reaction to being reunited with his own wife:

> As soon as I entered the House, my Wife took me in her Arms, and kissed me; at which, not having been used to the Touch of that odious Animal for so many Years, I fell in a Swoon for almost an Hour. (*Prose Writings*, XI, 289)

If, like Arbuthnot, we can laugh at Gulliver, we shall have seen clearly that his perspective on humanity, on ourselves, is far from true. We shall successfully have read 'aslant' what he has written with unswerving loyalty to the maxim 'that I would *strictly adhere to the Truth*' (*Prose Writings*, XI, 292).

It is easy, though, to dismiss Gulliver. No reader today is likely to be misled into believing that Swift and Gulliver speak

with one voice. It is less easy, however, to see what view Swift
would have us take from the book if it is not Gulliver's. Many
critics, of course, still hold a hard line on Swift's opinions of
mankind, and wish therefore to retain what is essentially
Gulliver's Houyhnhnmland perspective while nevertheless
ruling out Gulliver himself as a reliable spokesman. Here is one
recent example.

> Had Gulliver been presented as sane, we should (since again
> there is no real alternative voice, and no firm norm is
> indicated) have had to identify him with the satirist behind
> the mask, and so have been enabled to reject both as totally
> outrageous. As it is, we reject what comes from Gulliver, and
> are left with that disturbingly uncertain proportion of it
> which comes from Swift. It is precisely Gulliver's distance
> from Swift that permits the Swiftian attack to look
> plausible.[14]

Such a view is persuasive. What it is inclined to overlook,
though, is the relationship that is gradually established
throughout the book between the satirist and the reader. There
may be 'no real alternative voice', but to need a voice to counter
Gulliver's own is to be guilty of reading 'from the Left to the
Right, like the *Europeans*'. Every time we laugh at Gulliver, be it
in company with the King of Brobdingnag or with the various
seamen who find the antics of the returning traveller amusing, or
even in the company of that 'secret freemasonry' of people who
laugh at this sort of thing, we are hearing an 'alternative voice',
and one that is quite clearly sanctioned by the satirist. Each
laugh, therefore, is another link in the chain that binds us to the
writer behind the work, to the man 'behind the mask'. By the
time we reach Houyhnhnmland our trust (which is the quality
Tillotson emphasizes as most characteristic of the reader's
relationship with Pope) should be firmly with Swift, with his
artistic control over his material (in contrast, of course, to
Gulliver's over his), and with his ability to continue to arouse
both our interest and our amusement – the interest which, at its
most basic level, keeps us in the book with Gulliver, and the
amusement which keeps us beyond it with Swift. Because Part IV
presents problems, critics seek the answers to those problems
also in Part IV, and look for humour at the expense of the

Houyhnhnms (which there is), or for some softening of attitude towards the Yahoos (which there is not). The way out of the problems has already been provided, if our eyes and ears have been properly 'opened', before the 'Voyage to the Country of the Houyhnhnms' begins – has been provided by the developing relationship we have been experiencing with Swift himself through the book he is pretending someone else has written.

There is, however, more to it than this. As Gulliver returns from his 'Voyage to Brobdingnag', Swift provides us (and it has to be Swift, for Gulliver himself dismisses the incident almost out of hand) with an instructive species of literary *clin d'œil*, and one which, as much as anything, should convince us of a firmer 'norm' – a surer way of reading – than Gulliver's own. We have had related Gulliver's trip to the Brobdingnagian coast, his being borne away in his box, as he supposes, by the great eagle, his fall into the sea and finally his rescue, box and all, by 'Captain, Mr. *Thomas Wilcocks*, an honest worthy *Shropshire* Man' and his crew (*Prose Writings*, XI, 143). Then, after a sleep 'perpetually disturbed with Dreams of the Place I had left, and the Dangers I had escaped' (*Prose Writings*, XI, 144), Gulliver converses with Captain Wilcocks.

> I asked whether he or the Crew had seen any prodigious Birds in the Air about the Time he first discovered me: To which he answered, that discoursing this Matter with the Sailors while I was asleep, one of them said he had *observed* three Eagles flying towards the North; but remarked nothing of their being larger than the usual Size; which I suppose must be imputed to the great Height they were at. (*Prose Writings*, XI, 145)

Almost immediately we find the suggestion from the captain that Gulliver is out of his wits: 'Whereupon he began again to think that my Brain was disturbed, of which he gave me a Hint, and advised me to go to Bed in a Cabin he had provided' (*Prose Writings*, XI, 145). We, too, surely, wonder for a moment whether Swift is hinting to us that Gulliver is already an insane fantastic, or at least, as Gulliver suspects at the beginning of Part IV, has been all the while dreaming – 'I rubbed mine Eyes often, but the same Objects still occurred. I pinched my Arms and Sides, to awake my self, hoping I might be in a Dream'

(*Prose Writings*, XI, 229). We have, after all, been through this experience with Gulliver, have accepted his reasoning on how his box could suddenly take flight (*Prose Writings*, XI, 140-1). That three eagles were seen is some confirmation of Gulliver's conjectures, and yet how can we doubt the *observation* of the sailor, coming as he does from the 'real' world, that they were of normal size? Only when we remember the box, which has been seen and entered by the crew, do we stop trying to reconcile the irreconcilable. What we should realise is that we are being invited to see both perspectives at one and the same time – that of Gulliver and the reading eye that has followed him through his travels, accepting the fiction for the interest of the narration; and that of the seamen whose observation corresponds to our everyday expectation of things as we know they are, and who have only to explain to themselves the unusual (but not much more than unusual) discovery of a large box with a man inside and, coincidentally, the quite unremarkable sight of three normal-sized eagles 'flying towards the North'. But with our eyes thus almost literally 'aslant', we find ourselves focusing on the unread but nonetheless very real presence of the satirist who is so sure of his own control that he can draw the reader's attention to himself and to that very control without risking our commitment to the story being narrated. The hand that has directed laughter within the book – the Queen's laughter at Gulliver wedged inside the marrowbone (*Prose Writings*, XI, 108-9), the laughter of the Brobdingnagian court at Gulliver's fierce threats to the monkey (*Prose Writings*, XI, 123-4) or at his leaping into the 'Cow-dung' (*Prose Writings*, XI, 124) – now beckons us to join him in a laugh on quite a different level, for it is an invitation to find amusing the whole business of constructing and directing the fiction, including our part in that construction by lending our interest, by our readiness to be partially deceived and to continue being so. We are given, for a moment, a glimpse of the satirist, approving our amusement and approving the perception of readers like us who can recognise the bestowing of a huge literary wink.

This acknowledgement between satirist and reader of each other's presence (and there are, of course, innumerable smaller touches of acknowledgement throughout the *Travels*) gains more point by comparison with Gulliver's return from Houyhnhnmland, where we find a more serious *clin d'œil*, or rather an effect which we should not regard as a *clin d'œil* at all were it not for the pattern established by the observation of the eagles. The meeting with Captain Mendez is carefully prepared by Swift, having Gulliver first encounter apparently hostile savages, then balancing the humanity of the Portuguese seamen with Gulliver's 'Fear and Hatred' of his own kind (*Prose Writings*, XI, 285), and finally letting him be tied with cords and 'heaved' into the boat lest he should attempt to flee (*Prose Writings*, XI, 286). Gulliver reflects upon the seamen's capacity for speech – a reflection fully in keeping with our growing doubts over the reliability of language.

> When they began to talk, I thought I never heard or saw any thing so unnatural; for it appeared to me as monstrous as if a Dog or a Cow should speak in *England*, or a *Yahoo* in *Houyhnhnmland*. (*Prose Writings*, XI, 286)

As with the return from Brobdingnag, Swift is firmly establishing Gulliver's own state of mind in the reader's eye before confronting him and us with dramatically conflicting evidence, here, of course, in the person of the captain himself.

> His Name was *Pedro de Mendez*; he was a very courteous and generous Person; he entreated me to give some Account of my self, and desired to know what I would eat or drink; said, I should be used as well as himself, and spoke so many obliging Things, that I wondered to find such Civilities from a *Yahoo*. (*Prose Writings*, XI, 286)

We momentarily forget, with the listing of Mendez's virtues, both the perspective which views all men as Yahoos and the state of mind of the man who holds such a view. The reminder, then, all the more forceful for the slip in memory, produces an effect strikingly similar to that of the eagles incident. We are being invited, in fact, to see a man at the same time as a Yahoo and not a Yahoo, as the creature Gulliver's recent experience proves him to be and as the decent human being we know by our ordinary experience to exist (and Mendez's virtues are ones we actually *observe* in operation: they are not mere '*Names*' of virtues which, like 'Honour, Justice, Truth, Temperance, publick Spirit, Fortitude, Chastity, Friendship, Benevolence, and

Fidelity', Gulliver in his final chapter remarks 'are still retained among us in most Languages, and are to be met with in modern as well as ancient Authors; which I am able to assert from my own small Reading' (*Prose Writings*, XI, 294)). Yet the wink is less literary than moral. Certainly, we are not invited to be amused. That comes a little later, and it is solely at the expense of Gulliver. The invitation, as before, is to exchange a glance with the satirist, but rather than to laugh as he laughs, we are requested to judge as he judges. We know the eagles were large. We also know they were of normal size. We know that man is a Yahoo, and know, too, that he is not. Gulliver himself, who 'remained silent and sullen' (*Prose Writings*, XI, 286) like the splenetic Yahoo who would 'retire into a Corner, to lie down and howl, and groan, and spurn away all that came near him' (*Prose Writings*, XI, 263-4), is hardly exempt from the charge. Gulliver can perceive this, but it is a perception which leaves him racked by anger and frustration and renders him as proud in his mad ranting against humanity as those whom he censures for 'this absurd Vice' on the last page of his *Travels* (*Prose Writings*, XI, 296). We should perceive the same, that Gulliver and all his kind are Yahoos, but our perception, too, that they are not Yahoos – are capable of generosity, courtesy, nobility and, as we move away from the crucial example of Pedro de Mendez, of self-sacrifice, love, creativity and many more virtues possessed neither by Yahoos nor by Houyhnhnms – should make the effect of our perceiving quite different from the effect on Gulliver. He, after all that he has been through, still reads 'from the Left to the Right', sees in one dimension only, says, relying upon common sense and memory (and we are often called upon to remember Gulliver's excellent memory[15]), 'if not that, then this'. We, with our learned capacity to read '*aslant*' and our readiness to judge in the light of what Swift makes us *observe*, see finally not in Gulliver's dimension but rather beyond it in the dimension of the satirist.

What we see in this dimension is what Pope would have us see in the portrait of Atticus: that we may laugh *and* weep at proud, vulnerable mankind, and that both responses are equally valid, and valid at the same time. Our seeing gives a perspective on the affairs of man which is both godlike and human, which passes judgment as it affirms the worth of that judged. Because we have been brought into a relationship with Swift, albeit obliquely, and shared brief acknowledgements that the fiction is a fiction, that the material is controlled, we judge with the 'lofty scrutiny' of an amused onlooker who is above and beyond the world of the book. Because we are human, because we are interested in Gulliver's travels and in his changing perceptions of them, we are ready to lament the exemplary loss of his gullible innocence, just as we lament the unwritten and so unread grief of Glumdalclitch or the vulnerable good nature of Lord Munodi and Captain Mendez. Yet our lamenting is also an affirmation that such things are so, and a hope that such simple virtue will continue to exist. To respond fully to *Gulliver's Travels*, to be the ideal reader, as Dryden describes Dorset, 'considering that there is nothing perfect in mankind', is to hold each reaction, amusement or lamentation, judgment or pity, in the acknowledgement that the other is equally right. The perspective is caught completely in the example of the King of Brobdingnag, whose 'Morality and Government' (*Prose Writings*, XI, 292) Gulliver himself, with his excellent memory, recalls for us in the final chapter of his book. The King, having heard from Gulliver of 'the Manners, Religion, Laws, Government, and Learning of *Europe*' (*Prose Writings*, XI, 106), then 'could not forbear taking me up in his right Hand, and stroking me gently with the other; after an hearty Fit of laughing, asked me whether I were a *Whig* or a *Tory*' (*Prose Writings*, XI, 107). The King's ensuing remarks to the 'first Minister' indicate clearly that his laugh is at (Brobdingnagian) mankind as a whole, and not merely at Gulliver: 'he observed, how contemptible a Thing was human Grandeur, which could be mimicked by such diminutive Insects as I' (*Prose Writings*, XI, 107). It is a laugh of genuine godlike scrutiny of human affairs. And yet his gentle 'stroking' of Gulliver (a 'stroking' which also accompanies the King's more notorious judgment on human affairs later in the voyage (*Prose Writings*, XI, 132)) expresses more eloquently than any 'Left to Right' account of his opinions could the tender concern he feels for the life he is mocking.

The laugh of the King of Brobdingnag is the ideal laugh, the laugh we should find ourselves brought to emulate through the experience of reading *Gulliver's Travels*, a laugh made not in partial ignorance, like Shaftesbury's Ethiopian, but with a full uncompromising awareness of what it means to be human. There is no buying-off of the reader here, no readiness to give false comfort with half a picture, but nor is this the kind of work which, like *Verses on the Death of Dr. Swift*, earns our laughter by bringing us close to our most basic fears. Rather, it is the laugh which means we have been brought close to our own human nature, seen its corruption, its absurdity, its tenderness, and now laugh not with contempt but in affirmation of its value and in the certainty that life, despite its corruptions and absurdities, will go on. Gulliver is indeed 'a happy man that at his age can write such a merry work'.[16]

In a note to the lines quoted a little earlier from his translation of *The Iliad*, Pope reflects upon the curious vision of Jupiter smiling at 'the discord of the Gods'. He was, he says, 'at a loss for the reason' until he found the answer in '*Eustathius*':

> *Jupiter*, says he, who is the lord of nature, is well pleased with the war of the Gods, that is of earth, sea, and air, & c. because the harmony of all beings arises from that discord: Thus earth is opposite to water, air to earth, and water to them all; and yet from this opposition arises that discordant concord by which all nature subsists. Thus heat and cold, moist and dry, are in a continual war, yet upon this depends the fertility of the earth, and the beauty of the creation. So that *Jupiter*, who according to the *Greeks* is the soul of all, may well be said to smile at this contention.
> (*Iliad*, XXI, 454n.)

We who respond with our smiles or laughter to the contention that is satire are likewise affirming a belief in the ultimate 'concord by which all nature subsists'. Our perception of particular satiric victims may be the initial cause of our laughter, but as soon as we laugh we find ourselves in a different dimension. Our laughter expresses not our contempt for a Cibber or our hatred for a Yahoo, but rather our faith in the flow of life to which the minor deviant, the Bentley, the Theobald, the Shadwell, is scarcely an irritant. We look, finally, not upon the individual when we judge with our laughter, but upon the kind, and as we laugh we give full physical expression to our faith in that kind, our celebration that life has continued, and our belief that mankind, somehow, will survive.

There, on the mountain and the sky,
On all the tragic scene they stare.
One asks for mournful melodies;
Accomplished fingers begin to play.
Their eyes mid many wrinkles, their eyes,
Their ancient, glittering eyes, are gay.

Notes

CHAPTER 1: THE UNEASY CHAIR

1. *Correspondence of Jonathan Swift*, ed. Harold Williams, 1963-5, II, 365; see also II, 366n.2.
2. Swift, *Correspondence*, II, 366, 367-8, 374.
3. Swift, *Correspondence*, II, 369-70.
4. Steele is one of fifteen characterised as 'ungrateful' in Swift's list of 'friends', printed by Sir Walter Scott in his 1814 *Memoirs* of Swift, Appendix VIII, p. xcviii, reprinted by Williams, *Correspondence*, V, Appendix XXX, p. 270. Addison, Congreve and Rowe do not appear in the list.
5. Swift, *Correspondence*, I, 348-9.
6. Bertrand A. Goldgar, *The Curse of Party: Swift's Relations with Addison and Steele*, 1961, charts in detail the growth and decline of the friendship. Chapter 2 deals with 'Swift's Change of Parties, 1709-1710'.
7. Swift, *Correspondence*, I, 351.
8. Swift, *Correspondence*, IV, 546.
9. Swift, *Correspondence*, I, 355.
10. Goldgar, p. 114.
11. See Swift, *Correspondence*, I, 354n.2.
12. Swift, *Correspondence*, I, 355-6.
13. One further letter each concludes this exchange, whereafter Swift and Steele apparently corresponded no more. Significantly, Steele is absent from Swift's 1729 list of 'Men famous for their learning, wit, or great employments or quality', a list in which he includes Addison, Congreve and Rowe (see *Correspondence*, V, Appendix XXXI, p. 271).
14. *Guardian* 29.
15. See especially Paul Elkin, *The Augustan Defence of Satire*, 1973, chapter 2, for the range of these works. A short general account of attitudes towards laughter and comedy can be found in the opening section of Ian Donaldson's essay on 'Drama from 1710 to 1780' in *Dryden to Johnson*, ed. Roger Lonsdale, 1971, pp. 190-225.
16. *Spectator* 182.
17. *Spectator* 525.
18. Swift, *Correspondence*, IV, 384.
19. See E. A. Bloom and L. D. Bloom, *Satire's Persuasive Voice*, 1979, for further discussion, especially chapter 3; also Elkin for a useful and thorough bibliography.

20. *On Poetry: A Rapsody*, ll. 319–20 (*The Poems of Jonathan Swift*, ed. Harold Williams, 2nd edn, 1958).
21. Rochester, *Satyr against Mankind*, ll. 133–6 (*Poems on Several Occasions*, 1680?, 1971 edn).
22. Hobbes, *Leviathan*, 1651, ed. Michael Oakeshott, n.d.; *The Elements of Law*, ed. Ferdinand Tönnies, 2nd edn, 1969.
23. *Leviathan*, p. 36.
24. *Elements of Law*, pp. 41–2.
25. *Elements of Law*, p. 14.
26. *Elements of Law*, p. vi.
27. *De Homine*, 1658, chapter XII, para. 7 (tr. as *Man and Citizen*, Charles T. Wood, T. S. K. Scott-Craig and Bernard Get, 1972, p. 59).
28. *Leviathan*, pp. 35–6.
29. *Leviathan*, p. 34.
30. *Leviathan*, p. 34.
31. *Leviathan*, p. 36.
32. *Leviathan*, p. 64.
33. *Leviathan*, p. 57.
34. *Leviathan*, p. 32.
35. *Leviathan*, p. 46.
36. *Leviathan*, pp. 47–8.
37. Shaftesbury, *'Sensus Communis'; An Essay on the Freedom of Wit and Humour*, Section III, in *Characteristics of Men, Manners, Opinions, Times*, 1711, Treatise II, ed. John M. Robertson, 1964, I, 46–7.
38. *'Sensus Communis'*, *Characteristics*, I, 48.
39. *'Sensus Communis'*, *Characteristics*, I, 98–9.
40. Shaftesbury, *A Letter Concerning Enthusiasm*, in *Characteristics*, Treatise I, I, 17.
41. *'Sensus Communis'*, *Characteristics*, I, 47.
42. *'Sensus Communis'*, *Characteristics*, I, 46.
43. *'Sensus Communis'*, *Characteristics*, I, 53.
44. *'Sensus Communis'*, *Characteristics*, I, 85.
45. *'Sensus Communis'*, *Characteristics*, I, 86; cf. *Letter, Characteristics*, I, 10.
46. *'Sensus Communis'*, *Characteristics*, I, 77–8.
47. *'Sensus Communis'*, *Characteristics*, I, 83.
48. *'Sensus Communis'*, *Characteristics*, I, 44.
49. *'Sensus Communis'*, *Characteristics*, I, 98.
50. *'Sensus Communis'*, *Characteristics*, I, 57.
51. *'Sensus Communis'*, *Characteristics*, I, 58.
52. Johnson, *The Vanity of Human Wishes*, l, 52.
53. Francis Hutcheson, *Reflections on Laughter*, Glasgow, 1750 (first published London, 1728) p. 27.
54. Anthony Collins, *A Discourse Concerning Ridicule and Irony in Writing*, 1729, ed. E. A. and L. D. Bloom, 1970, p. 12.
55. Elkin, p. 65. The reference is to Corbyn Morris, *An Essay Towards Fixing the True Standards of Wit, Humour, Raillery, Satire, and Ridicule*, 1744, p. 33.
56. Elkin, p. 66.
57. Bloom and Bloom, p. 19.

58. Dryden, *A Discourse concerning the Original and Progress of Satire*, 1693, in *John Dryden: Selected Criticism*, ed. James Kinsley and George Parfitt, 1970, pp. 208–9.
59. *Discourse*, pp. 210–11.
60. *Discourse*, p. 244.
61. *Discourse*, p. 238.
62. *Discourse*, p. 239.
63. *Discourse*, p. 248.
64. *Discourse*, p. 250.
65. *Discourse*, p. 252.
66. *Discourse*, p. 256.
67. *Discourse*, p. 257.
68. *Discourse*, p. 258.
69. Elkin, pp. 158–9.
70. Dryden, *Discourse*, p. 261.
71. *Discourse*, p. 264.
72. *Discourse*, p. 261.
73. *Discourse*, p. 262–3.
74. *Discourse*, p. 263.
75. See especially Elkin, chapter 4, 'Main Lines of Attack', and Bloom and Bloom, chapter 1, 'Intention: Satiric Mode of Feeling'.
76. *Spectator* 355.

CHAPTER 2: ACTS OF EXCLUSION

1. Irvin Ehrenpreis, *The Personality of Jonathan Swift*, 1958, p. 33.
2. Denis Donoghue, *Jonathan Swift: a Critical Introduction*, 1969, p. 207.
3. Deane Swift, *Essay upon the Life, Writings and Character of Dr. Jonathan Swift*, 2nd edn, 1755, in *Swift: The Critical Heritage*, ed. Kathleen Williams, 1970, p. 147.
4. Ehrenpreis, pp. 34–5, quoting 'various London newspapers of 13, 16, 23 and 27 June 1730' and Swift's *Correspondence*, ed. F. E. Ball, 1910–14, IV, 161–2.
5. Ehrenpreis, p. 36.
6. Henri Bergson, *Laughter: an essay on the meaning of the comic*, 1900 (tr. Cloudesley Brereton and Fred Rothwell, 1935, p. 69).
7. Bergson, p. 26.
8. Bergson, p. 28–9.
9. Bergson, p. 30–1.
10. Bergson, p. 4.
11. Bergson, p. 5.
12. Bergson, p. 143.
13. Bergson, p. 25.
14. Bergson, p. 19.
15. Bergson, p. 21.
16. Bergson, p. 197.
17. Sigmund Freud, *Jokes and their Relation to the Unconscious*, 1905 (*Psychological Works*, tr. James Strachey, VIII, 1960 p. 103).

18. Bergson, p. 134
19. Bergson, p. 198.
20. Freud, 'Humour', 1927 (*Psychological Works*, tr. Strachey, XXI, 1961, p. 161).
21. Freud, *Jokes* (*Works*, VIII, 100).
22. Freud, *Jokes* (*Works*, VIII, 103).
23. Freud, *Jokes* (*Works*, VIII, 133).
24. Freud, *Jokes* (*Works*, VIII, 133).
25. Freud, *Jokes* (*Works*, VIII, 189).
26. Freud, *Jokes* (*Works*, VIII, 199–200).
27. Freud, *Jokes* (*Works*, VIII, 189).
28. Freud, *Jokes* (*Works*, VIII, 209).
29. Freud, 'Humour' (*Works*, XXI, 162).
30. Freud, 'Humour' (*Works*, XXI, 163).
31. Freud, 'Humour' (*Works*, XXI, 163).
32. R. D. Laing, *Self and Others*, 1961 (1971 edn) pp. 98–9.
33. Laing, *Self and Others*, p. 136.
34. Laing, *Self and Others*, p. 86.
35. R. D. Laing, *The Divided Self*, 1960 (1965 edn) p. 39.
36. Laing, *The Divided Self*, p. 42
37. Laing, *The Divided Self*, p. 75.
38. Laing, *The Divided Self*, p. 113.
39. Laing, *The Divided Self*, p. 46.
40. Laing, *The Divided Self*, p. 47.
41. Martin Buber, 'Distance and Relation', *Psychiatry*, 20, in Laing, *Self and Others*, p. 98.
42. Laing, *Self and Others*, p. 100–1.
43. Laing, *Self and Others*, p. 101.
44. Laing, *Self and Others*, p. 106.
45. Laing, *The Divided Self*, p. 56.
46. Laing, *The Divided Self*, p. 76.
47. *Spectator* 355.
48. Laing, *The Divided Self*, p. 77.
49. Laing, *The Divided Self*, p. 82.
50. Robert C. Elliott, *The Power of Satire: Magic, Ritual, Art*, 1960 (1966 edn) pp. 283–4.
51. Elliott, p. 277.
52. Laing, *The Divided Self*, pp. 90–1.
53. See, for example, *Three Hundred Years of Psychiatry*, ed. Richard Hunter and Ida Macalpine, 1963; also Allan Ingram, *Boswell's Creative Gloom: A Study of Imagery and Melancholy in the Writings of James Boswell*, 1982.
54. Laing, *The Divided Self*, p. 116, citing Freud, *Beyond the Pleasure Principle*, 1920 (*Psychological Works*, tr. Strachey, XVIII, 1950, pp. 12–16).
55. Laing, *The Divided Self*, pp. 118–19.
56. But see Richard Boston, *An Anatomy of Laughter*, 1974, p. 140, on how the Chaplin costume, which included 'Fatty Arbuckle's trousers' and 'Ford Sterling's size 14 shoes', orginated in 1913.
57. Enid Welsford, *The Fool: His Social and Literary History*, 1935, esp. pp. 66–75.

58. Welsford, p. 243.

59. Freud, *Jokes* (*Works*, VIII, 199).

60. Herbert Davis, *The Prose Writings of Jonathan Swift*, II, 1966 edn, p. xii, points out that the *Answer to Bickerstaff* by 'A Person of Quality' was not included in Swift's works until Hawkesworth's quarto edition of 1765, and may have been written by Swift himself or by 'one of his friends'.

61. See Swift, *Prose Writings*, II, xiv.

62. Bergson, p. 14.

63. Bergson, pp. 15–16.

64. *An Essay upon the Taste and Writings of the Present Times, but with a more particular view to Political and Dramatic Writings. Occasion'd by a late Volume of Miscellanies by A. Pope, Esq: and Dr. Swift*. Inscribed to the Right Honourable Sir Robert Walpole. By a Gentleman of C—st C—h, Oxon, 1728, in Williams (ed.), p. 94.

65. Letter to Pope, 26 November, 1725, in Swift, *Correspondence*, III, 118.

66. Letter to Pope, 30 August, 1716, in Swift, *Correspondence*, II, 214.

67. See, too, the effective 'killing' of Steele and of William Wood, to give only two examples, by means of such remorseless punning on their names that neither is left with any shred of personality, the one in *The Importance of the Guardian Considered*, 1713 (Swift, *Prose Writings*, VIII, 1973 edn, p. 8), the other in *A Serious Poem Upon William Wood*, 1724.

68. *Part of the Seventh Epistle of the First Book of Horace Imitated*, l. 36.

69. Donoghue, p. 220.

70. Robert Martin Adams, *Strains of Discord*, 1958, p. 254.

71. William Wotton, *A Defence of the Reflections upon 'Ancient and Modern Learning', In Answer to the Objections of Sir 'W. Temple', and Others. With Observations upon 'The Tale of a Tub'*, 1705, reprinted in Swift, *A Tale of a Tub*, ed. A. C. Guthkelch and D. Nichol Smith, 2nd edn, 1958.

72. C. J. Rawson, *Gulliver and the Gentle reader*, 1973, p. 1.

73. See *The Twickenham Edition of the Poems of Alexander Pope*, V, *The Dunciad*, ed. James Sutherland, 3rd edn, 1963, pp. 248–50.

74. Colley Cibber, *A Letter from Mr. Cibber, To Mr. Pope, Inquiring into the Motives that might induce him in his Satyrical Works, to be so frequently fond of Mr. Cibber's Name*, 1742, p. 15.

75. Cibber, *Letter*, pp. 45–6.

76. Cibber, *Letter*, p. 50.

77. Cibber, *Another Occasional Letter from Mr. Cibber to Mr. Pope*, 1744, p. 15, cited by Sutherland, *Poems of Alexander Pope*, V, p. xxxiii.

78. Norman Ault, *New Light on Pope*, 1949, p. 302.

79. *The Correspondence of Alexander Pope*, ed. George Sherburn, 1956, IV, 415.

80. Pope, *Correspondence*, IV, 492.

CHAPTER 3: SHEWING THE TEETH

1. Charles Darwin, *The Expression of Emotions in Man and Animals*, 1872, intr. S. J. Rachman, 1979, pp. 202–3.

2. Pope, Swift, *et al.*, *Memoirs of the Extraordinary Life, Works, and Discoveries of Martinus Scriblerus*, 1741, ed. Charles Kerby-Miller, 1950, p. 133.
3. Darwin, p. 93.
4. Darwin, p. 121, quoting Sir C. Bell, *The Anatomy of Expression*, 1844, p. 140.
5. Darwin, p. 121.
6. Darwin, p. 130.
7. Darwin, pp. 75–6.
8. Darwin, pp. 132–3.
9. Darwin, p. 134.
10. Suzanne Chevalier-Skolnikoff, 'Facial Expressions in Nonhuman Primates', in *Darwin and Facial Expression: A Century of Research in Review*, ed. Paul Ekman, 1973, p. 83.
11. J. A. R. A. M. van Hooff, 'A Comparative Approach to the Phylogeny of Laughter and Smiling', in *Non-Verbal Communication*, ed. Robert A. Hinde, 1972, p. 212.
12. Van Hooff, pp. 212–13.
13. Van Hoof, p. 213.
14. Van Hoof, p. 215.
15. Van Hoof, pp. 215–16.
16. Van Hoof, p. 217.
17. Van Hoof, p. 217.
18. Van Hoof, p. 211.
19. Van Hoof, p. 239.
20. Chevalier-Skolnikoff, pp. 80–2.
21. Van Hoof, pp. 235–6.
22. Van Hoof, p. 236.
23. Bergson, p. 6.
24. Shaftesbury, *'Sensus Communis'*, *Characteristics*, I, 74.
25. Bergson, pp. 7–8.
26. Freud, *Group Psychology and the Analysis of the Ego*, 1921 (*Psychological Works*, tr. Strachey, XVIII, 1955, p. 98).
27. Freud, *Group Psychology* (*Works*, XVIII, 85) citing W. McDougall, *The Group Mind*, 1920, p. 45.
28. Freud, *Group Psychology* (*Works*, XVIII, 78) citing G. Le Bon, *Psychologie des foules*, 1895, tr. *The Crowd: a Study of the Popular Mind*, 1920, p. 62.
29. See in this connection Allan Rodway's comments on 'mithridatic comedy' in *English Comedy*, 1975, pp. 20–1.
30. Laing, *Self and Others*, pp. 39–40.
31. Laing, *Self and Others*, pp. 40–1.
32. Bloom and Bloom, p. 128.
33. Bloom and Bloom, pp. 128–9.
34. Elliott, p. 84–5, citing Hugh Dalziel Duncan, *Language and Literature in Society*, 1953, pp. 24–5.
35. Freud, *Group Psychology* (*Works*, XVIII, 117).
36. Bergson, p. 138.
37. Shaftesbury, *'Sensus Communis'*, *Characteristics*, I, 76–7.

38. This is a subject frequently returned to in *The Examiner*, and is particularly dealt with in paper 25.
39. Not, of course, an uncommon idea in Swift's work. See, for example, his poem 'To Mr. Delany' where he observes of 'Voiture' that 'Fools would fancy he intends / A Satyr where he most commends' (ll. 39–40).
40. Sheridan, *The Critic*, I, i (*The Dramatic Works of Richard Brinsley Sheridan*, ed. Cecil Price, 1973, II, 506–8).
41. Freud, *Group Psychology* (*Works*, XVIII, 86).
42. Freud, *Group Psychology* (*Works*, XVIII, 86–7).

CHAPTER 4: THE PLAYGROUND OF THE MIND

1. Freud, *Jokes* (*Works*, VIII, 103, 133).
2. Freud, *Jokes* (*Works*, VIII, 222–3).
3. Bergson, pp. 67–8.
4. Van Hooff, p. 210.
5. Freud, *Jokes* (*Works*, VIII, 146–7n.2).
6. William R. Charlesworth and Mary Anne Kreutzer, 'Facial Expressions of Infants and Children' in Ekman, p. 106.
7. Darwin, pp. 211–12.
8. Darwin, 'A Biographical Sketch of an Infant', *Mind*, 1877.
9. J. Y. T. Greig, *The Psychology of Laughter and Comedy*, 1923, p. 25ff.
10. Darwin, *Expression of Emotions*, p. 211.
11. Greig, p. 26 and notes.
12. Jean Piaget, from *Play, Dreams and Imitation in Childhood*, 1951, in *Play – Its Role in Development and Evolution*, ed. J. S. Bruner, A. Jolly and K. Sylva, 1976, p. 168.
13. Greig, p. 66.
14. Piaget, p. 168.
15. Piaget, p. 168–9.
16. Charlesworth and Kreutzer, p. 106–7.
17. Van Hooff, pp. 237–8.
18. Charlesworth and Kreutzer, p. 108.
19. J. Watson, 'Smiling, Cooing and "The Game"', from *Merrill-Palmer Quarterly*, No. 18, 1972, in Bruner, Jolly and Sylva, p. 272.
20. Charlesworth and Kreutzer, p. 109.
21. Jerome S. Bruner, 'Nature and Uses of Immaturity', from *American Psychologist*, vol. 27, no. 8, August 1972, in Bruner, Jolly and Sylva, p. 48.
22. Charlesworth and Kreutzer, p. 109.
23. Charlesworth and Kreutzer, p. 151.
24. Jerome S. Bruner and V. Sherwood, 'Peekaboo and the Learning of Rule Structures', in Bruner, Jolly and Sylva, p. 283.
25. Bruner, p. 48.
26. Freud, *Jokes* (*Works*, VIII, 227); see also *Beyond the Pleasure Principle* (*Works*, XVIII, 17).
27. Freud, *Jokes* (*Works*, VIII, 227).

28. N. G. Blurton Jones, 'Non-verbal communication in children', in Hinde, p. 281.
29. Blurton Jones, p. 280.
30. Van Hooff, p. 217.
31. N. G. Blurton Jones, 'Rough-and-tumble Play among Nursery School Children' from 'An ethological study of some aspects of social behaviour of children in nursery schools', *Primate Ethology*, ed. Desmond Morris, 1967, in Bruner, Jolly and Sylva, p. 357.
32. Simone de Beauvoir, *Memoirs of a Dutiful Daughter*, tr. James Kirkup, 1970, in Bruner, Jolly and Sylva, p. 586.
33. Greig, p. 57.
34. See, for example, Sylvia G. Feinburg, 'Combat in Child Art', 1974, in Bruner, Jolly and Sylva, pp. 589–93.
35. Freud, *Jokes* (*Works*, VIII, 125).
36. Ruth Weir, 'Playing with Language' from *Language in the Crib*, 1962, in Bruner, Jolly and Sylva, p. 610, citing Y. R. Chao, 'The Cantian idiolect', *Semitic and Oriental Studies* (1951), no. II; W. Kaper, *Einige Erscheinungen der kindl. Spracheswerbung*, 1959; K. Ohnesorg, *Fonetickà studie*, 1947; O. Jespersen, *Language: Its Nature, Development and Origin*, 1949; C. and W. Stern, *Die Kindersprache*, 1928; E. and G. Scupin, *Bubi's erste Kindheit*, 1907.
37. Bruner, Jolly and Sylva, p. 530.
38. Weir, p. 611.
39. Weir, p. 609.
40. Bruner and Sherwood, p. 282, citing K. Nelson, 'Structure and strategy in learning to talk', *Monographs of The Society for Research in Child Development*, No. 38 (1973) pp. 1–137.
41. Bruner and Sherwood, p. 283.
42. Freud, *Jokes* (*Works*, VIII, 125).
43. Weir, p. 611.
44. Weir, p. 611, citing G. Vinogradov, *Russkij detskij folklor*, 1930, and K. Chukovsky, *Ot dvux do pjati*, 1956.
45. Weir, pp. 611–12.
46. Bruner, Jolly and Sylva, p. 530.
47. Weir, pp. 614–15.
48. Weir, p. 617.
49. K. Chukovsky, 'The Sense of Nonsense Verse', from *From Two to Five*, 1963, in Bruner, Jolly and Sylva, pp. 601–2.
50. Laing, *The Divided Self*, p. 39.
51. Laing, *The Divided Self*, p. 39.
52. Courtney B. Cazden, 'Play With Language and Meta-Linguistic Awareness: One Dimension of Language Experience', paper presented to the second Lucy Sprague Mitchell Memorial Conference, *Dimensions of Language Experience*, New York City, 19 May, 1973, in Bruner, Jolly and Sylva, p. 603.
53. Cazden, pp. 604–5.
54. Johan Huizinga, *Homo Ludens: a Study of the Play Element in Culture*, 1939 (tr. R. F. C. Hull, 1949, p. 141).
55. Huizinga, p. 151.

56. Huizinga, p. 154.
57. Huizinga, p. 155.
58. Huizinga, p. 155.
59. Dryden, *Of Dramatic Poesy: An Essay*, 1668, in *Selected Criticism*, p. 73.
60. Pope, *The Dunciad in Four Books*, 1742 (*Poems of Alexander Pope*, V).
61. Laing, *The Divided Self*, p. 116.
62. Freud, *Jokes* (*Works*, VIII, 134).
63. See Huizinga, pp. 49–50, for his arguments that the *agon* and play should be taken as intimately related in Greek civilization.
64. Watson, p. 268.
65. Huizinga, p. 28.
66. Freud, *Group Psychology* (*Works*, XVIII, 22–3).
67. Freud, *Jokes* (*Works*, VIII, 120).
68. Darwin, *Expression of Emotions*, p. 202.
69. Bergson, p. 80.
70. Bergson, p. 73.
71. Bergson, pp. 80–1.
72. Geoffrey Tillotson, *On the Poetry of Pope*, 2nd edn, 1950, pp. 115–16.
73. Dryden, *Discourse on Satire*, in *Selected Criticism*, p. 272.
74. Huizinga, p. 38.
75. Huizinga, p. 198.
76. Dryden, *Discourse on Satire*, in *Selected Criticism*, p. 272.
77. L. S. Vygotsky, 'Play and its Role in the Mental Development of the Child', *Soviet Psychology*, vol. 12, no. 6 (1966) pp. 62–76, in Bruner, Jolly and Sylva, p. 541.
78. Bruner, p. 48.
79. Bruner and Sherwood, p. 284.
80. Freud, 'Humour' (*Works*, XXI, 161).
81. Freud, 'Humour' (*Works*, XXI, 164).
82. Freud, 'Humour' (*Works*, XXI, 166).
83. Freud, *Group Psychology* (*Works*, XVIII, 17).
84. Huizinga, p. 29.
85. Shaftesbury, '*Sensus Communis*', *Characteristics*, I, 90–1.
86. Thomas Carlyle, 'Jean Paul Friedrich Richter', *Critical and Miscellaneous Essays*, 1869 edn, I, 15, cited by Greig, p. 252.
87. Carlyle, I, 15–16, cited by Greig, pp. 252–3.

CHAPTER 5: GLORY, JEST AND RIDDLE

1. René Wellek, *A History of Modern Criticism: 1750–1950*, I, *The Later Eighteenth Century*, 1955, p. 107.
2. Shaftesbury, '*Sensus Communis*', *Characteristics*, I, 89.
3. Shaftesbury, '*Sensus Communis*', *Characteristics*, I, 90.
4. Shaftesbury, *Miscellaneous Reflections on the Preceding Treatises, etc.*, Miscellany II, in *Characteristics*, Treatise VI, II, 231.
5. Hobbes, *Leviathan*, pp. 47–8.
6. Hobbes, *Leviathan*, p. 48.

7. Joseph Conrad, *The Shadow-Line*, 1917 (1925 edn) p. 130.
8. J. S. Cunningham, 'On Earth as it Laughs in Heaven: Mirth and the "Frigorifick Wisdom"', in *Augustan Worlds: Essays in Honour of A. R. Humphreys*, ed. J. C. Hilson, M. M. B. Jones and J. R. Watson, 1978, p. 135.
9. Freud, 'Humour' (*Works*, XXI, 164 and 166).
10. See also Cunningham's comments on this passage, p. 137.
11. Cunningham, p. 147.
12. William Blake, *The French Revolution*, printed 1791, ll. 190–1 (*Complete Writings*, ed. Geoffrey Keynes, 1957).
13. Bloom and Bloom, pp. 123–4.
14. Rawson, p. 14.
15. See, for example, *Prose Writings*, XI, 20, 94, 161 and 292.
16. Arbuthnot to Swift, 5 November, 1726, in Swift, *Correspondence*, III, 180.

Bibliography

I WORKS WRITTEN BEFORE 1800

Addison, Joseph and Richard Steele, *The Spectator*, 1711–12, 1714.

An Essay upon the Taste and Writings of the Present Times, but with a more particular view to Political and Dramatic Writings. Occasion'd by a late Volume of Miscellanies by A. Pope Esq: and Dr. Swift. Inscribed to the Right Honourable Sir Robert Walpole. By a Gentleman of C—st C—h, Oxon, 1728, in Kathleen Williams (ed.), *Swift: The Critical Heritage*, London, 1970

Blake, William, *The French Revolution*, printed London, 1791, in *Complete Writings*, ed. Geoffrey Keynes, London, 1957.

Cibber, Colley, *A Letter from Mr. Cibber, To Mr. Pope, Inquiring into the Motives that might induce him in his Satyrical Works, to be so frequently fond of Mr. Cibber's Name*, London, 1742.

——, *Another Occasional Letter from Mr. Cibber to Mr. Pope*, London, 1744.

Collins, Anthony, *A Discourse Concerning Ridicule and Irony in Writing*, London, 1729, ed. E. A. and L. D. Bloom, Los Angeles (Augustan Reprint Society), 1970.

Dryden, John, *A Discourse Concerning the Original and Progress of Satire*, London, 1693, in James Kinsley and George Parfitt (eds.), *John Dryden: Selected Criticism*, Oxford, 1970.

——, *Of Dramatic Poesy: An Essay*, London, 1668, in Kinsley and Parfitt, *Selected Criticism*.

——, *Poems*, ed. James Kinsley, 4 vols., Oxford, 1958.

Hobbes, Thomas, *Leviathan: Or the Matter, Forme and Power of a Commonwealth Ecclesiasticall and Civil*, London, 1651, ed. Michael Oakeshott, Oxford, n.d.

——, *The Elements of Law, Natural and Politic*, published 1650 as *Human Nature*, ed. Ferdinand Tönnies, Cambridge, 2nd edn., 1969.

——, *De Homine*, 1658, tr. as *Man and Citizen*, Charles T. Wood, T. S. K. Scott-Craig and Bernard Get, New York, 1972.

Hutcheson, Francis, *Reflections on Laughter*, Glasgow, 1750, first published London, 1728.

Johnson, Samuel, *Poems*, ed. D. Nichol Smith and E. L. McAdam, Oxford, 1941.

Morris, Corbyn, *An Essay Towards Fixing the True Standards of Wit, Humour, Raillery, Satire, and Ridicule*, London, 1744.

Pope, Alexander, *Poems*, Twickenham edn, ed. John Butt *et al.*, 10 vols, London, 1954–67.

    II. *The Rape of the Lock and Other Poems*, ed. Geoffrey Tillotson, 3rd edn, 1962.

III i. *An Essay on Man*, ed. Maynard Mack, 2nd edn, 1961.

III ii. *Epistles to Several Persons*, ed. F. W. Bateson, 2nd edn, 1961.

IV. *Imitations of Horace*, ed. John Butt, 2nd edn, rev., 1961.

V. *The Dunciad*, ed. James Sutherland, 3rd edn, rev., 1963.

VII-VIII. *The Iliad*, ed. Maynard Mack *et al.*, 1967.

——, *Correspondence*, ed. George Sherburn, 5 vols, Oxford, 1956.

Pope, Swift, *et al.*, *Memoirs of the Extraordinary Life, Works, and Discoveries of Martinus Scriblerus*, London, 1741, ed. Charles Kerby-Miller, New Haven, 1950.

Rochester, John Wilmot, Earl of, *Poems on Several Occasions*, 'Antwerp' (London), 1680?, repr. Menston, 1971.

Shaftesbury, Anthony Ashley Cooper, 3rd Earl of, *Characteristics of Men, Manners, Opinions, Times*, London, 1711, ed. John M. Robertson, 2 vols, Indianapolis, 1964.

I. *A Letter Concerning Enthusiasm to My Lord* *****, 1708.

II. *'Sensus Communis'; An Essay on the Freedom of Wit and Humour in a Letter to a Friend*, 1709.

VI. *Miscellaneous Reflections On the preceding Treatises, etc.*, 1711.

Sheridan, Richard Brinsley, *Dramatic Works*, ed. Cecil Price, 2 vols, Oxford, 1973.

Steele, Richard, *The Tatler*, 1709-11.

——, *Guardian* 1713.

Swift, Deane, *Essay upon the Life, Writings and Character of Dr. Jonathan Swift*, London, 1755, in Williams (ed.), *Swift: The Critical Heritage*.

Swift, Jonathan, *Prose Writings*, ed. Herbert Davis *et al.*, 14 vols, Oxford, 1939-63.

II. *Bickerstaff Papers and Pamphlets on the Church*, ed. Herbert Davis, 1966 edn.

III. *The Examiner and other Pieces written in 1710-11*, ed. Herbert Davis, 1966 edn.

VIII. *Political Tracts 1713-1719*, ed. Herbert Davis and Irvin Ehrenpreis, 1973 edn.

XI. *Gulliver's Travels*, ed. Herbert Davis, 1965 edn.

XV-XVI. *Journal to Stella*, ed. Harold Williams, 1974 edn.

——, *A Tale of a Tub*, ed. A. C. Guthkelch and D. Nichol Smith, Oxford, 2nd edn, 1958.

——, *Polite Conversation*, ed. Eric Partridge, London, 1963.

——, *Poems*, ed. Harold Williams, 3 vols, Oxford, 2nd edn, 1958.

——, *Correspondence*, ed. Harold Williams, 5 vols, Oxford, 1963-5.

Wotton, William, *A Defence of the Reflections upon 'Ancient and Modern Learning', In Answer to the Objections of Sir 'W. Temple', and Others. With Observations upon 'The Tale of a Tub'*, London, 1705, in Swift, *A Tale of a Tub*, ed. Gutkelch and Nichol Smith.

II WORKS WRITTEN BETWEEN 1800 AND THE PRESENT

Adams, Robert Martin, *Strains of Discord*, Ithaca, 1958.

Ault, Norman, *New Light on Pope*, London, 1949.

Barnard, John (ed.), *Pope: The Critical Heritage*, London, 1973.
Beauvoir, Simone de, *Memoirs of a Dutiful Daughter*, tr. James Kirkup, Harmondsworth, 1970, in J. S. Bruner, A. Jolly and K. Sylva (eds), *Play – Its Role in Development and Evolution*, Harmondsworth, 1976.
Bergson, Henri, *Laughter: an essay on the meaning of the comic*, 1900, tr. Cloudesley Brereton and Fred Rothwell, London, 1935.
Bloom, Edward A. and Lillian D. Bloom, *Satire's Persuasive Voice*, Ithaca and London, 1979.
Blurton Jones, N. G., 'Rough-and-tumble Play among Nursery School Children' from 'An ethological study of some aspects of social behaviour of children in nursery schools', *Primate Ethology*, ed. Desmond Morris, London, 1967, in Bruner, Jolly and Sylva (eds), *Play*.
——, 'Non-verbal communication in children', in Robert A. Hinde (ed.), *Non-verbal Communication*, Cambridge, 1972.
Boston, Richard, *An Anatomy of Laughter*, London, 1974.
Brooke, Nicholas, *Horrid Laughter in Jacobean Tragedy*, London, 1979.
Bruner, Jerome S., 'Nature and Uses of Immaturity', *American Psychologist*, vol. 27, no. 8, August 1972, in Bruner, Jolly and Sylva (eds), *Play*.
Bruner, Jerome S. and V. Sherwood, 'Peekaboo and the Learning of Role Structures', in Bruner, Jolly and Sylva (eds), *Play*.
Bruner, Jerome S., Alison Jolly and Kathy Sylva (eds), *Play – Its Role in Development and Evolution*, Harmondsworth, 1976.
Buber, Martin, 'Distance and Relation', *Psychiatry*, 20, in R. D. Laing, *Self and Others*, London, 1961 (1971 edn).
Carlyle, Thomas, 'Jean Paul Friedrich Richter', *Critical and Miscellaneous Essays*, 3 vols, London, 1869 edn.
Cazden, Courtney B., 'Play With Language and Meta-Linguistic Awareness: One Dimension of Language Experience', paper presented to the second Lucy Sprague Mitchell Memorial Conference, *Dimensions of Language Experience*, New York City, 19 May, 1973, in Bruner, Jolly and Sylva (eds), *Play*.
Charlesworth, William R. and Mary Ann Kreutzer, 'Facial Expressions of Infants and Children', in Paul Ekman (ed.), *Darwin and Facial Expression: A Century of Research in Review*, New York and London, 1973.
Chevalier-Skolnikoff, Suzanne, 'Facial Expressions in Nonhuman Primates', in Ekman (ed.), *Darwin and Facial Expression*.
Chukovsky, K., 'The Sense of Nonsense Verse', *From Two to Five*, Berkeley, 1963, in Bruner, Jolly and Sylva (eds), *Play*.
Conrad, Joseph, *The Shadow-Line*, London, 1917 (1925 edn).
Cunningham, J. S., 'On Earth as it Laughs in Heaven: Mirth and the "Frigorifick Wisdom"', *Augustan Worlds: Essays in Honour of A. R. Humphreys*, ed. J. C. Hilson, M. M. B. Jones and J. R. Watson, Leicester, 1978.
Darwin, Charles, The Expression of Emotions in Man and Animals, London, 1872, intr. S. J. Rachman, London and New York, 1979.
——, 'A Biograpical Sketch of an Infant', *Mind*, 1877.
Donaldson, Ian, 'Drama from 1710 to 1780', *Dryden to Johnson*, ed. Roger Lonsdale, London, 1971.
——, *The World Upside-Down*, Oxford, 1970.

Donoghue, Denis, *Jonathan Swift: a Critical Introduction*, Cambridge, 1969.
——, (ed.), *Jonathan Swift: A Critical Anthology*, Harmondsworth, 1971.
Duncan, Hugh Dalziel, *Language and Literature in Society*, Chicago, 1953.
Ehrenpreis, Irvin, *The Personality of Jonathan Swift*, New York, 1958.
Ekman, Paul (ed.) *Darwin and Facial Expression: A Century of Research in Review*, New York and London, 1973.
Elkin, Paul, *The Augustan Defence of Satire*, Oxford, 1973.
Elliott, Robert C., *The Power of Satire: Magic, Ritual, Art*, Princeton, 1960 (1966 edn).
Farley-Hills, David, *The Benevolence of Laughter: Comic Poetry of the Commonwealth and Restoration*, London, 1974.
Feinburg, Sylvia G., 'Combat in Child Art', 1974, in Bruner, Jolly and Sylva (eds), *Play*.
Freud, Sigmund, *Psychological Works*, tr. James Strachey, 24 vols, London, 1953–74.
Goldgar, Bertrand A., *The Curse of Party: Swift's Relations with Addison and Steele*, Lincoln, 1961.
Grant, Mary A., *The Ancient Rhetorical Theories of the Laughable: The Greek Rhetoricians and Cicero*, University of Wisconsin Studies in Language and Literature, no. 21, Madison, Wisconsin, 1924.
Greig, J. Y. T., *The Psychology of Laughter and Comedy*, London, 1923.
Hilson, J. C., M. M. B. Jones and J. R. Watson (eds), *Augustan Worlds: Essays in Honour of A. R. Humphreys*, Leicester, 1978.
Hinde, Robert A. (ed.), *Non-verbal Communication*, Cambridge, 1972.
Huizinga, Johan, *Homo Ludens: A Study of the Play Element in Culture*, 1939, tr. R. F. C. Hull, London, 1949.
Hunter, Richard and Ida Macalpine, *Three Hundred Years of Psychiatry: 1535–1860*, London, 1963.
Hutchinson, Peter, *Games Authors Play*, London and New York, 1983.
Ingram, Allan, *Boswell's Creative Gloom: a Study of Imagery and Melancholy in the Writings of James Boswell*, London, 1982.
Johnson, Maurice, *The Sin of Wit: Jonathan Swift as a Poet*, Syracuse, New York, 1950.
Kernan, Alvin B., *The Plot of Satire*, New Haven, 1965.
Laing, R. D., *The Divided Self: An Existential Study in Sanity and Madness*, London, 1960 (1965 edn).
——, *Self and Others*, London, 1961 (1971 edn).
Le Bon, G., *Psycholgie des foules*, Paris, 1895, tr. *The Crowd: A Study of the Popular Mind*, London, 1920.
Lonsdale, Roger (ed.), *Dryden to Johnson*, London, 1971.
McDougall, W., *The Group Mind*, Cambridge, 1920.
Piaget, Jean, *Play, Dreams and Imitation in Childhood*, London, 1951, in Bruner, Jolly and Sylva (eds), *Play*.
Rawson, C. J., *Gulliver and the Gentle Reader*, London, 1973.
Rodway, Allan, *English Comedy*, London, 1975.
Swabey, Marie Collins, *Comic Laughter*, New Haven, 1961.
Tave, Stuart, M., *The Amiable Humorist: a Study in the Comic Theory and Criticism of the Eighteenth and Early Nineteenth Centuries*, Chicago, 1960.
Tillotson, Geoffrey, *On the Poetry of Pope*, London, 2nd edn, 1950.

Van Hooff, J. A. R. A. M., 'A Comparative Approach to the Phylogeny of Laugher and Smiling', in Hinde (ed.), *Non-verbal Communication*.

Vygotsky, L. S., 'Play and its Role in the Mental Development of the Child', *Soviet Psychology*, vol. 12, no.6 (1966), in Bruner, Jolly and Sylva (eds), *Play*.

Watson, J., 'Smiling, Cooing and "The Game"', *Merrill-Palmer Quarterly*, No. 18, 1972, in Bruner, Jolly and Sylva (eds), *Play*.

Weir, Ruth, 'Playing with Language', *Language in the Crib*, The Hague, 1962, in Bruner, Jolly and Sylva (eds), *Play*.

Wellek, René, *A History of Modern Criticism: 1750-1950*, 4 vols, I, *The Later Eighteenth Century*, London, 1955.

Welsford, Enid, *The Fool: His Social and Literary History*, London, 1935 (1968 edn).

Williams, Kathleen (ed.), *Swift: The Critical Heritage*, London, 1970.

Yeats, W. B., *Collected Poems*, London, 2nd edn, 1950.

Index